Communication in Mission

This fascinating and stimulating compendium has been shaped by contributors who probed deeply into missional communication initiatives that negatively impacted a gospel witness. Through insightful analysis and well-grounded suggestions, they move readers forward to consider fresh options for fruitful intercultural engagement. A particular strength is the breadth of contemporary spheres addressed, which invites readers from diverse areas of mission to examine their own (mis)communication experiences and seek more effective strategies. I heartily recommend this compendium for all desiring to communicate the gospel in relevant, winsome, and effective ways.

EVVY HAY CAMPBELL, PhD
Associate Professor, Intercultural Studies Emerita,
Wheaton College Graduate School

Communication in Mission is like fresh water and a rich meal. It is a gift to both contemporary missions scholars and practitioners, as well as the church at large. First, the book recognizes the role of communication as more than simply a tool, rather as a way of life, and more specifically the key to a life with great impact. Second, the compilation of authors offer micro (everyday) and macro (societal) nuanced understandings of how communication impacts missions and how missions impact communication. This book exceeded its goal of capturing my attention and speaking to my heart. May it do the same for you.

K. ARIANNA MOLLOY, PhD
Associate Professor, Department of Communication Studies,
Biola University

The world of missions is a complex entity, especially when it comes to cross-cultural communication. Fortunately, this well-researched and documented missiological compendium has emerged to guide cross-cultural workers in this complex task. The authors are not only scholars but also missional practitioners. Their work is refreshing because it emerges out of their personal mission experience. Readers will greatly profit from this treasure of missiological thought, which will stimulate increasingly effective cross-cultural communication in their ministries, helping the advancement of the gospel.

CECIL STALNAKER, PhD
Professor Emeritus and Adjunct Professor, Intercultural Studies,
Tyndale Theological Seminary, the Netherlands

Communication in Mission offers a wide-ranging compendium—from storytelling to AI—that will expand your thinking and keep you current in the fast-changing world of communication.

TOM STEFFEN, DMiss
Professor Emeritus, Intercultural Studies,
Biola University

www.emsweb.org

The Evangelical Missiological Society (EMS) is a professional organization with more than four hundred members comprised of missiologists, mission administrators, reflective mission practitioners, teachers, pastors with strategic missiological interests, and students of missiology. EMS exists to advance the cause of world evangelization. We do this through study and evaluation of mission concepts and strategies from a biblical perspective with a view to commending sound mission theory and practice to churches, mission agencies, and schools of missionary training around the world. We hold an annual national conference and eight regional meetings in the United States and Canada.

Other Books in the EMS Series

No. 1 *Scripture and Strategy: The Use of the Bible in Postmodern Church and Mission* | David Hesselgrave

No. 2 *Christianity and the Religions: A Biblical Theology of World Religions* Edward Rommen and Harold Netland

No. 3 *Spiritual Power and Missions: Raising the Issues* | Edward Rommen

No. 4 *Missiology and the Social Sciences: Contributions, Cautions, and Conclusions* | Edward Rommen and Gary Corwin

No. 5 *The Holy Spirit and Mission Dynamics* | Douglas McConnell

No. 6 *Reaching the Resistant: Barriers and Bridges for Mission* Dudley Woodberry

No. 7 *Teaching Them Obedience in All Things: Equipping for the 21st Century* Edgar Elliston

No. 8 *Working Together with God to Shape the New Millennium: Opportunities and Limitations* | Kenneth Mulholland and Gary Corwin

No. 9 *Caring for the Harvest Force in the New Millennium* Tom Steffen and Douglas Pennoyer

No. 10 *Between Past and Future: Evangelical Mission Entering the Twenty-First Century* | Jonathan Bonk

No. 11 *Christian Witness in Pluralistic Contexts in the Twenty-First Century* Enoch Wan

No. 12 *The Centrality of Christ in Contemporary Missions*
        Mike Barnett and Michael Pocock

No. 13 *Contextualization and Syncretism: Navigating Cultural Currents*
        Gailyn Van Rheenen

No. 14 *Business as Mission: From Impoverished to Empowered*
        Tom Steffen and Mike Barnett

No. 15 *Missions in Contexts of Violence* | Keith Eitel

No. 16 *Effective Engagement in Short-Term Missions: Doing It Right!*
        Robert J. Priest

No. 17 *Missions from the Majority World: Progress, Challenges, and Case Studies* | Enoch Wan and Michael Pocock

No. 18 *Serving Jesus with Integrity: Ethics and Accountability in Mission*
        Dwight P. Baker and Douglas Hayward

No. 19 *Reflecting God's Glory Together: Diversity in Evangelical Mission*
        A. Scott Moreau and Beth Snodderly

No. 20 *Reaching the City: Reflections on Urban Mission for the Twenty-First Century* | Gary Fujino, Timothy R. Sisk, and Tereso C. Casino

No. 21 *Missionary Methods: Research, Reflections, and Realities*
        Craig Ott and J. D. Payne

No. 22 *The Missionary Family: Witness, Concerns, Care*
        Dwight P. Baker and Robert J. Priest

No. 23 *Diaspora Missiology: Reflections on Reaching the Scattered Peoples of the World* | Michael Pocock and Enoch Wan

No. 24 *Controversies in Mission: Theology, People, and Practice of Mission in the 21st Century* | Rochelle Cathcart Scheuermann and Edward L. Smither

No. 25 *Churches on Mission: God's Grace Abounding to the Nations*
        Geoffrey Hartt, Christopher R. Little, and John Wang

No. 26 *Majority World Theologies: Self-Theologizing from Africa, Asia, Latin America, and the Ends of the Earth* | Allen Yeh and Tite Tiénou

No. 27 *Against the Tide: Mission Amidst the Global Currents of Secularization*
        W. Jay Moon and Craig Ott

No. 28 *Practicing Hope: Missions and Global Crises*
        Jerry Ireland and Michelle Raven

No. 29 *Advancing Models of Mission: Evaluating the Past and Looking to the Future* | Kenneth Nehrbass, Aminta Arrington, and Narry Santos

Communication in Mission

Global Opportunities and Challenges

Marcus Dean, Scott Moreau, Sue Russell,
and Rochelle Scheuermann, Editors

Evangelical Missiological Society Series no. 30

Communication in Mission: Global Opportunities and Challenges

© 2022 by Evangelical Missiological Society. All rights reserved.

No part of this book may be reproduced, stored in a retrieval system, or transmitted in any form or by any means—electronic, mechanical, photocopy, recording, or otherwise—without prior written permission from the publisher, except brief quotations used in connection with reviews in magazines or newspapers. For permission, email permissions@wclbooks.com. For corrections, email editor@wclbooks.com.

All Scripture quotations, unless otherwise indicated, are taken from the ESV® Bible (The Holy Bible, English Standard Version®), Copyright © 2001 by Crossway, a publishing ministry of Good News Publishers. Used by permission. All rights reserved.

Scripture quotations marked NIV are taken from the Holy Bible, New International Version®, NIV®. Copyright © 1973, 1978, 1984, 2011 by Biblica, Inc.™ Used by permission of Zondervan. All rights reserved worldwide. www.zondervan.com. The "NIV" and "New International Version" are trademarks registered in the United States Patent and Trademark Office by Biblica, Inc.™

Scripture quotations marked NLT are taken from the Holy Bible, New Living Translation, copyright ©1996, 2004, 2015 by Tyndale House Foundation. Used by permission of Tyndale House Publishers, Carol Stream, Illinois 60188. All rights reserved.

Published by William Carey Publishing
10 W. Dry Creek Cir
Littleton, CO 80120 | www.missionbooks.org

William Carey Publishing is a ministry of Frontier Ventures
Pasadena, CA | www.frontierventures.org

Cover and Interior Designer: Mike Riester

ISBNs: 978-1-64508-402-0 (paperback)
    978-1-64508-409-9 (epub)

Printed Worldwide

26 25 24 23 22   1 2 3 4 5   IN

Library of Congress Control Number: 2022945117

Contents

Preface *By Marcus Dean* ix

Part 1: Communicating the Gospel through the Language of Words and Art

Chapter 1: Preaching between Scylla and Charybdis: Sermons and the Task of Contextualization in the Twenty-First Century
By Jared E. Alcántara 3

Chapter 2: The Character of the Incarnation in Preaching with Translators: Principles and Practices
By John Cheong and Rochelle Scheuermann 15

Chapter 3: Missions Application of Translanguaging Theory and Methodologies: Leveraging Multilingualism to Increase Ministry Impact
By Timothy Hatcher 29

Chapter 4: Hidden Stories of Reciprocal Mission in the Glocal World: A Case Study *By Joy Kim* 41

Part 2: Communicating the Gospel in Global Settings

Chapter 5: Knowing When to Drink Coffee: A Case Study of (Mis)Communication in Intercultural Mission Partnership
By Phil Davis 53

Chapter 6: Contextualizing the Gospel in Australia: Empowering Christ to Communicate with an Aussie Accent
By Robert L. Gallagher 67

Chapter 7: Honor/Shame Culture: Analyzing Impact on Christian Women's Social Exchanges
By Kara L. Garrison 85

Chapter 8: Conversing with Unique Identities: American Muslim Youth in a Multicultural Religiously Plural World
By Matthew Henning 99

Part 3: Communicating Well in Mission

Chapter 9: Communicating a Decolonized Gospel
By Theon E. Hill 115

Chapter 10: Pursuing Textual Community with a Chinese House Church Movement
By Hannah Nation 127

Chapter 11: Communicating a Missions Theology through the Prism of the Black Church: A Case Study *By Linda P. Saunders* 137

Chapter 12: **Faithful Fundraising:** Communicating Needs without Sacrificing Dignity or Short-Circuiting Discipleship
By Jessica Udall   149

Part 4: Communicating Mission through Social Media

Chapter 13: **The Medium Is the Message:** Reflections on Disciple-Making in the Age of Social Media
By Michael Hamkin Lee   163

Chapter 14: **Communicating for the Frontiers:** How Communication in the Twenty-First Century Impacts Mission in Restricted-Access Contexts
By J. T. Matthews   177

Chapter 15: **Understanding the Written Word through Popular Culture in Japan**
By Song Joseph Cho   191

About the Contributors and Editors   203

Figures

Figure 2.1 Cross-Cultural Preaching: Triple Hermeneutic	17
Figure 2.2 Translated Preaching: Triple Hermeneutic, Maximized and Minimized	18
Figure 2.3 Incarnational Model of Translated Preaching	25
Figure 4.1 Bo Shi Self-Portrait	46
Figure 6.1 Features of Effective Mateship Evangelism	82
Figure 7.1 Hindrances to Trusting Relationships	88
Figure 7.2 Narrative Themes Regarding Implicit Hierarchy from Myanmar Christian Women	90
Figure 13.1 McLuhan's Tetrad: A Framework to Assess the Impact of Media	166
Figure 14.1 Data Visualization of Facebook Relationships	181
Figure 14.2 Adoption of AI Surveillance Practices by Global Regions	183

Tables

Table 3.1 Key Terms Comparison Chart: Justified (Headland 2013)	36
Table 6.1 Comparison of Christianity and Australian Culture (author created)	71
Table 6.2 Comparison of Anglicanism and Australian Culture (author created)	73
Table 6.3 Comparison of Anglicanism and Aussie Mateship (author created)	75
Table 6.4 Models of Mateship Evangelism (author created)	79

Preface

We live in a time in which we are bombarded by what we could call hyper-communication. From social media to a plethora of advertisements to around the clock TV and cable news, we are surrounded by communication. Someone or some company is continuously clamoring for our attention, usually for their economic gain. Perhaps due to the over-abundance of these communication efforts, the messages get louder and more brazen. Our senses can easily be overloaded! It becomes hard to communicate about what is really important.

In this environment, gaining people's attention with the good news of the Bible is an increasing challenge. In the missions task, we likewise face louder and more diverse competing messages that make the gospel seem like less than good news. The communicative approach of the church needs to become more meaningful and more effective than the efforts of our societies. I am reminded of Elijah's encounter with God in 1 Kings 19. As per Elijah's need, God was not in the loud wind, the earthquake, or the fire, but in a *gentle whisper* (1 Kgs 19:12 NIV, emphasis mine). God spoke softly to Elijah so that his message came through; today we must not only focus on the message of the gospel, but also on how it is delivered. Hence the theme from the 2021 EMS Conference: Communication(s) in Mission.

This compendium brings together a variety of voices that speak to global missions and the task of communication and mission. Some of the voices may seem like shouts and others like gentle whispers, but each has an important contribution for all who will listen and learn. While these chapters provide only a brief exploration of the theme, each author lays a foundation upon which others in the mission community can build so that the task of communicating God's love in our needy world will move forward with grace and greater relevance. It is the goal of the editors that through this volume the church will be better able to communicate the gospel in ways that capture attention and speak to the heart of each recipient. May the Holy Spirit guide our learning!

—Marcus Dean

Part 1

Communicating the Gospel through the Language of Words and Art

In these opening chapters the authors focus on the spoken word, whether through preaching, the use of translanguaging, or storytelling. Based on his plenary message, Jared Alcántara reminds the reader of the importance of our words when we preach the gospel. The sermon is a joint proclamation of the preacher and the church sharing a contextualized message with the community. Alcántara guides the reader in thinking not only about the need for contextualization, but the dangers of both syncretism (over-contextualization) and under-contextualization. The reader is challenged to find balance between culture and the good news, between the familiar and the transformational.

John Cheong and Rochelle Scheuermann present various aspects to be considered when preaching the gospel through a translator. These authors point out the breadth and depth of the dynamics of preaching including hermeneutics, the interaction of the preacher and interpreter, communication styles and context, and the role of the Holy Spirit.

Timothy Hatcher highlights the challenge found in multilingual communities, which use language differently than in monolingual contexts and even in standard translation between two or more languages. Multilingual people not only speak multiple languages, but often combine their languages to achieve a unique identity and style of communication. Those engaged in missions in a multilingual context need to learn to engage in translanguaging, the process of merging language experiences in real life contexts as the local speakers do.

Finally, Joy Kim discusses the importance of storytelling among immigrants and refugees. She shares stories from personal experiences that embody the truth of the gospel and connect with the arts, worship, and mission. Kim's goal is to illustrate the connection of the *missio Dei*, people on the move, and the body of Christ. Through this intersection we are better connected in the multilingual and multicultural story God is writing that reaches across cultures and extends around the globe.

—MARCUS DEAN

Chapter 1

Preaching between Scylla & Charybdis

Sermons and the Task of Contextualization
in the Twenty-First Century

Jared E. Alcántara

Homiletics concerns itself with the faithful and fitting proclamation of God's Word in service to God's people, the church, so that they might hear it, be transformed by it, and bear witness to it in the world. The ministry of proclamation features the preaching of the Word by a person but is not limited to that person's scope or office. The scope of proclamation extends beyond the event of public preaching since the Word announces good news whenever it is used as a wise teacher to the young or the old, as spiritual milk to the new disciple, as life and strength in small group communities, and as a comforting balm to those who suffer. Proclamation finds its center in and through the office of the preacher, even its catalytic spark, but it only achieves its ultimate aim when it belongs to the Body of Christ. The preacher's job is not so much to preach for the sake of the church as it is to help the church preach for the sake of the world. P. T. Forsyth (1970, 79) reminds us of this great responsibility in his famed 1907 Yale Beecher Lectures on Preaching when he exclaims: "The one great preacher in history, I would contend, is the Church. And the first business of the individual preacher is to enable the Church to preach."

Whether the task is proclamation in a general sense or preaching in a specific sense, a wise and skillful preacher knows how to chart a path between gospel fidelity and contextual propriety, between "faithfulness and fittingness," to use terms from homiletician Leonora Tubbs Tisdale (1997). One strives toward faithfulness to the gospel through rightly handling the Word that announces it while also striving to be fitting to the people to whom the Word is preached in a manner that is clear, accessible, and intelligible. The one who proclaims the Word must somehow honor God and reach people; otherwise, he or she has failed to love one or the other, the God of the gospel or the people to whom the gospel of God is preached. What is needed, Tisdale (1997, 31) argues, is a two-fold aim: "Preaching which not only aims toward greater faithfulness to the gospel of Jesus Christ but which also aims toward greater 'fittingness' (in content, form, and style) for a particular congregation."

No doubt, Tisdale's two-fold aim strikes a chord among those scholars, pastors, missionaries, and students who wrestle with the challenges of contextualization and who train themselves in the work of contextualizing. Exciting opportunities come about when Christians engage in fruitful discussions about this subject, especially when concrete decisions and actions follow. Alongside these opportunities, we also find the pain associated with failures to contextualize well. So much ground is lost in gospel work when people fail to be fitting to the spaces where they serve.

Tisdale's reminder to preachers to balance faithfulness and fittingness comes with much greater force in a similar warning about balance made by a leader in intercultural studies. This leader offers an admonishment to help practitioners appreciate what is at stake. In *A Word in Season*, Lesslie Newbigin (1994) warns against two opposing dangers which he refers to as "the Scylla and Charybdis between which one must steer" (67). Irrelevance lurks as a monster on one side, an under-contextualized approach that forsakes people. Syncretism lurks as a monster on the other side, an over-contextualized approach that forsakes orthodoxy. "Every missionary path," Newbigin writes, "must find the way between the two dangers. And if one is more afraid of one than the other, one will certainly fall into the opposite" (67).

But, how do we chart this path? How do we navigate the dangers between which we must steer? How do we preach "between Scylla and Charybdis"? To get at the answer, we need to understand the question better. Thus, at the outset, I will put the question into conversation with the larger modern contextualization conversation. Then, I will discuss the perils of under-contextualization and over-contextualization. Finally, at the end, I will imagine what preaching between Scylla and Charybdis might sound like now and in the future.

The Rise of Modern Contextualization Discussions[1]

In his seminal article, "Critical Contextualization," published in 1987, Paul G. Hiebert contends that most of the history of modern Western missions before 1950 is a history of under-contextualized witness (1987, 76; later as a book chapter in Hiebert 1994). In exceptional cases, the missionaries who prioritized contextualization encountered resistance, whether it was a hermeneutic of suspicion from those who opposed their work or under-appreciation

---

[1] Some paragraphs in this section have been adapted from my 2020 article in *Trinity Journal* (Alcántara 2020, 185–98). See pp. 190–92 in particular.

from those who believed that their work was second order to gospel work. Among Roman Catholics, Hiebert mentions Jesuit missionaries to India who had their efforts to contextualize challenged and undermined by Franciscan missionaries who said that the Jesuits had forsaken the gospel in their attempts to contextualize. Among Protestant missionaries, Hiebert mentions those who labored to learn Indian languages, and who later wrote dictionaries, booklets, and hymns in English and German. Their work played an important role in the cross-cultural learning and interest that followed, but their names were not lifted up as heroes to emulate. Hiebert could have mentioned other names as positive examples, such as Hudson Taylor or William Cameron Townsend. However, his larger point was this: under-contextualization was more the norm and good contextualization the exception (Hiebert 1994, 76).

After 1950, a number of important discussions emerged both in Roman Catholicism and Protestantism. Post-Vatican II, three Catholic theologians—Robert Schreiter (1997, 2007), Aylward Shorter (1988), and Stephen Bevans (2002)—advanced important discussions about "inculturation," the term they preferred to "contextualization." In more recent years, the Latinx Catholic theologian Orlando Espín (2007) has advanced the conversation, opting for "interculturality" over inculturation. It should be noted here that while Bevans' work advanced discussions on contextualization, some of his models also leaned toward a syncretistic and over-contextualized approach to mission.

In the 1950s and into the 1960s, Protestants usually used the language of adaptation or inculturation to describe cross-cultural work, language that gave way later to terms such as indigenization and indigeneity in the late 1960s and early 1970s. However, in 1972, Taiwanese theologian Shoki Coe (1972, 21) challenged scholars to adopt the language of contextualization, which he said was "a more dynamic concept which is open to change and which is future oriented." That same year, the Theological Education Fund argued for the same term, contextualization, which they described as a "theological necessity demanded by the incarnational nature of the Word" (Theological Education Fund Staff 1972, 20).

Since that time, a number of models of contextualization have emerged, such as Charles H. Kraft's "dynamic equivalence" model in the 1970s, David Hesselgrave's work on communicating Christ cross-culturally, also in the 1970s, Paul Hiebert's work on critical cultural contextualization in the late 1980s, and Lamin Sanneh's translation model in the late 1980s (Kraft 1973; Hiebert 1987; Hesselgrave 1991; Sanneh 2009). In the last thirty years, other theorists also made significant contributions, such as Dean Gilliland, Tite Tiénou, Marc Cortez, Charles Van Engen, Andrew F. Walls,

Orlando E. Costas, and A. Scott Moreau, though it should be noted that some of them were integral to the conversations that took place in the 1970s and 1980s (e.g., Orlando Costas' work at the Lausanne Congress in 1974).[2]

A growing body of research on contextualization in homiletics has also emerged over the last fifty years. The first trajectory of scholarship is *congregational studies*. Through interviews, surveys, and other forms of evaluation and assessment, those who have published works in congregational studies have focused on what listeners hear and experience during sermons (Howe 1967; Allen 2004; McClure et al., 2004). In so doing, homileticians have sought to lessen the gap between the sender and the receiver in communication. A second trajectory is *minoritized voices* speaking out with greater frequency and fervency about preaching in minoritized preaching traditions. In addition to making original contributions to advance the field, these publications forced majority-culture homileticians to recognize, one, that preaching is neither monolithic nor univocal and, two, that some of the claims made about the pulpit and the pew do not necessarily apply when we interrogate White normative assumptions about preaching (Mitchell 1990; Taylor 1977; Arrastía 1992; González and Jiménez 2005; Kim 1999). The final trajectory concerns itself with the *process of contextualization*. By process I mean the *how* of contextualizing in light of the forces that shape the beliefs, attitudes, habits, and practices of listeners. One of the more popular resources in evangelicalism is Timothy J. Keller's *Preaching: Communicating Faith in an Age of Skepticism* (2015). Keller challenges pastors to contextualize by engaging the secular mind and heart of the non-believer, interrogating the secular web of beliefs to which believers and non-believers are held captive, and presenting the gospel of Christ as the antidote both to irreligion and to religion. One of the more popular resources in mainline liberalism is Leonora Tubbs Tisdale's *Preaching as Local Theology and Folk Art* (1997). Tisdale encourages pastors to become local ethnographers of their congregations, students of context and its sources. These and other resources like them have advanced discussions in homiletics in recent decades.

The Dangers of Under- and Over-Contextualization

Now that I have traced the development of modern contextualization discussions both in intercultural studies and homiletics, I will deal with the Scylla and the Charybdis, that is, the dangers of under-contextualization and over-contextualization, perils that preachers must navigate in order to be faithful in preaching and witness.

---

[2] For an excellent summary of the various models that have emerged, see Moreau 2012.

Under-Contextualization

First, we will consider the Scylla of under-contextualization. Perhaps a story taken from cultural anthropology will help us recognize what under-contextualization looks like in cross-cultural mission. Drawing on his work with the Aguaruna people in northern Peru, Robert J. Priest (2006) tells an apocryphal tale about a young missionary named "Dave," a tale that is intended to be hyperbolic and that will be paraphrased here.

Dave has just graduated from a North American seminary, and he goes at once to northern Peru as a missionary to serve the thirty-five thousand Aguaruna people. On the one hand, Dave is prepared. He has a good handle on Scripture and knows how to exegete biblical texts. He has a firm grasp of Christian doctrine. He has helpful frameworks for thinking and acting theologically in concrete situations. Perhaps he has even taken courses in psychology and anthropology at seminary that no doubt will assist him in communicating cross-culturally.

On the other hand, Dave is *not* prepared at all. In seminary, he learned about foundational Christian doctrines such as the "nature of sin, its origins, its transmission, its extent, and its effects," but he departs for northern Peru with little to no "corresponding understanding of Aguaruna moral discourses and sensibilities" (Priest 2006, 186). When he arrives, Dave searches for a word in the Aguaruna language that captures all the nuances that the English word "sin" captures, but he does not find it. As a result, he does what many others do: he talks about sins in the plural instead of sin in the singular, and then searches for evidences of sins in the communal life of the Aguaruna. The problem is that the Aguaruna do not see the public sins that he identifies as morally reprehensible. If these were, in fact, sins, then why would the Aguaruna be so public about them? Would not the natural impulse be to hide them? Dave believes that his monogamous marriage and refusal to imbibe the powerful alcoholic drink *nijamanch* communicate that he is living a morally virtuous lifestyle. However, the Aguaruna interpret his monogamy as a failure to care for vulnerable women in the society and his abstaining from *nijamanch* as an anti-communitarian and self-serving act. As Priest (187) puts it, they do not "see these as virtues and may judge him morally deficient on other grounds."

In a show of hospitality, Dave's hosts invite him to a communal meal in which people crouch down in a circle and eat from the same common plate. Unlike in his home context in the United States, he now lives in a society where food is in short supply, especially protein like meat. Dave's hosts have not eaten meat for two days, but they do something that is both virtuous and generous. They share their meat with him. Every Aguaruna child learns from an early age that one is supposed to eat small amounts of meat and larger amounts of manioc, a starch that Dave thinks is flavorless. But, Dave does just the opposite. He eats large amounts of meat and small amounts of manioc. Not only are his actions considered juvenile—parents scold their children for eating too much meat—they are also considered immoral. As Priest (187) puts it, "Dave is likely to be seen as the worst kind of glutton, an *estsemjau*, a 'meat glutton.'" Dave thinks he is living as a *tsadiq*, in Hebrew, a "righteous person." However, his refusal to drink *nijamanch*, his public display of meat gluttony, along with many other cultural faux-pas communicate to the Aguaruna that he is not a morally virtuous person at all. He wants to warn the Aguaruna about the dangers of sin, but almost everything he does among them communicates that he is a sinful and dangerous person, even if he intends otherwise. Dave comes across as anti-community, gluttonous, sexually immoral, anti-women, stingy, and inhospitable. More important, Dave's failure to contextualize incapacitates his mission in northern Peru, and it erodes his legitimacy among the people he feels called to serve. Dave does not need an under-contextualized framework that separates mission from theology or theology from mission, but rather a more synthetic approach, what Priest (195) refers to as "missional theologizing."

> Many of today's preachers assume that the behaviors that make sense to them will automatically make sense to those to whom they minister.

Although the apocryphal tale about Dave is meant to be hyperbolic, one could argue that the same proclivities that reveal themselves in Dave's witness to the Aguaruna in Peru also arise among preachers in North America. Call them family resemblances. Usually because of naivete and sometimes due to arrogance, many of today's preachers assume that the behaviors that make sense to them will automatically make sense to those to whom they minister, that the language they speak in the pulpit is the same language that people speak everywhere, that the frameworks they have are the frameworks that are most accessible, that knowledge of how things operated in the ancient world is the same as discernment for how to live wisely in the modern world, or that a preoccupation with sins in the plural is the same as a robust doctrine of sin in the singular.

In his book *Preaching: A Kind of Folly*, Ian Pitt-Watson (1978) draws much-needed attention to this gap, especially in communication. According to him, most preachers speak the "language of Canaan," but most people speak the "language of Babylon." The language of Canaan does play an important role, but what is needed now more than ever is for preachers to speak better Babylonian (Pitt-Watson 1978, 52). The problem with under-contextualized sermons,

Haddon Robinson (2014, 47–48) claims, is that they use "coded language never heard in the marketplace, [they] dabble in great biblical concepts, but the audience feels that God belonged to the long ago and far away."

Believers in Christ understand that God does not belong to "the long ago and far away." Under-contextualized preaching, however, tries to locate God there rather than here. It concerns itself more with the fact that Jesus lived than the hope that Jesus lives. It wrestles with, "*Did* Jesus walk on water?" when the question most listeners ask is, "*Does* Jesus walk on water?" Robinson (2014, 47–48) puts it this way: "Expositors must not only answer the questions our fathers and mothers asked; they must wrestle with the questions our children ask."

Over-Contextualization

Now that we have discussed the Scylla of under-contextualization, we will consider the Charybdis, that is, over-contextualization—the opposite danger to be confronted in order to be faithful in preaching and witness. Here, Newbigin's thoughts on the matter will assist us. Upon returning to England after decades of missionary service in India, Newbigin discovered that the England he returned to was far more syncretistic than Christian. It just so happens that syncretism is not just a Southern and Eastern problem; it is also a Northern and Western problem. In his description of English theology, Newbigin (1994, 67) writes: "Ours is an advanced case of syncretism ... instead of confronting our culture with the gospel, we are perpetually trying to fit the gospel into our culture." By the phrase "our culture," Newbigin means a post-Enlightenment, scientific, and secular framework that separates fact from value and public knowledge from private faith, a way of seeing and being that is not so much a worldview as it is an ideology. Ironically and tragically, in the spaces where it is announced that Jesus is the Messiah, new messiahs inevitably appear. Wherever there is a distortion of the gospel, an uptick in ideology will follow. Here is how Newbigin (1989, 122) puts it in *The Gospel in a Pluralist Society*:

> The coming into the world of the promise of total salvation, of a radically new age, precipitates at the same time the appearing of those who offer salvation on other terms. Therefore it will not only be the old paganisms that fight against the Church, but also the new messianisms. Wherever the gospel is preached, new ideologies appear—secular humanism, nationalism, Marxism—movements which offer the vision of a new age, an age freed from all the ills that beset human life, freed from hunger and disease and war.

So, what is the point here? Yes, we find ideologies in every space in which the gospel is preached and, yes, we find syncretistic versions of the faith in every hemisphere. But, Newbigin seems to have a special interest in challenging over-contextualized versions of the faith in Western Christianity, perhaps because he is so troubled by the subtlety and perniciousness of it. Western Christianity, he claims, has succumbed to a form of "cultural captivity" that cannot be remedied without serious effort and ongoing intercession. Western society is not so much a secular society as it is a pagan society born out of a rejection of Christianity and an embrace of pseudo-gospels in its place (Newbigin 1994, 66). A society like this, he argues in *Foolishness to the Greeks*, is "far more resistant to the gospel than the pre-Christian paganism with which cross-cultural missions have been familiar. Here, surely, is the most challenging missionary frontier of our time" (Newbigin 1986, 20).

If Newbigin is right, then Christian preachers have their work cut out for them. We should learn to speak better Babylonian, but we should also steer clear of the seductive power of trusting in Babylonian gods as a result. We should wrestle with the questions our children ask, yes, but we should also take seriously the expectation of Psalm 78:4 (NIV): "We will tell the next generation the praiseworthy deeds of the Lord; his power, and the wonders he has done."

Without a balance, we might succumb to syncretistic preaching. It comes in many forms. Syncretistic preaching displays *theological* distortions. H. Richard Niebuhr predicted much of what we see today back in 1959. In his book *The Kingdom of God in America*, Niebuhr (1959, 193) describes our theologies in this succinct statement: "A God without wrath who sent man without sin into a kingdom without judgment through the ministrations of a Christ without a cross."

Syncretistic preaching has *political* distortions. This is another way of saying ideology tied to political allegiance. When a preacher does this, he or she sounds more like Amaziah the priest defending the king of Bethel's reputation than the prophet Amos defending God's reputation (Amos 7:10–17). One cannot be a faithful preacher and a sycophant of the state at one and the same time.

We find *nationalistic* distortions in various ideologies such as colonialism, imperialism, racism, and ethnocentrism. If you want to find concrete examples of nationalistic syncretism, just type in "Christian worship service and the Fourth of July" into Google, and you will find all the examples that you need. In all seriousness, how can there be contextually faithful preaching in spaces where national, cultural, or ethnic superiority reigns supreme? Lamin Sanneh, in his book *Translating the Message* (2009), claims that such a stance contradicts the spirit of the gospel itself. He writes: "The gospel demands frontier crossing for its wider transmission, and it is contradictory to its spirit to invoke cultural hegemony as the prerequisite of conveying God's truth" (Sanneh 2009, 34).

Lastly, we find *culture-commodifying* distortions. In a preacher's quest to be popular, he or she could fail to be faithful. Too many preachers prioritize branding, promotion, and celebrity, often in ways that are subtle enough to remain hidden. They demonstrate a form of popular relevance through familiarity with pop culture, but they often lack the interpersonal investment required to be the pastors that God has called them to be. They might have gifts as dynamic communicators but, in the end, they do not utilize these gifts to say much about God. They spend little time opening the one book that matters most; their sermons sound more like TED Talks than the faithful and fitting proclamation of God's Word. If I might paraphrase the well-known Lutheran preacher Paul Scherer (1965, 7), the problem with meeting people where they are at is that usually they are in the wrong place.

Preaching between Scylla and Charybdis

So, where do we go from here? Now that we have discussed the second danger, that of over-contextualization, we will turn back toward the question that we posed earlier: "How do we preach between Scylla and Charybdis?" Put more precisely, how do we strive toward contextually responsive preaching that is both faithful to the gospel and fitting to the situation? I will offer at least a provisional answer to promote deeper thought and further reflection.

First, contextually responsive preaching sounds like sermons that are both *rational and rhetorical.* Of course, we still need preaching that gives people reasons for their faith, that appeals to their minds, especially since some of the most powerful secularizing forces in North America are housed in our universities. That stated, we also need preaching that takes seriously the significance of language, that honors the force of sacred eloquence in service to Christ. We live in a society marked by testimony, story, poetics, and secondary orality. Some preaching already accesses these domains, often in minoritized contexts. If we do not engage people at these levels, then they will find their most compelling stories and songs somewhere else.

Second, contextually responsive preaching sounds like sermons that are both *identificational and transformational.* Here, I borrow language from Dean Flemming in *Contextualization in the New Testament* (2005). In his study of the apostle Paul's preaching in the book of Acts, Flemming observes that Paul opted for both identification and transformation rather than one or the other. Paul was able to find a magnificent balance between, on the one hand, an *identificational* approach that proclaims the gospel in ways the audience can understand and, on the other, a *transformational* approach that resists compromising the gospel's integrity in a pluralistic world. *This is a challenge that every preacher must face.* (Flemming 2005, 86, emphasis added)

To say that the gospel is identificational is to say that it can reach anyone and everyone everywhere by the grace of God and through the diligence of people who will do anything short of sinning to reach people with the gospel. To say that the gospel is transformational is to claim that it challenges our false allegiances and alliances, calls for rejection of our idols, and expects radical repentance and transformation not only in individuals but also in systems, structures, and nations.

Third, contextually responsive preaching sounds like sermons that are both *locally contingent and interculturally competent*. At the local level, we need preaching that is contingent to our time and place, to the people to whom we are preaching. Call it a local accent, if you will, a manner that makes our language more accessible and intelligible in the place where we minister. The well-known homiletician Fred Craddock (1985, 98, emphasis added) puts it better than I could when he writes, "Whatever may be provided a preacher by any and all resources, it is only when *local soil* has been added that the sermon will take root and flourish." But, we also need preaching that engages at the intercultural level. We need sharp increases in intercultural competence by which I mean "the cultivation of knowledge, skills, and habits for effectively negotiating cultural, racial, and ecclesial difference" (Alcántara 2015, 30). Preachers who cultivate intercultural competence are willing to do the hard work of interrogating their own cultural values and blind spots, calling into question their syncretistic proclivities and, most important to the work of global Christianity, challenging themselves to become border crossers in obedience to Christ. We belong first and foremost to God, but we also belong one to another. We belong to the communion of saints, past and present. Until we learn to speak to one another, we will continue to speak past one another.

Conclusion

The challenge is as it has always been, to navigate between extremes rather than to let the tide pull us too far in one direction or the other. In the challenge, we also find a potential opportunity, one that many early Christians embraced in seeking to build outposts of heaven, spaces that were faithful and fitting, timeless and timely. The anonymous writer of the *Epistle to Diognetus,* describes them this way: "every foreign land is to them a fatherland and every fatherland a foreign land" (Radford 1908, 63). Perhaps the challenge is an opportunity after all.

References Cited

Alcántara, Jared E. 2015. *Crossover Preaching: Intercultural-Improvisational Homiletics in Conversation with Gardner C. Taylor.* Downers Grove, IL: IVP Academic.

Alcántara, Jared E. 2020. "Sermons with 'Local Soil': Cultivating Contextually Responsive Preachers." *Trinity Journal* 41: 185–98.

Allen, Ronald J. 2004. *Hearing the Sermon: Relationship, Content, Feeling.* St. Louis: Chalice.

Arrastía, Cecilio. 1992. *Teoría y Práctica de La Predicación.* Miami: Editorial Caribe.

Bevans, Stephen B. 2002. *Models of Contextual Theology.* Maryknoll, NY: Orbis.

Coe, Shoki. 1972. "Contextualizing Theology." In *Third World Theologies*, edited by Gerald H. Anderson and Thomas F. Stransky, 10–24. Grand Rapids, MI: Eerdmans.

Craddock, Fred B. 1985. *Preaching.* Nashville: Abingdon.

Espín, Orlando O. 2007. *Grace and Humanness: Theological Reflections Because of Culture.* Maryknoll, NY: Orbis Books.

Flemming, Dean S. 2005. *Contextualization in the New Testament: Patterns for Theology and Mission.* Downers Grove, IL: InterVarsity Press.

Forsyth, P. T. 1907. *Positive Preaching and the Modern Mind.* London: Hodder & Stoughton.

González, Justo L., and Pablo A. Jiménez. 2005. *Púlpito: An Introduction to Hispanic Preaching.* Nashville: Abingdon.

Hesselgrave, David J. 1991. *Communicating Christ Cross-Culturally: An Introduction to Missionary Communication.* Grand Rapids, MI: Zondervan.

Hiebert, Paul G. 1987. "Critical Contextualization." *International Bulletin of Missionary Research* 11, no. 3 (July): 104–12.

Hiebert, Paul G. 1994. *Anthropological Reflections on Missiological Issues.* Grand Rapids, MI: Baker.

Howe, Reuel L. 1967. *Partners in Preaching: Clergy and Laity in Dialogue.* New York: Seabury.

Keller, Timothy. 2015. *Preaching: Communicating Faith in an Age of Skepticism.* New York: Penguin.

Kim, Eunjoo Mary. 1999. *Preaching the Presence of God: A Homiletic from an Asian American Perspective.* Valley Forge, PA: Judson.

Kraft, Charles H. 1973. "Dynamic Equivalence Churches: An Ethnotheological Approach to Indigeneity." *Missiology: An International Review* 1, no. 1 (January 1): 39–57.

McClure, John S., Ronald J. Allen, Dale P. Andrews, and L. Susan Bond, eds. 2004. *Listening to Listeners: Homiletical Case Studies.* St. Louis: Chalice.

Mitchell, Henry H. 1990. *Black Preaching: The Recovery of a Powerful Art.* Nashville: Abingdon.

Moreau, A. Scott. 2012. *Contextualization in World Missions: Mapping and Assessing Evangelical Models*. Grand Rapids, MI: Kregel.

Newbigin, Lesslie. 1986. *Foolishness to the Greeks: The Gospel and Western Culture*. Grand Rapids, MI: Eerdmans.

Newbigin, Lesslie. 1989. *The Gospel in a Pluralist Society*. Grand Rapids, MI: Eerdmans.

Newbigin, Lesslie. 1994. *A Word in Season: Perspectives on Christian World Missions*. Grand Rapids, MI: Eerdmann.

Niebuhr, H. Richard. 1959. *The Kingdom of God in America*. New York: Harper & Row.

Pitt-Watson, Ian. 1978. *Preaching: A Kind of Folly*. Philadelphia: Westminster.

Priest, Robert J. 2006. "'Experience-Near Theologizing' in Diverse Human Contexts." In *Globalizing Theology: Belief and Practice in an Era of World Christianity*, edited by Craig Ott and Harold A. Netland, 180–95. Grand Rapids, MI: Baker Academic.

Radford, Lewis Bostock, ed. 1908. *The Epistle to Diognetus*. New York: SPCK.

Robinson, Haddon W. 2014. *Biblical Preaching: The Development and Delivery of Expository Messages*. Grand Rapids, MI: Baker Academic.

Sanneh, Lamin. 2009. *Translating the Message: The Missionary Impact on Culture*. Maryknoll, NY: Orbis.

Scherer, Paul. 1965. *The Word God Sent*. New York: Harper & Row.

Schreiter, Robert J. 1997. *The New Catholicity: Theology Between the Global and the Local*. Maryknoll, NY: Orbis.

Schreiter, Robert J. 2015. *Constructing Local Theologies*. Maryknoll, NY: Orbis.

Shorter, Aylward. 1988. *Toward a Theology of Inculturation*. Maryknoll, NY: Orbis.

Taylor, Gardner C. 1977. *How Shall They Preach? The Lyman Beecher Lectures and Five Lenten Sermons*. Elgin, IL: Progressive Baptist Publishing House.

Theological Education Fund Staff. 1972. *Ministry in Context: The Third Mandate Programme of the Theological Education Fund* (1970–77). Bromley, England: Theological Education Fund Staff.

Tisdale, Leonora Tubbs. 1997. *Preaching as Local Theology and Folk Art*. Minneapolis: Fortress.

Chapter 2

The Character of the Incarnation in Preaching with Translators
Principles and Practices

John Cheong and Rochelle Scheuermann

There are many mission books on Bible translation, interpretation, and cross-cultural communication (e.g., Hesselgrave 1991; Kraft 2005; Moreau, Campbell, and Greener 2014; Sanneh 2009), fewer on cross-cultural preaching, but none on a theology and missiology of preaching with translators, even though interpreted preaching is practiced worldwide every week. The same is true in homiletics, with few works on sermon translation or interpreting, and none fully addressing the theology and social dynamics of working with translators in multicultural congregations, even though multiculturalism is growing in today's societies (Downie 2014, 1). Of the few cross-cultural preaching textbooks, most are relatively dated and written from a homiletical rather than missiological perspective. Two recent works, Matthew Kim's *Preaching with Cultural Intelligence* (2017) and Jared Alcántara's *Cross-Over Preaching* (2015) dialogue with partners largely from 2000 to 2006. Little else spans the field. With regards to interpreted preaching, Parish (2018, 231) says research is "largely focused within the disciplines of linguistics and interpretation" and, thus, has "failed to explore the preacher's role in co-producing the sermon or to consider the theological and homiletical implications of what is happening in this shared preaching space" (30). She identifies Downie (2014) as the first to consider the homiletical importance of interpreted preaching. His 2016 doctoral research draws on some homiletical concepts but overall remains within linguistics and intercultural studies. Parish's study is "the first in-depth research undertaken in theology and specifically with a focus on interpreted preaching in a mission context" (2018, 190). In this chapter, we draw from Downie and Parish's arguments that interpreted preaching has a distinct theology and practice of homiletics, and integrate these with missiological insights on communication, translation, and culture.

Interpreted preaching, according to Parish (2018, 1–2) "encapsulates and embodies a greater sense of what is occurring in the preaching act," conveying "the complex interplay that takes place when two (or more) people share the preaching space." Historically, interpreted preaching often preceded or stimulated new church plants since many people groups did not have a written language prior to missionaries' arrival (Parish 2018, 8). Today, we use translators when there is/are 1) a missionary not fluent in the many languages spoken, 2) a large refugee population, 3) occasional travel to nearby places without having language fluency, or 4) short-term missionaries or visiting speakers asked to preach (Kuligin 2008, 1). In every case, an interpreter is used and viewed as "a by-product of the nature of global missions" (Parish 2018, 182).

We do not advocate using translators in *all* cross-cultural preaching nor minimize the importance of language-learning. We write to address those who must work with translators due to the reasons above and to ameliorate the theological deficits in the missiology and homiletics of interpreted preaching.

In our chapter, we argue that the preaching-translating dynamic is rooted and reflected in the character of the incarnation and its relation to communication in mission. The incarnation has been used to provide theological support for missionary identification, holistic ministry and liberation, contextualization, inculturation of the church, and manifesting the life of Christ (Ott 2010, 98–102). Our missiological and homiletical basis for interpreted preaching will relate to all these senses of incarnation except for holistic ministry.

Situating Translation within Cross-Cultural Communication

In a mono-cultural preaching event, the preacher interprets the Scriptural text, then encodes a message which the audience must decode or interpret. When the audience understands the message the preacher intended, communication successfully occurs. While many factors enhance or detract from message transmission (word choice, tone, volume, non-verbal language, environment, etc.), when preacher and audience share more dimensions, meaning is easier to transmit and receive.

In cross-cultural preaching, preachers shoulder the added responsibility of minimizing communication loss or distortion by encoding the message in a way that best matches the audience. Such "receptor-oriented" (Kraft 2005, 67) preaching requires sufficient cultural knowledge about the audience's language, values, beliefs, and worldview, and sufficient socio-cultural relationship between preacher and audience. Receptor-oriented practices include 1) using language and imagery that enables the audience to more easily decode the intended message, 2) honoring cultural practices, values, beliefs, and worldviews as much as possible, 3) connecting with everyday life experiences of the audience, 4) displaying culturally appropriate body language, dress, and emotion, and 5) honoring the audience's ideal sermon, preacher, and approach to the Bible (see Cathcart 2011; Anderson 2012; Cathcart 2012; Choi 2012; Kim 2017; Priest 2012; and Tarr 2012). For the message to be received, the preacher engages in a triple hermeneutic. First, she engages the text such that the message she intends to communicate accurately reflects the intended Scriptural message. This is a cross-cultural reading because the preacher must bridge the "distance between the biblical texts and [the preacher's] own world and perspective" (Brown 2007, 125). Next, the preacher translates the intended Scripture message into the audience's language and culture, minimizing the effort the audience must expend to decode the message so that as much of the intended message gets across as possible (see figure 2.1). Most of this translation process takes place in and through the preacher.

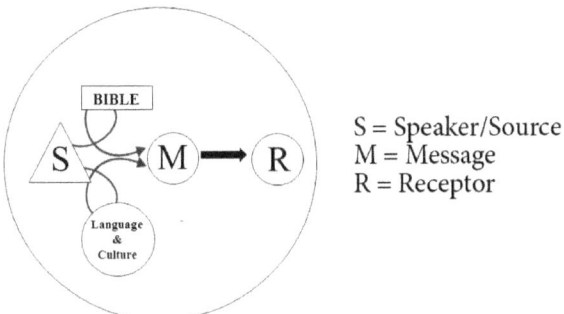

Figure 2.1 Cross-Cultural Preaching: Triple Hermeneutic
(used with permission from Robert J. Priest)

Preaching-translation changes the cross-cultural communication flow because, while the preacher still engages in receptor-oriented practices, the linguistic and cultural barriers between preacher and audience produces "cultural gaps ... where the preacher is not able or is unaware to contextualize the culture-specific elements of the sermon" (Parish 2018, 45). The translator steps into this space, interpreting the preacher's (verbal and non-verbal) message and making requisite adjustments to it to "prevent misunderstandings, or smooth them" (Parish 2018, 45 citing Tison), thereby enabling the audience to comprehend the intended message. This leads the preacher toward what we call a *minimized* triple-hermeneutic (see figure 2.2) since the preacher is limited in her cultural and linguistic engagement. This also leads the translator toward a *maximized* triple-hermeneutic because the translator not only interprets and encodes the preacher's full verbal and non-verbal message for the audience, the translator also needs sufficient Scriptural knowledge to ensure coherence between the Scriptural message, the preacher's message, and the translator's encoded message. Giving space for adjustments during the encoding process to prevent and respond to misunderstandings is, thus, "an important element of sermon interpreting that challenges traditional views of interpreters who are expected to repeat word for word or the 'sense' of what is said" (Parish 2018, 45).

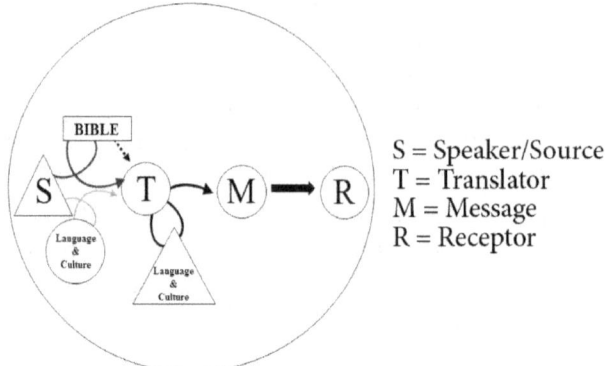

Figure 2.2 Translated Preaching: Triple Hermeneutic, Maximized and Minimized
(Adapted from Robert J. Priest with permission)

The Character of the Incarnation in the Preaching-Translating Dynamic

Christ's incarnation (John 1:14) is the singular epochal event in human and cosmic history where the transcendent God condescended to reveal himself in flesh to humans. In Christ, God *translated* his divinity into human form in three ways: he became *embodied* in the translation process, he *entrusted* himself to human culture and expression even as Christ was *empowered* by the Holy Spirit for his mission on earth. This theological triad frames our discussions on the character of the incarnation for preachers and translators in the preaching event.

Embodied Communication: Enlivening and Emoting the Preacher

When the Word became flesh, Jesus became the best translator for God by embodying God in human form and "decoding" divinity for humanity, making the invisible known through this enfleshment (John 14:7). In translating the divine, Christ's actions harmonized with the Father's in perichoresis, the "divine dance" of the inner life of the Trinity where the love of the Father flows into the Son and the love of the Son in turn to the Father (Seamands 2005, 143–44). Consequently, when we see Jesus, we see the Father made visible in Jesus' embodied and expressive life.

Entrusted Content: Embracing and Enjoying the Translator

With everything entrusted to Jesus by the Father (Matt 11:27), when Jesus spoke he fully communicated in accordance with the Father's will (John 4:34;

5:19; 6:38). In this relationship, the Father and Son "empty themselves into each and receive each other's fullness" (Seamands 2005, 80 citing Wainright). By doing so, their "distinctive identities as persons are exhibited *primarily* [italics original] in their ways of being dependent upon one another" in this mutual self-giving (Seamands 2005, 80). When we self-surrender, embrace, and enjoin our plans and message to another, we reflect the life of God in our ministry.

Empowered Commitment: Enlightening and Edifying the Preacher-Translator

God's Spirit is foundational in Christ's life because the "incarnation necessitates the trinity [and] speaks of the Holy Spirit as the means through which God continues the mission of Jesus ... therefore linking the Spirit-centered incarnation with a Spirit-centered Christian mission" (Langmead 2004, 45). The Holy Spirit functions as "the source of Jesus's authority—the sense that God's Spirit was ready to act through him ... His awareness of being uniquely possessed and used by divine Spirit was the mainspring of his mission and the key to its effectiveness" (Dunn 1975, 54). Unsurprisingly, the "*authority* (italics original) of his preaching can be said to derive from his sense of being Spirit-inspired" (66). When Jesus left, he gave the same Spirit and authority he had to his disciples to do his works (Matt 28:18–20; John 16:7; Acts 1:8).

Embodied Communication

Enlivening the Preacher

Communication involves the "dynamic, interactive process of encoding and decoding verbal and nonverbal messages within a defined cultural, physiological, relational, and perceptual environment" (Neuliep 2021, 10). When cultures are not shared, communication requires applying cultural understanding more intentionally to the encoding/decoding process. Preachers working with translators depend on the latter to encode/decode communication with the assumption that translators come from the receptor culture and thus are perfect intermediaries (Nida 1990, 39).

Though word choice in translation is vital, interpreted preaching, as an embodied experience, cannot overlook the importance of perception and behavior. Perception includes everything from "culturally specific" items like social categorization, worldview, values, and cognition, to "culturally personal" things such as attitude and adaptability. Behavior includes verbal and nonverbal processes like chronemics, kinesics, and proxemics (Nida 1990, 39). Haddon Robinson (2001, 202) suggests: "voice and gestures strike the audience's senses first" and "inflections and actions transmit ... feelings and attitudes more accurately than ... words." The translator as mediator between speaker and listener must "assess the intention of the speaker and transform what is being spoken at all levels of communication, including intentions and implicature" (Parish 2018, 32, citing Musyoka). Embodied translation becomes even more significant when a spoken language sermon is interpreted into sign language. Here, "the outcome may be similar to on stage interpreting of spoken languages, depending on the interpreter's position and the extent to which the preacher involves them in their sermon" (Downie, 2014, 3).

For interpreted preaching, "the role of nonverbal communication becomes more significant than perhaps any other form of preaching" (Parish 2018, 191) because close alignment between the preacher's and interpreter's nonverbal communication yields better "understanding and connection with the material being presented" for listeners (194). If interpreters "instinctively translate from a first person 'I' perspective, so too, they translate the body language and vocal inflections (where possible) of their co-preacher" (196). Not mimicking the preacher's gestures can actually change the meaning of the message. This is critical because often, "the congregation is watching and expects to see the interpreter match the preacher's movements" (121).

Because the translator also *interprets* culture, the event becomes an *interpreted performance*. Emotions and body language are circumscribed by cultural rules and interpreted differently in every context (Priest 1994, 295–96). Since nonverbal gestures are culturally variable and convey different meanings, a person must be careful in one's interpretation (Parish 2018, 195). Preachers should "use body language with cultural awareness" and not gesture unwittingly (176). However, for translators, "authenticity [appears] to be more important than imitation" (25, cf. Vigouroux 2010, 364). In cross-cultural situations, "the use of nonverbal communication transcends culture and even if one's own culture is traditionally more inhibited in bodily gestures, it does not prevent them from enjoying seeing others use them" (Parish 2018, 145).

When preachers and translators interact with one another in a more-or-less synchronized rhythm of embodied, nonverbal mimicry of one another's body expressions, it is a collaborative event (Parish 2018, 83), a "verbal and bodily animation of narrative characters in the sermon" (Vigouroux 2010, 361). "In a perichoretic team, as a result of indwelling together in God and one another, there is a collaboration and synergy that enables the individual members to transcend their own limitations" so that the sum is greater than their parts (Seamands 2005, 154). When preachers and translators flow together, "the sermon and its interpreted version together form a single performance of what God is doing in the church" (Downie 2014, 3).

Unsurprisingly, by approaching interpreted preaching as "a PERFORMING GENRE" rather than "a communicative activity ... bridging a linguistic gap"

(Vigouroux 2010, 365), preachers and interpreters can *embrace* the event and *enjoy* the moment together (Parish 2018, 135). This shared preaching moment also includes sharing space at the pulpit (Parish 2018, 172).

When this sense of sharedness occurs, this shifts the interpreters' role to that of "partners with the preacher in the performance of the sermon" (Downie 2014, 3) and even co-creators in "a new style of preaching" (Parish 2018, 206). When preachers see interpreters as partners and co-creators in a "homiletic dance … they are more likely to establish a rhythm that makes their task easier" (Parish 2018, 220), working to understand and attenuate "the cognitive and performative challenges involved in interpreting" (Downie 2014, 4). They will give more advance thought to the sermon's length and structure, building interpretation pauses into the sermon with adequate time for interpreting (Parish 2018, 159). Lack of preparation places "the burden of effective communication with the interpreter" (159). However, preachers and interpreters find pleasure when they are attuned to one another (156). In the best moments, "the interpreter's communicative action … is *context-renewing*; i.e., it produces a new context for the next speaker's (the pastor's) subsequent action … that helps shape the Pastor's sermon" (Vigouroux 2010, 361).

Emoting the Preacher

A second aspect of embodiment is how translators emote preachers. In "religious contexts, where interpreting is usually carried out by volunteers instead of professionals … the interpreter's ideal role seems to be that of a fully involved participant (including social, interactional, and spiritual involvement) [in] sharp contrast with many other professional interpreting practices," where an impartial objective interpretation is ideal (Hokkanen 2017, 2; cf. Parish 2018, 5).

In communication theory, meaning, ultimately, "results from *what* is said and *who* says it" (Dodd 1998, 21). Here, affectations enter translation because "emotions are about the ways in which the social world is one in which *we* are involved" (Dodd 1998, 21). Unsurprisingly,

> interpreters in religious settings have been observed to be involved on at least three levels: (1) socially, by having kinship and other close relations to the other participants or by being members of the religious community in which they interpret; (2) interactionally, by being involved in the co-construction of the interpreted sermon or other speech act; and (3) spiritually, by personally receiving and supporting the religious messages they interpret. (Hokkanen 2017, 5)

The expectation of emotionally involved translators and preachers arises because listeners expect a sermon delivered with heart and content. If preachers merely read without passion from a written text, a sermon can bore people. Exceptions do exist. For example, the great preacher Jonathan Edwards was known to "read" from his sermon notes. When he preached "Sinners in the Hands of an Angry God," his reading evoked great fear among his listeners. However, times change. Today, listeners expect preachers to preach with passion and be (somewhat) animated, but that expectation varies according to denomination, tradition, and culture.

As a form of interpretation, translation is not "mechanical, code-switching operations [where] literalness is equated with fidelity and for which knowledge of the languages concerned is sufficient to guarantee quality" (Parish 2018, 4 f.9, citing Valero-Garcés and Martin). Rather, "the interpreting activity" becomes "a communicative resource to shape the pastor's sermon and convey the Holy Spirit to the audience. Through his emotional display the interpreter illustrates how the Spirit moves through the preacher and his sermon" (Vigouroux 2010, 342). In many cases, the pastor can use "the interpreter's bodily participation as a narrative resource to convey his intense emotional experience" (362). In some churches, "'good' interpreting … is evaluated less on the basis of the interpreter's linguistic competence than on his ability to engage on the same emotional level as the pastor" (361–62). When the enlivened and emotional senses are carried through and performed by the translator, "interpreters have 'personal religious experiences'" during the preaching event (Parish 2018, 39).

Entrusted Content

Embracing the Translator

Preaching entails high responsibility because preachers are entrusted to communicate and deliver God's word faithfully. A translator enters a maximized triple hermeneutic when the preacher entrusts his words to her. Unless the preacher understands the translator's interpreted language, he has no direct access to the interpreter's "animation of his words" nor "control over the interpreter's entextualization …" (Vigouroux 2010, 356–57).[1] "For a text in another language," Kuruvilla (2009, 86) says, "it is the translator that becomes the hermeneutic intermediary between text and audience."

At the same time, "responsible *translators* … are those who speak a new language in the new context, thus faithfully proclaiming what is affirmed by the text and its transworld conceptual core" (Kuruvilla 2009, 88). Thus, "translation … implies that although we are speaking in a different language, we are still saying the *same thing*'" (87, italics original). It is only in attempting "to say the

---

[1] By using "entextualization," Vigouroux likely means contextualization though he does not define this term in his paper.

'same thing' to a contemporary audience, [that] the translated product … [can] be faithful to the source text, thereby bearing its authority" (Kuruvilla 2009, 87 citing Hordem).

In this dynamic, several layers of trust surface. First, preachers trust that "the interpreters are 'insiders' in their church and culture" (Parish 2018, 47 citing Tison) and expect they will "be experienced and proficient in interpreting" (Parish 2018, 101). Second, to serve well together, interpreters must also trust preachers. Lastly, congregations must trust "that the interpreter [is] saying what the preacher [has] said" (Parish 2018, 203).

Enjoying the Translator

Trust between preachers and translators begins with "building a relationship and rapport … before the preaching event" (Parish, 2018, 203-4). This is essential because preachers, when preaching in another cultural setting, are just like missionaries who are "at the mercy of indigenous presuppositions" (Sanneh 2009, 213). The preacher must surrender control and power of the message to the translator. This "position of powerlessness may evoke an uncomfortable response for the preacher especially if they are used to being in control in the preaching space" (Parish 2018, 5). This loss of control comes when they "find their competence in preaching that has been practiced and cultivated is frustratingly no longer in evidence" (6) or through "the loss of a base of familiarity or common stock of memories that facilitates a sense of belonging and intimacy" (6, citing Lamb).

If Jesus fully speaks only what the Father has entrusted him to (Matt 11:27) then the interpreter is obliged to translate as fully as possible the preacher's message. This interpretive freedom extends only to the degree they faithfully convey the clarity of the preacher's message as best as they can—they should not add to or subtract from the essence of the preacher's message.

Struggle for control surfaces in several ways. A common example is when the preacher interrupts and breaks down the translator's rhythm (Vigouroux 2010, 356), being "impatient for the interpreter to finish so that the preacher can … carry on preaching or … add further details" (Parish 2018, 210). When the translator speaks, the preacher should pause because the pause:

> is a crucial time in the interpreted preaching moment. It needs to be used with consideration and valued as part of the interpreted preaching dynamic. What is a void for the preacher is actually the moment of fullness and clarity for the congregation. (209)

If preachers proactively work with their interpreters to pause at the right moments, it will enable them to experience a better preaching pace with the interpreter and, as a result, find the experience less frustrating and disruptive to the preaching rhythm (211). Another benefit is that the "preacher can use this time to gauge [and] look for the congregational response they expected and gauge the effectiveness of the message" (214).[2]

The struggle for control also emerges when translators modify the sermon because they "[have] their own agenda for the congregation, they may disagree with what the preacher is saying, they may realise that what is being said would not translate to the congregation and their context, or they may not understand the preacher and therefore give a sermon of their own" (25). Here, "the guest preacher has no control over any of these possible outcomes and trusts that the message they have prepared is essentially the message that is transmitted to the congregation" (25). When this occurs, "the interpreter may take their role as gatekeeper to mean they should modify the content of the preacher's message or deliver a completely different sermon altogether, especially if they also have a pastoral role in the congregation" (24).[3]

If a preacher does not know what the interpreter said and is unsure if the latter translated what she has verbalized, the sense of mistrust may be mutual because most "interpreters desire to be accurate and faithful in their interpreting, and any variation to the sermon is done to convey meaning not for another agenda such as to assume power" (110). When interpreters sense that preachers mistrust their translation, emotional or psychological discord enters into the preaching-translating dynamic.

Parish (3) notes, "The final transmitted sermon is ultimately the product of the interpreter not the preacher." If preachers can entrust and surrender the sermon to interpreters and embrace their effort, they "may discover a fresh new preaching rhythm endowed with the Spirit's power" (6). However, even when the preacher and translator work in perfect tandem, they are insufficient without relying fully on the Holy Spirit.

Empowered Commitment

Enlightening the Preacher-Translator

Acts 2 recounts the birth of the church and her mission and it is here we find interpreted preaching "initiated and made possible" (26).[4] Interpreted preaching "embodies the Pentecost belief that all peoples should hear the good news in their heart language communicated through preachers and interpreters empowered by the Holy Spirit" (Parish 2018, 241). God empowers speaker

---

2 For extended discussions on the "pause" in translation, see Parish (2018, 209–15).

3 For other reasons interpreters do not fully translate the preacher, see Parish (2018, 116–17).

4 The Holy Spirit does more in preaching. Space delimits this discussion, but for more, see Parish (2018, 26–27).

and listener, and, for the interpreter, the Holy Spirit also helps "join together the phrases not exactly the words that have been said … bringing out … rich meaning [and] are arriving at the same destination" even without using similar words or interpretations as the preacher (Parish 2018, 123).

The same Spirit that empowers preachers and translators also inspires the Word (2 Tim 3:16) they deliver, enabling them to communicate it authoritatively so listeners are convicted of sin, righteousness, judgment, and truth (John 16:8–13). Neither the preacher nor the translator stands alone, but in the Spirit's accompanying and empowering presence whose role is envisioned in the dynamics laid out in figure 2.3:

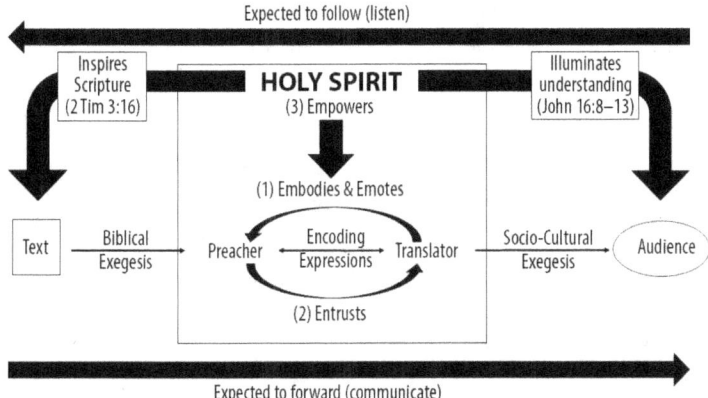

Figure 2.3 Incarnational Model of Translated Preaching (Cheong and Scheuermann)

Because of the Spirit's role in the entirety of the interpreted sermon, preachers and translators can trust God to continue speaking long after the preaching is over (Newbigin 1998, 36).

Edifying the Preacher-Translator

When partners pray together to function well together, they invite God's Spirit into the shared mutuality of the preacher-translator relationship and become uniquely joined as one, even if it lasts only for that time. This is another perichoretic moment (Seamands 2005, 152–54). By inviting and working with the Spirit in this way, preaching becomes a triadic relationship between God, the preacher, and the translator. As preachers are moved by the Spirit to deliver God's Word to the listeners through the interpreters, the latter point listeners back to the preacher and her message, rather than drawing attention to themselves. This mirrors how the Spirit's witness points back to Jesus' message (John 16:14).

Without the Holy Spirit, preaching and translation descend to mere human techniques reliant on the mechanics of delivery, rhetoric and translating for success. We do all we can to honor the Word and proclaim its meaning faithfully in the preaching event, but only the Holy Spirit can surpass our best efforts to magnify God and his Word, point us to Christ, and produce deep changes in the hearts of believers.

Conclusion

We have argued that the preaching-translating dynamic is firmly rooted and reflected in the character of the incarnation and its relation to communication in mission. How these principles and practices emerge and are expressed will vary by context. However, wherever interpreted ministries are, these foundations—centered on the character of the incarnation—remain the same. When we attend to these embodied and entrusted dimensions in our task and rely on God's empowering Spirit, we serve God more faithfully as we reflect the character of the incarnation in communicating God's Word to the people in his mission. If the preaching-translation dynamic patterns itself in this way, is enabled by the continuing power of the incarnation, and joins in the ongoing mission of God, it can be said to be incarnational as well (Langmead 2004, 219).

References Cited

Alcántara, Jared E. 2015. *Crossover Preaching: Intercultural-Improvisational Homiletics in Conversation with Gardner C. Taylor*. Downers Grove, IL: IVP Academic.

Anderson, Victor D. 2012. "Tuning Sermons for Different Ears: Help for Sermon Design from Socio-Linguistics." *Trinity Journal* 33 (2): 223–33.

Brown, Jeannine K. 2007. *Scripture as Communication: Introducing Biblical Hermeneutics*. Grand Rapids, MI: Baker Academic.

Cathcart, Rochelle L. 2011. "Preaching and Culture: An in-depth analysis of the engagements with culture in the sermons of Rob Bell, Timothy Keller, and Michael Pfleger." PhD diss., Trinity Evangelical Divinity School.

Cathcart, Rochelle L. 2012. "Culture Matters: How Three Effective Preachers (Tim Keller, Rob Bell, Father Pfleger) Engage Culture in the Preaching Event." *Trinity Journal* 33, no. 2: 209–22.

Choi, Woosung Calvin. 2012. "A Multiperspectival Approach: Preaching to the Multiethnic Congregation." *Trinity Journal* 33, no. 2: 273–84.

Dodd, Carley H. 1998. *Dynamics of Intercultural Communication*, 5th ed. Boston, MA: McGraw-Hill.

Downie, Jonathan. 2014. "Towards a Homiletic of Sermon Interpreting." *Journal of the Evangelical Homiletics Society* 14, no. 2: 1–9.

Dunn, James D. G. 1975. *Jesus and the Spirit: A Study of the Religious and Charismatic Experience of Jesus and the First Christians as Reflected in the New Testament*. London: SCM.

Hesselgrave, David J. 1991. *Communicating Christ Cross-culturally: An Introduction to Missionary Communication*. 2nd ed. Grand Rapids, MI: Zondervan.

Hokkanen, Sari. 2017. "Experiencing the Interpreter's Role: Emotions of Involvement and Detachment in Simultaneous Church Interpreting." *Translation Spaces* 6, no. 1: 62–78.

Kim, Matthew D. 2017. *Preaching with Cultural Intelligence: Understanding the People Who Hear Our Sermons*. Grand Rapids, MI: Baker Academic.

Kraft, Charles H. 2005. *Communication Theory for Christian Witness*. Maryknoll, NY: Orbis.

Kuligin, Victor. 2008. "The Pros and Cons of Preaching with an Interpreter." *Missio Nexus*, January 1.

Kuruvilla, Abraham. 2009. "Preaching as Translation via Theology." *Journal of the Evangelical Homiletics Society* 9, no. 1: 85–97.

Langmead, Ross. 2004. *The Word Made Flesh: Towards an Incarnational Missiology*. Lanham, MD: University Press of America.

Moreau, A. Scott, Evvy Campbell, and Susan Greener. 2014. *Effective Intercultural Communication: A Christian Perspective*. Grand Rapids, MI: Baker.

Neuliep, James W. 2021. *Intercultural Communication: A Contextual Approach*. 8th ed. Thousand Oaks, CA: Sage.

Newbigin, Lesslie. 1998. *Trinitarian Doctrine for Today's Mission*. Carlisle, UK: Paternoster.

Nida, Eugene. 1990. *Message and Mission: The Communication of the Christian Faith*. Rev. ed. Pasadena, CA: William Carey.

Nida, Eugene. 1999. "Communication and Social Structure." In *Perspectives on the World Christian Movement: A Reader*, 3rd ed., edited by Ralph D. Winter and Steven C. Hawthorne, 429–37. Pasadena, CA: William Carey.

Ott, Craig, Stephen J. Strauss, and Timothy C. Tennent. 2010. *Encountering Theology of Mission: Biblical Foundations, Historical Developments and Contemporary Issues*. Grand Rapids, MI: Baker Academic.

Parish, Teresa. 2018. "A Homiletic for Interpreted Preaching." PhD diss., Charles Sturt University.

Priest, Robert J. 1994. "Missionary Elenctics: Conscience and Culture." *Missiology* 22, no. 3: 291–315.

Priest, Robert J. 2012. "Building a Bridge to Somewhere." *Trinity Journal* 33, no. 2: 175–79.

Robinson, Haddon W. 2001. *Biblical Preaching: The Development and Delivery of Expository Messages*. 2nd ed. Grand Rapids, MI: Baker Academic.

Sanneh, Lamin. 2009. *Translating the Message: The Missionary Impact on Culture*, 2nd ed., revised and expanded. Maryknoll, NY: Orbis.

Seamands, Stephen. 2005. *Ministry in the Image of God: The Trinitarian Shape of Christian Service*. Downers Grove, IL: IVP.

Tarr, Del. 2012. "Narrative: Tripping the Memory Banks of the Audience." *Trinity Journal* 33, no. 2: 247–56.

Vigouroux, Cecile B. 2010. "Double-Mouthed Discourse: Interpreting, Framing, and Participant Roles." *Journal of Sociolinguistics* 14, no. 3: 341–69.

Chapter 3

Missions Application of Translanguaging Theory and Methodologies

Leveraging Multilingualism to Increase Ministry Impact

Timothy Hatcher

The Friday night youth group at the Alpha and Omega Church in Miami, Florida, draws more than four hundred students. The worship band offers a blended musical style incorporating pop, rock, and salsa music to communicate the gospel to English-dominant Hispanic youth "*con el sabor latino*" ("with a Latin flavor"). This weekly service freely uses "Spanglish," a blend of English and Spanish (Rodriguez 2012, 437). Martin Ortiz (1993, 62) defines Spanglish as "a new functional language that incorporates both Spanish and English by juxtaposing Spanish grammatical structure on English-based words, thereby permitting US-born Latinos *to develop an identity unique from those of their parents or the dominant group*" (emphasis added). Ortiz's definition is important because it recognizes the connection between the free blending of languages and dynamic, hybridized identities. In this example, students blend English and Spanish for two reasons: the negotiation of meaning and the construction of social identity.

Logic would suggest that missions work is complicated by the presence of multiple languages but is simplified and made more efficient by using single languages. Historically and currently, mission organizations prefer to interact with the smallest set of languages possible. "How many languages must a missionary learn in order to minister effectively?" some wonder. One multilingual educator describes the way multiple languages are often viewed by businesses and governments like this: "the economics of monolingualism is such that two languages are a nuisance, three languages are uneconomic, and many languages are absurd" (Pattanayak 1981, xiv). However, Pattanayak does not stop here. She challenges this assumption by focusing on the way multilingual communities conceptualize and use language: "where many languages are a fact of life and a condition of existence, *restrictions on the choice of languages* is a nuisance and one language is not only uneconomic, but absurd" (Pattanayak 1981, xiv, emphasis added).

Fortunately, multilingual educators have explored the ways multilinguals think and live. They have pioneered new teaching methodologies that leverage the full linguistic resources of multilingual communities in ways that do not require educators (or missionaries) to learn every minority language represented in their field of service. Considering the tendency of missions to default to monolingual methods of delivery in highly multilingual contexts, it is critical for missions to develop increased understanding of emic perspectives of multilinguals. Cross-cultural workers who learn more than one language often come from societies where their home language is a dominant language. They assume that their experience with multiple languages mirrors those of people who have grown up in pervasively multilingual societies. Those from multilingual societies use and view language quite differently. Church planters, Bible school trainers, and Bible agencies need fresh multilingual approaches that fit more naturally with the ways multilinguals conceptualize language. Mission agencies need to discover and model multilingual engagement strategies for host communities. By using translanguaging (i.e., language blending) theory and methodologies, missions workers can leverage multilingualism in simple ways to increase ministry effectiveness.

Monolingual Answers to Multilingual Questions

Multilingualism is not new—Jesus lived in a multilingual society and was himself multilingual, speaking Aramaic, Hebrew, Greek, and Latin (Ong 2015). Mission agencies are increasingly aware of the phenomenon of multilingualism and its accompanying complexities. The interconnectedness that results from the forces of migration, globalization, ease of travel, and enhanced digital communication make this a unique moment (Hatcher 2011). The nature of multilingualism has changed dramatically with more language groups in close contact with one another than at any previous time in history. Individuals and social groupings increasingly adopt hybridized identities due to their transnational, translocal, and transcultural life experiences. While multilingualism is a historically common phenomenon, multilingualism is manifesting itself in new ways.

Unfortunately, mission agencies from largely monolingual societies continue to emphasize international languages, sometimes called gateway languages. Often the assumption is that if multilingual members of a community have some facility in a language of wider communication (LWC), then it is most efficient to provide access to Scripture in that LWC; it is assumed that it is labor-intensive and inefficient to minister in a number of smaller mother tongues. In contrast, some minority-language-focused ministries, like Bible translation agencies, promote vernacular languages but do so with a monolingual mindset that prioritizes vernacular languages. Both approaches are appropriate in certain contexts, but in multilingual communities, multilingual approaches are sometimes more effective. The flawed question of both these ministry approaches is: "What is the best language in which to minister?" In many multilingual contexts, a better question is: "What language or mix of languages is best for ministry?"

The challenge with multiple languages is that it appears less efficient to individuals from more monolingual cultures. Rather than seeing multilingualism as a resource that can be leveraged easily, it is viewed as an obstacle to overcome. Missionaries do not wish to spend all their time learning numerous minority languages to a level that they could plant churches or teach Bible school curriculum in them.

There are hopeful solutions to this dilemma arising from the world of multilingual education, particularly translanguaging methodologies. Many educators have long noted how monolingual instruction is an enormous impediment to learning for multilinguals. Governments and schools think they save a great deal of money, which may be true in the short run, if they can offer educational instruction in only one language. Many studies demonstrate that the quality of learning and student satisfaction both rise when educators ongoingly utilize all a students' languages—their full linguistic resources. To maximize these new methodologies, it is critical to understand first the way multilinguals in multilingual societies view language.

The Way Multilinguals View Language

SIL member Sangsok Son (2018) notes differences between grassroots bilinguals (Mohanty 2006) and elite bilinguals. Elite bilingualism is the voluntary learning of a language for individual reasons that is done in largely monolingual societies. Mother tongue speakers of English in the United States may learn a second language well if they want to, but there is rarely any compulsion to do so outside of school. Such Americans have options. They may learn Spanish, French, or German. They may branch out and learn Japanese, Mandarin, or Russian. With the recent exception of Spanish, they will find few native English speakers who speak their second language outside of educational or business circles. Most missionaries are elite bilinguals.

Contrastingly, grassroots bilinguals are multilingual from a young age, and many or most of the members of their society will be multilingual in the same language(s) they are. Take for example my Ugandan friend, Fredrick N., who speaks English and Swahili but also speaks his mother tongue and three other related but distinct languages well. Language learning for him was not a hobby or connected to international business or to academic use. He learned these languages to be able to interact with his neighbors, go to school, work, and even participate in courtship. His grassroots multilingualism had a far more immediate and everyday use than does the elite bilingualism of individuals from highly affluent countries. These differences in the way elite multilinguals obtain, use, and even conceptualize language limit our ability to recognize simple and effective multilingual methods that can increase ministry impact.

Multilinguals often do not recognize solid boundaries between different languages. A Puerto Rican woman living in Tulsa, Oklahoma, serves as a professional interpreter for governmental, educational, and professional counseling services and maintains high fluency in both Spanish and English. In describing her experience with language, she said, "I don't speak two languages. I speak one language with many words." Her understanding of language and identity sees them as a unified whole. Being a professional interpreter, she understands the nuanced differences between the languages better than most. In terms of identity and preference, she likes to blend languages. Like many multilinguals, she prefers to use all of her linguistic resources blended together rather than abiding by rigid language boundaries. Grassroots multilinguals delight in the creative blending of all their vocabulary instead of being limited to a small percentage of their linguistic repertoire.

Translanguaging and Understanding

Translanguaging is the process by which bilinguals leverage and blend their various language resources (vocabulary) in everyday interactions. Ofelia García (2009, 128) defines translanguaging as "the act performed by bilinguals of accessing different linguistic features to maximize communicative potential." Translanguaging has implications for effective ministry practices just as it has for effective educational practices. Not using people's full linguistic repertoire limits their ability to engage with Scripture. For example, an individual who knows two languages does not know 100 percent of both languages. Their vocabulary may be 63 percent from their mother tongue and 37 percent from the language of wider communication. When ministry only occurs in this person's mother tongue, it does not access 37 percent of the person's vocabulary. If that ministry is in an LWC, the person is unable to use 63 percent of their vocabulary in that process. A more multilingual engagement strategy allows multilinguals to engage with Scripture, church, and other forms of ministry without these limitations of meaning. Using the full vocabulary allows them to understand concepts more fully and to express their identities more authentically.

> Not using people's full linguistic repertoire limits their ability to engage with Scripture.

Translanguaging and Identity

Some minority communities work hard to retain their ethnic group identity. Others embrace the identity of the dominant culture. Still others blend elements of their ethnic culture with those of their new location. These choices are reflected linguistically. Groups may retain their native languages, shift to the language of the dominant community, or blend these languages together. Robert Le-Page and Andrea Tabouret-Keller (1985) recognize that when speakers choose which language to speak, they are performing an "act of identity," audibly projecting the identity they wish to claim. When minority groups blend languages, this is a reflection of their hybridized identities. Sam George (2020, 178–79) describes hybridized individuals and communities as "double voiced and double accented ... [and] double languaged" as an expression of their "duality of personhood." Blended identities are by no means fixed; rather they are always negotiated in each given dialogic context and are thus dynamic and complex.

Translanguaging provides a foundation for innovative multilingual teaching methodologies that leverage multilingualism for ministry but do not require missionaries, church planters, Bible school teachers, or indigenous pastors to learn more languages. The section that follows will highlight a series of translanguaging teaching methodologies for church planters, Bible schools, and established churches.

Translanguaging Ministry Methodologies for Church Planters

One of the most natural settings to accommodate translanguaging is in discovery Bible studies, whether these groups are part of a church planting strategy or a discipleship strategy within an existing church. In these settings, Bible passages are presented in *both* the LWC and the vernacular language. Participants are free to discuss the passage in whichever language or mix of languages they prefer. This can be done in any modality, including text, audio, or oral performance. Many translanguaging communities have pioneered this approach themselves. In his dissertation research in Cameroon, Joel Trudell (2004, 136) describes the functioning of a translanguaging Bible study in the Lamnso language group. The leader asks a group member to read the selected passage in an English version, and then the leader reads the same passage from the Lamnso New Testament. After that, everyone closes their Bibles and recounts the passage in their own words. The Bible study leader primarily uses Lamnso to give instructions, and participants respond mostly in Lamnso, although a few answer in English. The Lamnso are free to use whichever language or languages are meaningful to them in terms of content or identity. Notice how this Bible study does not restrict Bible reading, listening, or discussion to one language. It uses both languages. This approach does not limit participants to a small percentage of their linguistic repertoire but allows them to leverage their full linguistic resources.

In East Aurora, Illinois, Pastor Obe Arellano leads Community Christian Church, a predominantly Hispanic congregation. Arellano has long been committed to small groups and to bilingual ministry. Initially, they started bilingual Bible studies, but these failed. It proved impractical for monolingual Spanish speakers and monolingual English speakers to navigate a Bible study together. Too much time was spent interpreting what everyone said, which was particularly problematic when a person shared something deeply emotional and then had to wait while someone else interpreted. It was clear that a different approach was needed.

However, Arellano later began translanguaging Bible studies—Spanglish Bible studies where Scripture was read in both English and Spanish and participants discussed texts in whichever language or mix of languages felt comfortable for them. Arellano uses this method only when all group participants are bilingual. This approach has proven to be very effective (Jackson 2014). Notice that translanguaging Bible studies like this one help in several ways. They help with comprehension—people can use all of their vocabulary and not just a part. They also appeal to people's preferred blended identities, not requiring them to be fully Spanish or fully English. People are given the freedom to connect with God and each other in ways that are most natural to them. This mirrors the way people use language in everyday life.

Translanguaging Approaches for Multilingual Bible Schools

Perhaps no other context is more challenging in accommodating vernacular languages than the Bible school setting. It is not uncommon for Bible school professors to teach a classroom with a dozen minority languages represented. Bible school teachers cannot possibly speak all these languages. Nor can the Bible school provide vernacular language textbooks or other instructional materials. Fortunately, multilingual educators around the world have pioneered excellent methodologies that significantly enhance student learning with little or no cost or inconvenience to instructors or institutions.

Concept Literacy

Boakye and Mbirimi (2015, 155) report an andragogical approach at the University of Cape Town in South Africa called *concept literacy*. This involves the development of multilingual glossaries for heteroglossic students of economics and law. This is necessary because legal and economic terminology are challenging to translate into Zulu, Xhosa, Sepedi, SeSetho, Setswana, and Afrikaans. Such glossaries are used in a scaffolding approach where students progressively deepen their understanding of the English technical terminology through progressive explorations of the concepts in students' "primary language." The main goal is to empower future lawyers to be able to communicate legal concepts to their clients. The unexpected benefit of this approach is that the students themselves develop a deeper understanding of the legal concepts through utilizing these glossaries. They understand the concepts more fully than they do when teaching is conducted exclusively in English. Bible college professors could similarly allow students to compile glossaries of key theological terminology in their own languages. This process itself is highly instructive.

Many resources already exist for the Bible school classroom. In many languages, Bible translators have completed New Testaments, prepared introductions and glossaries, and sometimes have compiled full dictionaries. These supports are quite helpful in a classroom with multiple languages represented and are also increasingly available digitally making access simple.

Language Grouping

Multilingual educators have also found that encouraging students to sit in groups by language enhances their ability to learn and to obtain proficiency in the LWC. Students can discuss concepts in their mother tongues to clarify meaning and enhance understanding of difficult concepts. This is not a transitional activity but one that should be continued at all levels of education. For centuries, educators have held to the mistaken notion that isolating students from their mother tongues and exposing them exclusively to an LWC is the fastest, most effective way to help them learn the language and thus grasp the teaching content. Decades of research in multilingual education has proven the opposite to be true. Ongoing first language support provides students with a deeper understanding of learning concepts and more rapid acquisition of instructional languages.

Key Terms Workshops

In 2005, Paul and Edna Headland designed a *Key Terms of the Bible* short course for a Bible school in Colombia that attracted students from multiple minority language communities.[1] The Headlands prepared key terms comparison charts of various Scripture selections both in Spanish and in the students' mother tongues.[2] Each chart focuses on a different key term. Key terms are important

---

[1] The full course materials are available in English, Portuguese, and Spanish: https://scripture-engagement.org/content/key-terms-bible-course/.

[2] To prepare the faculty of the Bible school, the Headlands first presented the key terms course using various translations of the Bible in Spanish, which helped the instructors see the value in comparing translations. They also began teaching the students using the Spanish translations and then introduced the comparisons across languages.

words that are used throughout the Bible and contain theological concepts that are critical for understanding the teaching of Scripture.

Below (see Table 3.1) is a sample of the key terms comparison chart for the term "justified" (Headland 2013). Each row has a different Bible verse that contains the term "justified" or a variation of it. The first column is a national language translation, and each subsequent column uses a different language represented in the Bible school. The verses are also glossed in national languages so that the meaning of each can be compared between the students from different linguistic backgrounds.

The Bible school students are accustomed to reading and discussing theological terms only in Spanish. Dusting off their mother tongue Bibles and using them to explore the meanings of important biblical terms helps them to understand these terms more deeply and prepares them to be able to use their mother tongue in ministry. For example, one of the students objected to the translation of "justified" in their mother tongue, exclaiming, "That's not what "justified" means!" The Headlands patiently asked the student to explain what 'justified' mean. The student discovered that he did not know until that day as he read it in his mother tongue.

The Bible school students give extremely positive feedback about the key terms course, but it is the Bible school teachers who are most enthusiastic. They find that it is "an excellent way to teach doctrine" and ask for permission to teach the course every year (Headland 2013).

Ref & NASB	Bukidnon Manobo	Kankanaey	Tagbanwa	Otomi	Uma	Yakan
Luke 7:29 When all the people and the tax collectors hear this, they acknowledged God's justice	Said, "How very proper are the customs of God."	Acknowledged that what God had done was correct	Acknowledged as true what God has caused to be said by Juan		Heart the words of Yesus	Really listened to Isa
Rom 5:1 Having been justified by faith ...	God considers us to be righteous as if we had never sinned	God counts us as righteous		Our sins are cleared	We have become straight in God's sight	We (incl.) have been forgiven and considered straight by God
Rom 8:30 whom He called, He also justified	Considered us also to be righteous	Counted them as righteous		Have been cleared of sin	Definitely made us straight in his sight	Considered straight

Table 3.1 Key Terms Comparison Chart: Justified (Headland 2013)

Bible Reading Assignments

Another simple translanguaging exercise is to require students to read all Bible passages in both the LWC and their mother tongues. With the pervasiveness of digital distribution, it is simple for students to access their mother tongue Scriptures where they exist.[3] If they do not have the full Bible in their mother tongue, perhaps a related or regional language could be enriching depending on the student's proficiency. This assignment enables students to deepen their understanding of Bible readings and requires little to no modification of the school's teaching approaches.

The methods listed above do not require Bible school teachers to gain any proficiency in any additional languages or for Bible schools to spend any money. Yet, they greatly enhance student learning. Students understand topics more fully and gain fluency in the LWC more quickly. These approaches also affirm students' ethnic identities—empowering them to leverage their own languages and identities for the sake of the kingdom rather than restricting them to languages of wider communication.

Translanguaging in Multilingual Churches

Many multilingual churches already engage in rich translanguaging practices. Often, churches preach in multiple languages. The sermon is delivered in one language and is interpreted into one or more other languages. During sermons, it is common for bilingual pastors to incorporate words and phrases from other languages, a translanguaging approach to sermons. Listeners will, at times, listen to the sermon in the first language and anticipate how the interpreter will render it. Sometimes, members of the congregation will suggest words to interpreters during the sermon. These kinds of social interactions are often lively and dynamic.

Scripture engagement research in two hundred Bible translation programs has revealed some interesting patterns in church language use (Hatcher 2018). Prayers, songs, and other parts of the service are frequently presented in various languages, though there is a great diversity of practice among churches and Christian groups. Bible readings are an exception to this pattern of variety. In multilingual contexts, over 90 percent of churches read the Bible only in the LWC even when most other aspects of the service may use both languages or

---

[3] Comprehensive listings of resources, including multimedia resources, in every language can be found at Find.Bible. All SIL translations, including fuller listings of multimedia resources, can be found at scriptureearth.org. Many audio versions of the Bible can be found at the Faith Comes by Hearing: https://www.faithcomesbyhearing.com/audio-bible-resources. While YouVersion does a good job of keeping up with new translations, many other Scripture apps are available, especially for translations in resistant contexts.

the vernacular language. In the midst of otherwise pervasive translanguaging activities, direct engagement with vernacular Scripture often lags behind. This provides an opportunity for mission agencies to advocate for the use of translanguaging practices in Scripture readings.

In some contexts, pastors are assigned to churches outside their language groups and do not know much of the vernacular language where they are pastoring. Thus, they are unable to read the vernacular language Bible during a service even if they are motivated to do so. Sometimes, interpreters perform well but lack literacy skills in their mother tongue to be able to read the Bible publicly. Several churches in such contexts have found ways to remedy these challenges by leveraging existing resources. These churches identify readers who can perform vernacular language Bible readings from existing translations during the service. This provides a much more faithful and accurate rendering of Bible readings than spontaneous interpretations do.

Diglot Bible Translations, Apps, and Audio Players

Another common translanguaging practice or tool is diglot, or multiple-language publications of the Bible, which allow multilinguals to switch between languages in ways that feel the most natural to them and to find the most meaningful terms across languages. Diglots are important because translanguagers often do not understand both languages at the same level. Diglots allow translanguagers to freely pivot between languages in order to negotiate meaning.

Apps have provided a low-cost way to present multiple languages together, creating an electronic diglot. While the cost of publishing diglot books is significant, apps provide diglot options at little or no additional cost. Audio Scripture on mobile phones can also be accessed easily in more than one language. These kinds of supporting materials empower translanguaging communities to leverage their full linguistic repertoires to engage with Scripture.

Advocating for Translanguaging Engagement with Scripture

The tendency of indigenous pastors to favor the LWC in preaching is due to the previous policies of missions agencies and does not necessarily reflect the most effective practice for communicating gospel content. Missions agencies have traditionally modeled monolingual approaches to engaging with Scripture. They have modeled monolingual church services and Bible schools. They have modeled monolingual Bible studies, audio listening groups, and oral storying groups. Modeling translanguaging as an option provides host communities the agency to make their own linguistic choices for engaging with the Bible in more meaningful ways.

It is important to model translanguaging ministry options: translanguaging Bible studies, Sunday school classes, audio listening groups, and oral storying fellowships. Such relational Scripture engagement settings are more flexible and adaptable to innovations. Advocating for translanguaging options in sermons can be helpful, whether through interpreters or pastors using a mix of languages that everyone understands during sermons (even if it is only a few words in another language sprinkled throughout at appropriate moments). Songs and prayers are other church domains in which multiple languages can be used easily. Often, churches have not embraced these kinds of approaches simply because they have not seen them modeled. This provides Scripture engagement advocates an opportunity to offer options to churches in participatory and experiential ways.[4]

Conclusion

Elite multilinguals who encounter this presentation are usually intrigued. It is a new idea with interesting vocabulary. Grassroots multilinguals who hear or read this presentation are often enthusiastic. They frequently exclaim, "This is how we use language; this is how we think about language!" A translanguaging—or blended language—approach is not essential everywhere, but elite multilinguals should not be the ones who set language policies in multilingual communities; grassroots multilinguals should set the language policies for ministry. We should not restrict multilinguals to national or international languages for our own convenience when so many resources and approaches exist to empower them. We should also not require missionaries to learn an endless number of languages to minister. Instead, missionaries should model translanguaging methods and provide our multilingual brothers and sisters the option to creatively explore the most impacting ways to approach their ministry contexts.

References Cited

Boakye, Naomi, and Vimbai Mbirimi-Hungwe. 2015. "Multilingual Pedagogy in Higher Education: Lecturers' Perceptions of Translanguaging in Promoting Academic Literacy." In *New Directions in Language and Literacy Education for Multilingual Classrooms*, edited by Leketi Makalela, 153–74. Cape Town: CASAS.

---

4 Many practical workshops for pastor training workshops are available in *Translating the Bible into Action: How the Bible Can be Relevant in All Languages and Cultures* (Hill and Hill 2010). Particularly relevant to translanguaging are Chapter 6—"Using Scripture in Multilingual Churches" and Chapter 7—"Helping Interpreters Perform Well."

García, Ofelia. 2009. "Education, Multilingualism and Translanguaging in the 21st Century." In *Multilingual Education for Social Justice: Globalising the Local*, edited by Ajit Mohanty, Minati Panda, Robert Phillipson, and Tove Skutnabb-Kangas, 128–45. New Delhi: Orient Blackswan.

George, Sam. 2020. "Coconut Generation, Hybridity, and Hybrid Missions." In *A Hybrid World: Diaspora, Hybridity, and Missio Dei*, edited by Sadiri Joy Tira and Julie Lee Uytanlet, 173–86. Pasadena, CA: William Carey Publishing.

Hatcher, Timothy. 2011. "Bible Translation and Diaspora Missiology." BT Conference, Dallas, TX.

Hatcher, Timothy. 2018. "Testing Wayne Dye's Eight Conditions of Scripture Engagement Model in Cross-Cultural Bible Translation Programs." PhD diss., Assemblies of God Theological Seminary.

Headland, Edna. 2013. "Key Terms of the Bible Course: A Student's Manual for Scripture Use." https://scripture-engagement.org/content/key-terms-bible-course/.

Hill, Harriet, and Margaret Hill. 2010. *Translating the Bible into Action: How the Bible Can Be Relevant in All Languages and Cultures*. Carlisle, UK: Piquant Editions.

Jackson, Amy. 2014. "Small Groups in a Bilingual Church." Smallgroups.com, October 20, 2014. https://www.smallgroups.com/articles/2014.

LePage, Robert, and Andree Tabouret-Keller. 1985. *Acts of Identity: Creole-Based Approaches to Language and Ethnicity*. New York: Cambridge University Press.

Mohanty, Ajit K. 2006. "Multilingualism of the Unequals and Predicaments of Education in India: Mother Tongue or Other Tongue?" In *Imagining Multilingual Schools: Languages in Education and Globalization, Linguistic Diversity and Language Right*, edited by Ofelia García, Tove Skutnabb-Kangas, and Maria Torres-Guzman, 262–83. Clevedon, UK: Multilingual Matters.

Ong, Hughson T. 2015. *The Multilingual Jesus and the Sociolinguistic World of the New Testament*. Leiden: Brill.

Ortiz, Martin. 1993. *The Hispanic Challenge: Opportunities Confronting the Church*. Downers Grove, IL: InterVarsity Press.

Pattanayak, Debi Prasanna. 1981. *Multilingualism and Mother Tongue Education*. Delhi: Oxford University Press.

Rodriguez, Daniel A. 2012. "Hispanic Ministry Where Language Is No Barrier." *Missiology: An International Review* 38, no. 4 (October): 432–43.

Son, Sangsok. 2019. "Translanguaging, Identity, and Education in Our Multilingual World." In *Language and Identity in a Multilingual, Migrating World*, edited by Stephen J. Quakenbush and Gary F. Simons, 123–42. Dallas: Pike Centre/SIL International.

Trudell, Joel. 2004. "Bible Translation and Social Literacies Among Four Nso' Churches in Cameroon: An Ethnographic Study." PhD diss., University of Edinburgh.

Chapter 4

Hidden Stories of Reciprocal Mission in the Glocal World
A Case Study

Joy Kim

My case study presents stories from Clarkston, Georgia, a city known as "the most diverse square mile in America," which I call home. You may think it is an exaggerated or overrated title for a city, but it is not. Over the past thirty years, Clarkson has been welcoming refugees from around the world, especially from countries where conflict, violence, or persecution drove them out of their home.

The globally displaced refugee population has expanded nearly 50 percent since 2013 (Pew Research Center 2017). I have met some of these refugees in my city. They are now my neighbors, my favorite restaurant owners, and my dear friends. In my neighborhood's 1.4 square miles, there are over sixty languages spoken, with people from more than fifty countries (which includes more than ninety different ethnic groups) having resettled in this small town. The diversity flourishing in this compact area has been a great blessing to my family and we have come to love and build community with these people on the move. And in this multicultural setting I work with Proskuneo Ministries, whose mission is to "help the body of Christ see, live, and share the vision of multicultural, Jesus-centered worshiping communities among all peoples on earth as in heaven."

My story starts in South Korea where I was born and raised. I never imagined that I would live in a country other than my home country, which is still dear to my heart today. One day, my parents decided to leave for Australia, a place I knew nothing about. I had no part in that decision and felt like I was forced to leave all I had loved and known behind to move to a strange place. The move was very abrupt, and happened so fast that I did not even have a chance to pack my own bag. For the next decade or so in my teen years and in my twenties, I felt shocked, lost, and confused in so many ways as I tried to adjust to new cultures, languages, and peoples all around. To this day in my forties, I still struggle with a lingering question of asking who I truly am. I call this the never-ending identity crisis (it might have evolved into a mid-life crisis). Having no control over life events, disasters, and crises is not new to human experience, but if a move is somewhat traumatic in the way it happens, or why it happens, it not only takes years just to come to your senses and be aware of the impact, but it also takes more years to process and resolve the emotions and the traumatic effects on your brain that you might even have come to accept as part of yourself over time. In this long-term process of healing and restoration, through the arts (especially through music), I have found ways to express suppressed and trapped emotions and buried thoughts. I have also experienced the part the arts play in the process of trauma healing and self-discovery with my community in Clarkston. I have gained a new appreciation for the arts and have realized how they are connected to our well-being and how they can transform the ways we view and engage with ourselves, others, and God. I say this not to ask for pity or sympathy but to promote understanding of what this huge population of people on the move might go through, internally and externally, and how their moves significantly shape who they are today.

It is only very recently that I began to see the value of my own story and where I come from. For a long time, I did not own my story nor my culture. On the contry, I sought to deny those parts of myself. Now I know what hindered me from valuing or owning my story. It was because of the minority experience I have had over the years and how I internalized the messages that were communicated from that experience. The messages say that "you don't belong here" and "you will never be one of us," whatever that means at the moment. "You can be what we want you to be to fit in here, but you are not welcome to bring yourself (your own ideas or values) here." These messages are basically demanding me to deny who I am. I am not here to blame anyone for the messages I received. I simply bring to our awareness that messages received by different people are not always the same messages a sender expected or intended to communicate. Also, what appears on the surface to have been received on the end of the receiver may not truly reflect what they actually internalize within. I suspect what is embodied in the communication speaks louder than what is actually said verbally. In other words, what may be communicated to the receiver could be totally different from what a sender intended and, in fact, it is very possible to send the opposite message to the receiver, especially in a context where cultural values clash—not just between two cultures but multiple cultures all at the same time. In this context, finding one best way of communication that would work for all is just impossible. The messages that I internalized may have been affected by this complexity in communication.

Going back to my story, I do not have time to expound what minority experience is all about, but one thing I see that is related to our topic of communication and mission is that minority experience can seriously hinder a person from participating actively in reciprocal communications and relationships, especially with those they perceive as belonging to a majority group in society—majority not just in number, but also in terms of socially privileged groups in the center with more access to resources. Minorities often find themselves in the margins, in the "them" category in the "us vs. them" paradigm, and are often not considered fully human with immense abilities to create, to contribute with resources, and to communicate as equals. They are often in a position to receive and to follow rather than to give and to lead. Adrian Pei, in his book, *The Minority Experience* (2018, 131), states that minorities internalize this pain, "which takes the form of shame and self-doubt." This explains my own internal struggles over the years and still today. Interestingly, in my multicultural community, I find my experiences as a minority in the US are not too different from the experiences of minority individuals who came from other cultures, especially from the countries that were historically colonized by the West. The common threads that I find in our experiences are not just the hardships and suffering of our journeys, but also the internalized messages that cause us to believe that our identities, our stories, and the cultures we come from are not valuable enough to be recognized, considered, and respected, especially in Christian settings. Why is this happening? In this situation, how can reciprocity be cultivated in our communities?

Now, I present four short stories of my friends whom I met in my city, Clarkston. Through these stories, I hope you will glimpse what reciprocal mission looks like and see how reciprocal relationships are essential for all of us who are involved in God's mission.

Abraham came to the US when civil war broke out in Sudan in his twenties. His father was a general of the army in the south part of Sudan, and he told Abraham to leave the country. Abraham fled first to Egypt, then to Syria, and ended his journey in Clarkston as a refugee in the 1990s. He shared so many stories of being persecuted because he was a Christian in a Muslim country. One time, he was imprisoned in the desert for three days; singing worship songs kept him alive. Like the jailor who was transformed by Paul and Silas, the guard was amazed at his singing and asked Abraham about his God. In Clarkston, Abraham planted a church for Sudanese refugees, settled here, and became an American citizen. He joined Proskuneo as a staff member when he came back after another devastating tribal conflict in South Sudan. He had gone back to his country to celebrate the independence of South Sudan, but then people who fought against the north began to kill one another over the tribal conflicts. He wanted to take the multicultural Proskuneo team back to

South Sudan for his evangelistic outreach conference in Wau, South Sudan because he saw that God could bring different peoples together in worship by learning and singing one another's songs. In this war-torn area, when they sang a song (called "Arroboya") in one of the tribal languages, people came near the stage and started dancing with one another (Proskuneo Ministries 2020). It was not a common practice to sing a song from a minority group in Christian worship, especially in multi-tribal settings. Abraham wanted to demonstrate that it was truly possible to worship together in a way that honors the cultures and stories of peoples who share different cultural and social standings. The leaders of this outreach who were from different tribes in serious conflicts in the past came together intentionally to cultivate reconciliation and hope in the city. You know how significant it is in a top-down, hierarchical culture for leaders to demonstrate what is possible. When we sang "Arroboya" to the grandmother of Abraham's wife, she was in tears listening to the song. One of the highlight moments was when the local leaders and Proskuneo team members got together in the house where they all stayed to sing a song in the different languages they spoke. The song brought them together to cross cultural and language barriers and form the bond of connections and friendships.

The world is glocal, and diasporas can be connectors between continents to exchange new ideas and practices, and to form true reciprocal partnerships and friendships between their homelands and wherever they were scattered and planted like a seed by God, as described in the literature of diaspora missiology. Abraham is a bridge-builder between different peoples and communities in two different continents. He pursues and practices true reciprocal missions here and there and all around wherever he goes. Songs travel around the world. "Elai Yesu" (Proskuneo Ministries 2009), the song Abraham taught us, came here with Abraham to Clarkton, then traveled to Korea, Thailand, and many other places and then back to South Sudan with so many added languages of those with whom he worshiped with along the way. Languages are strong identity markers. Artistic traditions are also strong identity markers, almost as much as languages are. When I heard my Sudanese friends sing "Elai Yesua" in my language, I felt accepted and honored in my identity and connected to them like family, something I have never experienced before. Now I ask, who is doing the mission to whom? Who is communicating the gospel to whom?

Dareen and Chadi lived in Saudi Arabia for many years before they came to Clarkston and applied for asylum. Born in Damascus, Syria, they often tell me how proud they are of their Christian traditions and where they come from.

When they share their insight on the Middle Eastern culture in which the Bible was written, we do not need commentary to learn the cultural background of the text we are reading. Their Christian history and tradition goes back thousands of years and we, our worshiping community, are often amazed by how rich and refreshing it is when their cultural insight leads us to a new understanding of the stories in the Bible. When Chadi teaches the Bible on our house worship nights, he brings the Bible characters alive and makes them so real because of his understanding of the context in which they lived. We often lead worship together, make music and create new arts together, and homeschool and raise our children together. Dareen and Chadi are both musicians, storytellers, and multi-talented artists. Proskuneo produced a song of peace called "Salam" (Proskuneo Ministries 2020b) that Dareen co-wrote with one of our community members. Dareen and Chadi have been here in the United States for about seven years now, and, in contrast to the usual low expectations society has towards refugees and immigrants, they contribute so much to our community in so many ways: through their artistic expressions that enrich our worship; through their understanding of the Bible and a Muslim context that forms a bridge to that part of the world; through their glorious food and abundant hospitality; through their connections to the Arabic-speaking communities in the US and other countries where these diasporic communities are found; and through their generosity to give and share all they are and all they have with our community. When Dareen and I sat together to share tears and lament the death of her aunt who was killed in front of her sister by a bomb in her own house, I saw God sit with us in our suffering and grief. Her many traumatic memories surface my own traumatic memories, and together we are walking into healing and restoration in community. Again I ask, who is doing the mission to whom? Who is communicating the gospel to whom?

Meh Sod came to Clarkston as a refugee at the age of twelve with her family. From the first moment I met her, we were connected by a desire to tell our own stories and share our struggles to find our ethnic identities as bicultural, bilingual people living as minorities in the US. Med Sod had just lost her mother the year before, and this significant loss urged her to discover her own identity and story in order to ground herself with deep roots. Identity becomes an important issue in multicultural contexts, especially for those who come from minority groups. We ended up starting a documentary film project, "The Sound of Kweh" (Proskuneo Ministries 2021), that told her story and the stories of her Karen people in Clarkston, embedded in various artistic expressions. In this project, it was important for Meh Sod to tell stories of the

Karen people from their own perspectives with their own voices, unlike all other documentaries made about Karen people. From her perspective, since the Karen people lost their own land and country as one of the most persecuted minority groups in Myanmar, it is all the more important to preserve something of their own and express themselves in their own ways. And for Meh Sod, it was the artistic expressions that she identified as her own most strongly. As she discovers the beauty of her stories and culture in the weaved clothes, the blowing of the Karen horn, and the traditional tune and dance that bring memories of her childhood in the refugee camp, she feels that she finally finds her voice and feels the value of her own story and culture. For Karen-Americans, a new art and culture with a new identity emerges in hybrid forms that include the whole story of their journey from the refugee camp to Clarkston. Their identities are being shaped and formed as they embrace different cultures around them on the journey. Meh Sod has a compassionate heart and a burning desire for the next generation of Karen-Americans to see the image of God in themselves and in their community. She wants the Karen people to be able to connect with others in the multicultural community they live in now beyond their cultural and ethnic boundaries. She is part of God's mission to her own people, as well as to all the others around her who benefit from her invitation to see the world from her perspective, and from her bridge-building contribution to the community as a whole.

When Bo Shi first came to our Proskuneo school of the arts, he did not know how to speak English, but he knew how to speak a language of art (see figure 4.1).

Figure 4.1 Bo Shi Self-Portrait (used with permission)

In his self-portrait, he tells his story through images that show his life's journey of displacement. From the traumatic memories of war to his inner turmoil of confusion and loss on the way to where he is now, he speaks clearly and powerfully through his art piece. He also speaks a language of music through his guitar and his original music. Peoples in Myanmar have gone through unspeakable atrocities under the Burmese military dictatorship in place since a military coup took control of the country in February of 2020. In response, young people from different minority tribes who were once enemies came together to write a song of protest against injustice and violence and for peace and reconciliation among the peoples of Myanmar. In the music video of this song, "We Will Win" (Proskuneo Ministries 2021b), Bo Shi's guitar solo is a testament not only to his passion to see his people healed and restored from suffering from generation to generation, but also his hope for his people to come together in unity and diversity for the good of all peoples in Myanmar. It does seem hopeless and helpless if you focus on just the situation right now, but through this song the musicians communicate a strong message of hope and reconciliation to themselves and to the world. Bo Shi went back to the refugee camp as part of the Proskuneo team and became a bridge-builder for all who are involved in the mission. He said, "I want to go back and continue to help my Karen people. I know that God will refresh my soul as I work there. My journey has not ended. I am truly honored to be a part of this team." (Bo Shi, Facebook message to author, January 5, 2018). Again I ask, who is doing the mission to whom? Who is communicating the gospel to whom?

When our multicultural community comes together to co-create new arts, it leads us to create a new culture of reciprocal communication, contribution, and collaboration regardless of the social status, financial status, and cultural background of those who are involved. In the co-creating process, each one of us is a piece of the puzzle that we are putting together. Everyone brings their own beauty and together we create something new that reflects all of us. It forms an incredible bond of fellowship and friendship that overflows into the sharing of our lives and our resources on another level, because the reciprocal trust and relationship is formed and shaped through the process. Samuel Cueva (2015, 311), in his book, *Mission Partnership in Creative Tension* describes collaboration in mission as "a reciprocal relationship in freedom of sharing, reciprocal trust, truth in the gospel, unity in diversity, respect for dignity, and common goals for God's glory." We as a community can testify that reciprocity is the key for any meaningful transformation to happen in relationships and missions.

Diaspora groups have such rich resources such as cultural knowledge and insight, the connections they have to their homelands and to diaspora communities all around the world, artistic expressions, and so on. They have much to contribute to the process of building community through the arts. Art forms are a mirror to our own culture and worldview and a window to another. In the world of missions, the practice of looking into a culture's art forms to learn about its values and worldview has been acknowledged recently and is gaining more credibility, but the impact of this practice is not just for local artists but also for all those (church planters, Bible translators, educators, etc.) who are involved in God's mission. This is because the arts, in vastly different cultural forms, are gifts from God which help all of us to embody a message (which is the person of Jesus Christ) that communicates powerfully to the whole being of a person. In other words, art can help us experience the story or the message. It can truly embody the message in a way that words alone cannot contain. In a multicultural context which demands border-crossing to co-create and collaborate artistically, what is created together, as a result, is the embodiment of who each individual is and also who they are together: their collective identity is shaped in the co-creating process. It creates a new "us" which directly counters the "us vs. them" paradigm and traditional social power dynamics. Co-creation cultivates a new culture of reciprocal collaboration as participants are encouraged not only to contribute their own cultural expressions, but also embrace expressions of others. In John 17:21, Jesus prayed for us to be one as he is one with the Father. Co-creation is a way to reflect the image of our Triune God in perfect unity in diversity, and a multicultural community creating, collaborating, and living as one is a powerful witness to the world. And yes, it is true that it is our context that calls for diversity, but unity in diversity does not happen without much intention, pursuit, and care.

> In John 17:21, Jesus prayed for us to be one as he is one with the Father.

When we talk about reciprocal mission, we cannot overlook reciprocal transformation. When we engage in missions, we often think about those who are in need of transformation through the gospel and focus all our attention and resources on bringing about that transformation. In reciprocal mission, all members of the community are mutually transformed by the encounters they experience together: encounters with God, others, and even with themselves. Creative collaboration and co-creation position all who are involved into a learning posture which increases the self-awareness, cultural awareness, and community development that we all gain in the process. The ripple effect of these real encounters which cross cultural, ethnic, geographical, religious, socio-economic, and linguistic boundaries bring different peoples together and transform all of us in community closer to God's image. I have witnessed that God is truly carrying out his mission through his peoples who are created in his image, in all places and in all directions. Adrian Pei (2018, 180) confirms this truth and says, "The message of God is that history is not random, but purposeful, and that he is weaving the events of this world together like a master storyteller." God is writing his meta-narrative and preparing the church as his bride through all peoples. This includes people on the move who are often hidden in the sight of those actively involved in cross-cultural missions because we consider them to be recipients of missions rather than missionaries. I am the one who has been transformed so much by these encounters and received so much from those who are considered as "the least of these." They are my true friends who know me, and help me feel seen and heard, and who give love and receive love well. And together we participate in God's mission in ways that I have never imagined.

The world that needs the gospel is here, there, and everywhere. The peoples who are called to God's mission are here, there, and everywhere. I dare to say that the way forward for cross-cultural/multicultural encounters in this glocal world is a reciprocal, creative collaboration and co-creation with all peoples everywhere in every direction. I have witnessed this through collaborative, creative, community-oriented arts. True reciprocal communication is possible and it can move all of us toward a flourishing, abundant, interdependent unity in diversity that is beautifully reflected in our Triune God.

References Cited

Cueva, Samuel. 2015. *Mission Partnership in Creative Tension: An Analysis of the Relationships in Mission within the Evangelical Movement with Special Reference to Peru and Britain between 1987 and 2006.* Cumbria, UK: Langham Monographs.

Pei, Adrian. 2018. *The Minority Experience: Navigating Emotional and Organizational Realities.* Downers Grove: InterVarsity Press.

Pew Research Center. 2017. "Where Refugees to the U.S. Come From." https://www.pewresearch.org/fact-tank/2017/02/03/where-refugees-to-the-u-s-come-from/.

Pew Research Center. 2017b. "U.S Resettles Fewer Refugees, Even as Global Number of Displaced People Grows." https://www.pewresearch.org/global/2017/10/12/u-s-resettles-fewer-refugees-even-as-global-number-of-displaced-people-grows/.

Proskuneo Ministries. 2009. "One and Only (with Elai Yesua)." Produced by Proskuneo Ministries. Lyric video, 5:04. https://www.youtube.com/watch?v=DgWTQE37rxo.

Proskuneo Ministries. 2020a. "Arroboya | (COVER) Worship Song in Moro Language." Produced by Proskuneo Ministries. April 3, 2020. Lyric video, 1:54. https://www.youtube.com/watch?v=Te-CmsWQypk.

Proskuneo Ministries. 2020b. "Salaam (Official Audio and Lyric Video) // Proskuneo Ministries." Produced by Proskuneo Ministries. October 19, 2020. Lyric video, 6:18. https://www.youtube.com/watch?v=9Jr2ka18FpI.

Proskuneo Ministries. 2021a. "The Sound of Kweh | Karen Story Project." Written and Directed by Meh Sod Paw. August 14, 2021. Documentary film, 21:15. https://www.youtube.com/watch?v=Lfn8VMGjLXs&t=26s.

Proskuneo Ministries. 2021b. "We Will Win | #the myanmarproject." Directed by Proskuneo Ministries. July 1, 2021. Music video, 8:51. https://www.youtube.com/watch?v=ARGcyBXeDpw.

Part 2

Communicating the Gospel in Global Settings

In this section the authors engage the reader in thinking through the dynamics of communication in a variety of missional contexts. Phil Davis presents a case study that explores intercultural (mis)communication between ex-patriot missionaries and indigenous church workers. A crisis brought about by a new missionary leader reveals deep levels of differences in values and expectations that become evident through verbal and non-verbal communication. The commonality of history and a shared language (that of the ex-patriots) does not compensate for the perceived affronts to the relationships in this mission setting.

Robert Gallagher reflects on the contextualization of the gospel in contemporary Australian society. He discusses the background of the majority Anglo-Celtic culture (his own), and how that has shaped attitudes and feelings towards the Anglican Church and Christianity. He demonstrates the need to look at current cultural values, beliefs, and behaviors inherent in *mateship*, for example, in order to contextualize the Christian faith for Australia today.

Through a case study of Myanmar Christian women, Kara Garrison explains the ways in which traditional social exchanges based on honor/shame are a barrier to developing trusting relationships, even in the church. She challenges the missions community and the church to develop communication patterns that will replace fear, judgment, and shame with acceptance, trust, and honor. This will enable the church to become a safe place of healing both within the church and in the local community.

Part 2 ends with Matthew Henning's exploration of the difficulties that Muslim Youth face in North America. Because they are developing hybrid identities that are shaped by the tensions of being in a multi-cultural and religiously plural context, they are often not able to identify fully with any of the competing voices—whether from their tradition or their host culture—that they hear. By understanding the tensions these youths face between their families' cultures and the ones to which they are adapting, the church has an opportunity to communicate the message of Christ more clearly. —MARCUS DEAN

Chapter 5

Knowing When to Drink Coffee
A Case Study of (Mis)Communication in Intercultural Mission Partnership

Phil Davis

"If he came to teach me rather than learn from me, then we do not want him!" The loud, shaking voice on the phone—which belonged to the characteristically soft-spoken Pastor Shareek—underscored a jarring reality. Over just a few days, smoldering cross-cultural tension had caught fire, igniting a four-alarm blaze that was engulfing an entire organization.

The ministry had started more than a decade earlier as a partnership between a Western denominational expression and its sister body in a Middle Eastern context. Founding partners had seen provision, growth, and witness that surpassed even their boldest prayers. However, all this blessing had come with challenges, as rapid growth also accelerated this initiative's relational, professional, financial, and spiritual demands. As burnout and health concerns fueled attrition across the organization, local church leadership, the local ministry board, and the US agency agreed: more experienced leadership and increased structure were urgently needed.

After an extensive search and following local ministry board approval, the US denomination appointed Mike, a seasoned professional with international experience. Recognizing that linguistic and cultural hurdles presented formidable challenges, Mike began reading recommended books and conversing with ministry personnel to begin culture-specific preparation. However, as the ministry's leadership was fluent in English and had a long history of working with Westerners, there was reason to be optimistic.

Mike's initial reception featured the customary displays of hospitality. Pastor Shareek welcomed his new American partner to his home, where they exchanged gifts and mutual affirmations. A few days later, the ministry staff also served a welcome meal, introducing new colleagues and the host culture's delicacies at once. Mike's new coworkers greeted his first forays into the Arabic language and dishes with cheers and laughter, and the first business meetings began.

Within days, organizational leadership was uneasily backchanneling with other American personnel attached to the ministry to express concerns. Having been accustomed to Western partners who joined the work after years in the region or, at the very least, intensive language and cultural preparation, personnel felt jolted by the "rudeness" of their new boss. "He walks right by me without even greeting me!" "He is always laughing! Does he think we are stupid?" "He just sits in his office alone and never talks! Doesn't he want to get to know us?" "He's always talking about how he did things in America. Why does he think he is better than us?" A particularly animated concern: "He refuses to drink coffee with us!" The new leader's American colleagues followed up with pointers for their fresh coworker and encouraged staff members to extend grace.

All parties encouraged the new leader to greet and get acquainted with the staff. Since Mike was anxious to observe the organization in action, he welcomed this task. He also believed that it would give him a chance to address the layers of bureaucracy that separated him from most employees. He walked the halls and greeted staff in their offices, asking them their names and responsibilities. Other senior leadership responded with dismay at Mike's meddling with their reports. Clearly, he did not trust them and intended to circumvent their leadership. Why had he come with such a negative impression? Why was he poking his nose into every corner? If he wanted to know about employees' roles, he should have asked their bosses!

In the eyes of many, their American leader's relational distance, his silent smiles, and his suspicious sleuthing could only indicate the plotting of a jealous, rival group seeking to take control. Following a disagreement over an employee's performance evaluation, a top leader—who had hired the employee—resigned. He could not work for someone who showed no trust in him or respect for his position. He would not stand by to witness this hostile takeover in which the wealthy Americans provided the muscle for a competing group.

The following days were a whirlwind of activity. Staff threatened Mike and banned him from the building. Personnel organized a strike, blockading the offices and demanding their leader's return. Pastor Shareek, who believed that this new leader was tearing apart the ministry he spent years building and for which he was responsible, declared himself the sole decision-maker.

What had started as interpersonal conflict spread throughout the institution and, eventually, throughout much of the Christian community. The two "sides" occupied islands of meaning, rooted in interpretive frameworks that provided opposite gestalts that appeared self-evident to each side. To some, the new leader came with a critical judgment, intent on forcing a foreign system on his new charges and wresting control from the current leadership. To others, current leaders refused to engage in the leadership and accountability their situation demanded, placing their honor and tribal commitments above the organizational mission and its eternal purposes.

Mediating attempts seemed only to worsen the situation, as the mediators' projected neutrality puzzled and infuriated entrenched stakeholders. Discussions routinely centered on the ministry's original vision, standards of Christian behavior, and the characteristics of healthy leadership. These conversations pointed to still more challenging conflicts under the surface, as early partners expressed competing viewpoints of the project's purpose and its metrics of evaluation. Written documents, which were few, were unearthed and re-evaluated. Attempts to crystalize the partnership's nature and vision in greater detail cycled endlessly, repeatedly stalling as the process would near any formal, written, corporate affirmation.

During the debate, parties voiced conflicting expectations of each other, as key leaders' apparent clarity of purpose seemed instead to point to shared vocabulary associated with rather distinct conceptions. Perhaps no word was more regularly or passionately employed than *partnership*. Many asked: "Is *this* how they treat a *partner*?" If there was one thing everyone could agree on, their partners had painfully failed them in their time of need. The relational fallout from these many perceived failures was enormous.

Case Analysis

This case analysis will highlight several communications issues demonstrated in the above case, including several for which participants had been theoretically prepared. Indeed, both Mike and his new coworkers had a working familiarity with the variation of values and communication patterns across cultures before their interaction, which points to intercultural communication's inherent difficulty. While cross-cultural preparation equips the learner with useful generalities, it does not predict intercultural capacity, nor does it inevitably produce immediate success in intercultural communication. This analysis will suggest that historical frameworks, assumptions drawn from a shared language, and contrasting understandings of persuasion, leadership, and relational structures contributed to the communication crisis described above.

History

History provides essential interpretive context for communication, and many participants in the case posited their interpretations and expectations on historical foundations. In particular, the nature and role of oral tribal histories and the impact of a colonial past provide historical context in this case study.

A critical aspect of history in the tribal context is the fluid, polemical nature of historical recountings in the tribal milieu. Andrew Shryock's (1997) insightful, complex account of the tensions between Balga tribes in Jordan helpfully illustrates this dynamic. Shryock found that, though tribal oral histories are factually rooted in historical experience, they remain fragmented and contentious. They function to express collective identity, supporting the honor of each tribe against the challenges of others. Furthermore, because of the inherently competitive nature of these histories, Shryock's audience often opposed his attempts to integrate them in writing, seeing the exercise as dangerous (locs. 265–310).

Similarly, attempts to retell the ministry's early history and commitments became mired in conflicting narratives that mirrored the conflict's interpretive impasses. The oral performance of the past supported group honor and identity in the present. Just as in Shryock's experience, attempts to write an integrated history in the environment of power challenge were received coldly by most parties.

The introduction of Western workers into the ministry and conflict also arguably introduced the history of colonialism in this complex context. The perceived sudden critique and intervention by Mike—a Western leader sent by a Western organization—mirrors colonial experience, in which colonial powers granted a degree of local autonomy but retained *de facto* control (Funkshmidt 2002, 558). Rowe (2009) asserts that Majority World participants in mission partnership often cite this pattern of abuse of power, wherein final financial and strategic control remains with the powerful (often Western) party (153).

Arab denominational leadership engaged the conflict with another historical reference point: their shared history with the American sister body. Church leadership's strongest stances were not about money, biblical commitments, or any number of other factors in the crisis; their communications centered on loyalty to the denominational expression that had brought them the gospel. Stories of missionaries' sacrifice and service over more than a century formed the standard response to accusations of abuse and immaturity. Whereas present realities influenced the exercise of oral histories in the conflict, past corporate experience also provided interpretive aids—both positive and negative—for the present.

Language and Culture

The initial conflict in this case study was likely exacerbated by an overemphasis on the role of spoken language in intercultural communication, especially as compared to communication patterns, cultural symbols, and values. Though both sides cited verbal communication as inflammatory during conflict resolution, the nonverbal communication, as received from the interpreters' cultural frames of reference, seemed to cause the most profound offense.

Doerre (2001) describes nonverbal miscommunications in American-Syrian interactions on archaeological digs in Syria, giving particular attention to the influence of the actor's gender on audience interpretation. She notes that miscommunication occurs "as much from misinterpretations of posture and gesture as from a mutual lack of fluency in a common spoken language;" patterns of behavior carry implicit contextual meanings that elicit automatic responses (255). The digs' cultural context, Doerre observes, conditioned visceral reactions to practices such as sitting, shouting, smiling, joking, and even participating in physical work. Critical facets of this complex context escaped the perception of American participants, frustrating their engagements even when they attempted to respond adaptively to perceived positive feedback (256-61, 264).

In this case study, shared language, including common focal terminology and a familiar professional environment, likely presented even more significant obstacles to Mike's ability to interpret his actions in the eyes of his audience. However, just as in Doerre's examples, Mike's violations of nonverbal norms continued to elicit automatic responses, as exemplified in the perception of the leader's rejection of coffee—a symbol of broken relationship or even war. His internationally experienced peers may have happily adapted that symbol, but they were unprepared for him to reject it flatly. Similarly, the leader's choices to work in isolation were viewed as an unnatural form of work explainable as a rejection of relationship.

The shared language and experiences of participants also masked verbal communication challenges. Staff comfortability with the English language, Western education and management, and American culture seemed likely to ease the new leader's entry. However, as Suchan (2014) notes, "Patterns of thinking and action created by a person's primary language and culture strongly influence the strategies that person uses in a second language" (297). Analyzing an intercultural business meeting between US and Jordanian firms, Suchan details numerous misinterpretations that stemmed from linguistic and cultural patterns operating under the surface of English engagement. Although these underlying patterns were acute enough to derail negotiations, they were subtle enough to escape third-party mediators' immediate perception (293–97). Similarly, when Mike failed to employ English that corresponded to Arabic forms in his greetings and conversational structures, this linguistic conflict was veiled by the surface-level analysis of shared English fluency.

The staff's experience with Western management and cultures may also have increased their expectations of Mike's capacity for cross-cultural adaptation. Glowacki-Dudka, Usman, and Treff (2008) express this dynamic in their case study of an intercultural relationship engaged in both the United States and Saudi Arabia. Glowacki-Dudka, a participant in the case, experienced a warm relationship with her Saudi friend, AJ, in the US. However, she was shocked at AJ's behavioral transformation upon reentering a Saudi Arabian workplace (48–51). Glowacki-Dudka later realized that her friend had resumed her familiar social patterns and presumably expected her American friend to adapt similarly. This unrecognized, uneven capacity for code-switching appeared to significantly contribute to their mutual misinterpretation (51–54).

Persuasion and Authority

Suchan (2014) points to emotion, metaphoric language, and repetition—especially of "established truths"—as key strategies in Arabic persuasion (284–89). In this case study, contrasting strategies of persuasion appeared to confuse and frustrate both sides of the disagreement, as the conflict's intensity amplified contrasting views of authority and exacerbated miscommunication.

Emotion ran high throughout the narrative, and different parties appeared to display and interpret emotions in distinct ways. Lutz and White (1986) stress emotion's cognitive, social, and communicative functions. Across cultures, people employ emotional language to describe danger, relational loss, violations of expectations or mores, receipt of resources, and social connection, with emotion driving culturally influenced engagement with these life events (420–22, 427–31).

Pastor Shareek's uncharacteristic animation likely corresponded to senses of danger and violated mores, but it also served a powerfully persuasive communicative function. Suchan (2014) argues that "emotional resonance" is a critical part of eloquence in Arabic culture, and eloquence is instrumental to persuasion (288). Noer, Leupold, and Valle (2007) correspondingly found that emotional engagement—rather than American culture's characteristic emotional detachment—played a significant role in coaching practices even among managers from technical backgrounds in Saudi Arabia (275, 282, 284). In the case study, Mike not only appeared to be emotionally and relationally detached, but his emotional expressions—chiefly his smiles—ran counter to cultural norms. Graham (2014) notes that offenses of such deeply held norms are often attributed to an internal flaw in the offender and elicit hostility (533). By contrast, Pastor Shareek's uncharacteristic emotion was instrumental in solidifying group identities and rallying support.

When asked specific questions, Pastor Shareek often repeated his broad positions and reiterated his grievances, sometimes through eruptions of anger. To Mike, these reactions seemed irrational, immature, and evasive, much as the American participants in Suchan (2014) complained of the Jordanians "bombastic" and "unprofessional" behavior (295, 299). However, as he summarizes, "To protect individual and organizational honor … perceived challenge [has] to be met with power, emotion, and strong language" (298). Notably, Arab leaders coaching American personnel in the present case study often encouraged them to take more animated, less nuanced stands in their engagement in the conflict; equivocating was only eroding honor and further fueling suspicion.

In addition to oral persuasion, the written word took on added emphasis as the crisis deepened. Early in the partnership, both sides forewent written documentation in deference to the oral characteristics of the host context. Participants similarly deflected subsequent attempts to formalize organizational documents by appealing to historical relationships and oral recourse. However, several Arab leaders encouraged a written agreement as an absolute priority after the conflict's onset. As one leader stated, "If we can write this down and agree on it, it will become almost like the Bible to us. It will be nearly impossible to change." Indeed, extant written documents took center stage in the conflict, as Pastor Shareek often responded to questions by reciting them, occasionally after circulating written copies. By reciting what he considered definitive support—rooted in his status and the group ownership of these statements—Pastor Shareek was arguably engaging the conversation fully from his cultural frame of reference. He likely did not share the American leader's cause-and-effect enumeration of truth claims that exist independently of their social enactment.

Intercultural Leadership

Intercultural leadership played a central role in this case study, evidencing the influence of leadership expectations on interpretations of behavior. Power distance, honor, and collectivism were particularly significant.

Leadership in Arabic contexts navigates a tension between egalitarian values concurring with high power distance (Noer, Leupold, and Valle 2007, 275). A strong hierarchy in rule-based organizations coexists with demonstrations of humility and equality within groups and administrative layers. The leader ideally attains influence within the group through "persuasion, moral example, and goodwill," which are enhanced through displays of honor and generosity (Greaves 2012, 109, 112). Through personal skill and acts of performative honor, leaders gain the status necessary to lead as the "first among equals" (Khuri 1990, 11–12).

In this study's context, collective identities impacted how participants engaged and interpreted the workplace. Western participants often noted the difficulty of completing tasks alongside constant social demands. By contrast, Arab employees gathered to work. This gathering was implicitly linked to accountability, as it drove action and provided the opportunity for stakeholders to influence the result. When Mike chose to work independently, he may have therefore signaled disinterest in accommodating the positions of other stakeholders along with relational distance. From interpretations shared later in the crisis, it also became clear that Mike's independent work confirmed onlookers' suspicions of outside actors; it appeared more plausible that he was secretly working with another group than that he was working alone.

> In this study's context, collective identities impacted how participants engaged and interpreted the workplace.

The unequal social status between groups also influenced perception as Mike engaged and instructed individuals without understanding their group identities. Mike hoped to model accessible, engaged leadership. However, because he possessed high status, Mike's interjections across the institutional hierarchy unintentionally brought shame to supervisors and upset relationships among equals. In Glowacki-Dudka's engagement in Saudi Arabia, she similarly disrupted her workplace hierarchy by independently engaging her friend AJ's leaders in discussions about work. This perceived betrayal played a role in ending their friendship, and AJ's loss of face in the workplace led to her resignation (Glowacki-Dudka, Usman, and Treff, 2008, 49–51). By contrast, American volunteer leaders on Doerre's digs in Syria who did not intervene in work assignments were able to passively preserve extant social structures and their associated productivity (2001, 258).

Although Mike's view of leadership was individualistic and idea-centric, his new social environment supplied an interpretive frame for his behaviors that included unintended meanings. Robert Schreiter (1996) notes that receivers in intercultural communication use analogs to comprehend messages. These interpretive aids may or may not closely correspond to the sender's intended meaning (231). Accordingly, "Any message, when it crosses a boundary, both loses and gains information" (234). In this case, tribal analogs of leadership in an environment of honor-driven, collectivist power challenges served as interpretive frameworks for Mike's attempts at individual inclusion. For example, employees perceived Mike's attempts to include the voice of a "quiet" or "shy" individual—a member of a subordinate group—as a bid to enhance the relative power of the rival group. By contrast, Mike perceived the subordinate's detachment as a response to bullying and indicating low self-esteem. His analog was rooted in values of individual freedom and expression, values which his leadership choices sought to bring to full expression.

Intercultural Partnership and Patronage

Just as in the interpersonal context, familiar conversations conducted in shared terminology at the corporate level between partner organizations obscured widely divergent meanings influenced by unspoken values, social identities, and relational expectations. Because culture influences even the most basic concepts of mutual endeavor, underlying relational frameworks merit careful consideration.

From an individualistic perspective, relationships are often fluid and emphasize individual choice. Partnerships tend to construct similar relationships at a corporate scale, with organizations choosing to collaborate until the completion of a task that serves the purposes of both parties. However, relationships in collectivist cultures stress mutual obligations (Dean 2013, 281). In cultures that emphasize honor and exhibit high power distance, patronage structures tend to order these relational obligations. Patronage structures integrate inequality in a fluid, communal tapestry of reciprocity; the patron enhances their status by providing resources to the client, who reciprocates with loyalty to the patron (Georges 2019, 10–16, 27). Because intercultural partnerships have historically aimed to reduce inequality and dependency (Dean 2013, 273–74), especially in post-colonial relationships between the global North and South (Funkschmidt 2002, 568–71), partnerships pursued in patronage contexts present inherent challenges to both parties.

In this case study, the Western denomination's failure to recognize the dominant influence of patronage on the partnership may well have initiated Mike's collision course. Participants often discussed corporate interactions in contractual language, naming partners, negotiating agreements, drafting job descriptions and bylaws, and even referencing the procedures of synods. However, as the crisis demonstrated, these activities did not carry the same weight or meanings in the host context. The distinction between contractual partnerships and networks of patronage is particularly acute in perspectives of autonomy. Individualistic cultures value autonomy, often linking the concepts of maturity and independence. In this ministry partnership, the

Western denomination expressed this value by seeking to limit the duration of its involvement and constantly reforming its engagement to encourage the ministry's independence.

Although both parties verbally agreed on the importance of "independence," this word likely carried a different meaning to the two agreeing parties. Western mission has historically idealized ecclesial independence in terms of Venn and Anderson's three selves, and engagement in this ministry exemplified the pursuit of self-supporting structures. However, the dynamics of patronage in this unequal relationship relied on continued interdependence. Leaders like Pastor Shareek enhanced their honor-dependent leadership platforms through their global connections and the displays of generosity they supported, even as donors, churches, and mission organizations welcomed the opportunity to generously participate in an impactful, inspiring ministry. However, though financial independence was not idealized locally, independence in decision-making—taking a place as first among equals—was highly valued.

In the framework of patronage, both corporate entities existed in constant interpretive tension. As a financial patron, the Western denomination and its representatives struggled to decrease reliance on outside funding without diminishing their relationships and status by appearing stingy. As ministry clients dependent upon Pastor Shareek as a benevolent host, Western missionaries struggled to engage the crisis or even deeper ministry discussions without bringing him shame through perceived disloyalty and ingratitude. This tension built to a painful crescendo in the depths of the crisis. In patronage, "reciprocity is a moral obligation;" loyalty in critical situations is essential reciprocation of an honorable patron's generosity (Georges 2019, 15–16). Where Pastor Shareek was a client, the patron he had long honored had turned stingy and overbearing. Where he was a broker, the patron he connected to others had done untold damage, bringing him shame and heartbreak. Where he was a patron, his client had refused to reciprocate his generosity with loyalty when he depended on it the most.

Lessons Learned

When viewed from inception to crisis, this experience of miscommunication in intercultural partnership points to a tension of two closely related yet distinct "coffees": the coffee of relationship and the coffee of agreement. As Mike's reception evidenced, without heartily accepting the coffee of relationship, true intercultural exchange never begins. However, unless would-be partners delay the coffee of agreement during partnership formation, the complex and uncomfortable task of genuine intercultural communication—of creating a foundation of shared values that exceed shared terminology and mutual goodwill—becomes increasingly challenging. The rigors of ministry, the pressures of publicity, and the invisible persistence of default roles and expectations all deter the strenuous, reciprocal communication that such intercultural agreement requires.

The categories of the analysis suggest several areas about which would-be partners should constructively contend. A sincere posture of mutuality should be the starting point for intercultural collaboration (Dean 2013, 274–75). Intercultural partnership provides an inescapable challenge to individualistic values of independence; diversity of resources, perspectives, and experience demand biblical interdependence (1 Cor 12:12–31). Patronage frameworks aid in acknowledging and even managing inequality in interdependent relationships, yet biblical relationships challenge this model by asking the patron to yield honor and power to the ultimate Patron, serving others in brokerage of God's blessings rather than personal benefaction. Yielding power also requires powerful parties to perceive power dynamics from the other's perspective (Gittins 1994, 398–99). However, in the face of persistent inequality and on the heels of colonial history, essential discussions of power are all-too-readily deferred.

Discussions of accountability press the topic of power to the fore, with significant communication encoded in the very topics that make the floor of discussion and receive passionate engagement. As Rowe (2009) observes, "People only want others to be accountable for the things that are important to them" (155). Western partners often emphasize fiscal accountability. Instead, Rowe suggests accountability primarily for loyalty, positing publicized commitments as a means of socially secured accountability (152, 157). His suggestion introduces important material but also cannot stand alone. As in this case study, the standard of loyalty to people can short-circuit essential intercultural communication when its value is supreme.

There likely is no singular system or value capable of providing a basis for intercultural accountability. Instead, it arguably demands a posture, one of reciprocally choosing to be held accountable for what the "other" values most in sacrificial love. Entering into accountability presents risks—risks to finances and social face, among others. Would-be partners must consider these risks before initiating a shared endeavor. Some potential collaborations exact costs from both parties that would reasonably cause them to decline the engagement. However, choosing to decline the second coffee with full awareness is preferable to reaching intractable value differences only after bridges of communication have been destroyed.

Sources of authority must be fully engaged in the process of shared value creation, leading to expression in the most deeply held medium. In this case study, textual authority is such a medium. There is perhaps no higher hurdle than asking a leader to put their honor and reputation behind a defined proposal for collective affirmation. In this partnership, this authoritative hurdle was met with resistance, arguably for the same reasons it was essential: it cut to the heart of authority and would therefore introduce the social risks of strenuous engagement. Could the would-be partners clear the hurdle of the written corporate covenant? Was the endeavor valuable enough to face this process' inherent risks? For the Western denomination, donor intent and financial accountability often represented the final authority. Could the organization relinquish fiscal and strategic control, choosing to be held accountable for loyalty to the relationship? Could they communicate this to their donors and accrediting bodies, who formed a *de facto* foundation for the denomination's corporate model and often stood in the place of final authority?

These were high-stakes conversations to precede, not follow, the second coffee. Though these conversations were made more uncomfortable by a colonial past, avoiding them ensured the interventionist colonial model's eventual, unwitting employment. In response to violations of their most deeply held cultural values, both parties found moral justification to marshal whatever power was at their disposal to mutually destructive effect.

Establishing shared meaning, pressing to genuine intercultural communication about those things held most deeply, is easier said than done, easier dreamed than achieved. As Schreiter (1996) affirms, there is "no supracultural place to stand from which to communicate interculturally" (235). Instead, intercultural communication takes place in the "interstitial zone" of mutual experience, the "antechamber" to culture (237). However, as Jones (2019) observes, forming such a space depends on "the interaction of individuals who are more committed to the relationship than to their cultural values" (102).

In the heat of the division of this case, it became clear that each party faced the difficult challenge of putting their spiritual identities—the foundation of their relational identity and commitment (John 1:12-13; Eph 2:14-22; Col 1:13)—over all other values and loyalties. In this way, intercultural mission partnership provides a profound opportunity for participant growth in Christ-centered discipleship. As Bonhoeffer (1954) argues, self-interest and abuses of power invariably pollute direct human relationships. Where "one soul operates directly upon another soul," people may be "overpowered, but not won over by the thing itself" (33). However, relating to others through Christ and serving them "for Christ's sake" releases the desire to dominate and yields to mutual service (34–36). Having the wisdom and love to persevere to a true expression of intercultural communication rather than settling for an easily celebrated superficial unity is such a mutual service. To mission partnerships and partners, and before the witness-watching world, this service is indispensable.

Reference List

Bonhoeffer, Dietrich. 1954. *Life Together: The Classical Exploration of Christian Community*. New York: HarperOne.

Dean, Marcus W. 2013. "Mutuality in Missions: The Western Christian in Global Ministry." *Missiology: An International Review* 41, no. 3: 273–85.

Doerre, Sharon. 2001. "Negotiating Gender and Authority in Northern Syria." *International Negotiation* 6: 251–68.

Funkschmidt, Kai Michael. 2002. "New Models of Mission Relationship and Partnership." *International Review of Mission* 91, no. 363 (October): 558–76.

Georges, Jayson. 2019. *Ministering in Patronage Cultures*. Downers Grove, IL: InterVarsity Press.

Gittins, Anthony J. 1994. "Beyond Hospitality? The Missionary Status and Role Revisited." *International Review of Mission* 83, no. 330 (July): 397–416.

Glowacki-Dudka, Michelle, Irianti Usman, and Marjorie Treff. 2008. "Intercultural Conflicts Between Close Friends: A Case Study of Power Relations in Continuing Education in Saudi Arabia." *Convergence* 41, nos. 2–3: 41–58.

Graham, Sarah Ellen. 2014. "Emotion and Public Diplomacy: Dispositions in International Communications, Dialogue, and Persuasion." *International Studies Review* 16: 522–39.

Greaves, Sheldon. 2012. "A Primer of Middle Eastern Leadership Culture." *Journal of Strategic Security* 5, no. 4 (Winter): 99–118.

Jones, Todd. 2019. "Moving from Cross-Cultural to Intercultural Collaboration in Missions." *Lutheran Mission Matters* 27, no. 1 (May): 100–106.

Khuri, Fuad I. 1990. *Tents and Pyramids: Games and Ideology in Arab Culture from Backgammon to Autocratic Rule*. London: Saqi Books.

Lutz, Catherine, and Geoffrey M. White. 1986. "The Anthropology of Emotions." *Annual Review of Anthropology* 15 (October): 405–36.

Noer, David M., Christopher R. Leupold, and Matthew Valle. 2007. "An Analysis of Saudi Arabian and U.S. Managerial Coaching Behaviors." *Journal of Managerial Issues* 19, no. 2 (Summer): 271–87.

Rowe, Jonathan Y. 2009. "Dancing with Elephants: Accountability in Cross-Cultural Christian Partnerships." *Missiology: An International Review* 37, no. 2 (April): 149–63.

Schreiter, Robert J. 1996. "Communication and Interpretation Across Cultures: Problems and Prospects." *International Review of Mission* 85, no. 337: 227–39.

Shryock, Andrew. 1997. *Nationalism and the Genealogical Imagination: Oral History and Textual Authority in Tribal Jordan*. Vol 23 of Comparative Studies on Muslim Societies. Berkeley, CA: University of California Press. Kindle Edition.

Suchan, Jim. 2014. "Toward an Understanding of Arabic Persuasion: A Western Perspective." *International Journal of Business Communication* 51, no. 3: 279–303.

Chapter 6

Contextualizing the Gospel in Australia
Empowering Christ to Communicate with an Aussie Accent

Robert L. Gallagher

Historic and Geographic Influencers

Australia is a society of immigrants with concepts and institutions transported primarily from Europe over the last 230 years. As European Australians began building their nation, harsh conditions confronted the first settlers. Most of these pioneers were convicts from the British Isles who developed a sense of mutual dependence, which was transplanted to subsequent generations, and fostered throughout their colonial history. For instance, the early settlers lacked doctors and hospitals, and were not only dependent on each other for necessities, but for survival itself. The industrial revolution mitigated/eliminated the harshness of these earlier outback experiences, but the shape of interdependence remains.

The ethnic foundations of the Australian nation were Anglo-Celtic with democratic social and political orientations. Its citizens/people were aware of the derivative nature of their society and were conscious of shaping their own distinctive national identity. The common experience of the Australian frontier, with its vast mileage of unmapped and undeveloped terrain, molded this uniqueness. The pioneering experiences of the inhospitable, desolate landscape with its persuasive mythology have contributed to many of the basic qualities that Australians share. According to Harvie Conn, "Myth functions on the deepest level of a culture's structure" (Conn 1984, 326).

Representative of this shared foundation is Dorothea Mackellar's poem, "My Country," first published in London's *The Spectator* (a British political magazine) in 1908. This poem epitomizes the deep feelings of pride and love most Australians have for their country. The second and fifth stanzas read, in part, "I love a sunburnt country, a land of sweeping plains, of ragged mountain ranges, ... I love her far horizons, I love her jewel-sea, ... Core of my heart, my country! Land of the Rainbow Gold, for flood, fire, and famine, She pays us back threefold ... ."

The uniformity of the forlorn scenery—the sameness of the inland desert and temperate coastal plains—and adaptation to this dry land has wrought an inner loneliness which persists throughout Australian history.

Another historic influence that shaped Australian society was the introduction of Christianity. The English navigator James Cook discovered the continent of the "Southern Land of the Holy Spirit" for Britain in 1770, making it an outpost of Anglo-Celtic civilization, and eventually reflecting the British Christian denominations with their Protestant Anglican majority and oppressed Irish Catholic minority. In 1788, Arthur Phillip led the First Fleet into Sydney Cove, New South Wales, and founded a convict settlement to relieve the teeming prisons of England. The Anglican evangelical Samuel Marsden who arrived in 1793 as the second penal chaplain, also served as a magistrate in the colony. As an early court administrator at Parramatta, west of Sydney, he earned the title the "flogging parson" because of his severity in sentencing prisoners. Until Governor Ralph Darling (1825–31), the Church of England clergy in New South Wales were often colonial judges, which, from the prisoner's point of view, linked the church with government suppression. Thus, religion in the early colony at Sydney had connections to convict punishment, which resulted in an almost total rejection of the Christian message (Hughes 1986, 1–18).

The Church of England was the overriding religious institution throughout Australia's early settlement. Even though the early colonial authorities had contempt for the "consolations of religion," they believed that the Anglican clergy were to improve "public morality" in the colony. They also shared the belief that "the Protestant religion and British institutions were the finest achievements of the wit of humanity for the promotion of liberty and a high material civilization." The Protestant ministers were viewed as the "natural moral police officers of society" and socially helpful to the convict colony for preaching against "drunkenness, whoring, and gambling" (Clark 2006, 13–14). According to Manning Clark, "Evangelical [Anglican] Christianity dominated the religious life of Protestant Christianity in Australia throughout the whole of the nineteenth century" (2006, 14).

Australians held their first Church of England synod in the diocese of Sydney in 1866, even though it continued to import bishops from England. Exactly one hundred years later, the first Australian-born archbishop, Marcus Loane, won elections in Sydney. This came about after the Australian Church became autonomous from England in 1962. It was not until 1981 that the Church of England in Australia changed its name to the Anglican Church of Australia (Gallagher 2012, 168–70). Shane Clifton maintains, "It has become a historical truism to suggest that Australian churches continue to face the legacy of early antipathy to church authority with writers citing in particular the close alignment of the church and the state and early examples of ecclesial oppression" (2009, 51).

Characteristics of Aussie Culture

The foundational attributes of the Anglo-Celtic Australian populace arose within the colonial milieu of religious distrust combined with the distinctive ethos that Australians developed because of the historic and geographic influences described. The question to be asked regarding the resultant characteristics of the people is, "How do Australians behave in a given situation and why?" Because of their historic beginnings, coupled with the challenges of the natural environment, the people of Australia are pragmatic and creative, placing little emphasis on intellectual and spiritual activities. They are flexible, gregarious, and straightforward in their manner. Concerning personal features, Australians are easy-going, friendly, humorous, and sardonic, with a highly developed appreciation of the art of deadpan understatement and sarcasm. Australians especially enjoy informal, spontaneous, self-deprecating humor that might appear inappropriate, disrespectful, and offensive. To relieve stress during misery, Australian humor often increases in its jesting and irony with the twist of a witty quip.

While viewing the basic characteristics of Anglo-Celtic culture, it is important to realize that these depictions are generalizations and are not evident in every Australian. This is especially true of new Australians (recent immigrants) and the indigenous people—who, although they are only three percent of the total population (721,000), have legal rights to 40 percent of the continent's land mass. The traits described are fundamental cultural qualities, which many Australians share with other Australians, yet they are not present to the same degree in each person. Beliefs and values might shape the worldview of people within a particular culture, but the influences on the genders are sometimes different. The qualities of Australians depicted in this chapter are often evident in both men and women. Nevertheless, they are more dominant in the males of the society. With these limitations in mind, the following section will expand on the matters of culture fundamental to the Australian psyche that directly affect Australians' outlook towards the Christian faith (see Renwick 1980; Smith 1987; Garvin 1992; Smith 1992; Mackay 1993; Bryson 2001; Clancy 2004; Fletcher 2007).

Conversational Manner

In conversation, Australians use few words, carefully selected, and speak casually, while conveying meaning through pithy slices of information, rather than tending towards loquaciousness. In this relaxed and informal way, they enjoy cynicism in speech, especially when arguing, and lean towards being terse and piercing, readily expressing negative feelings and opinions about both people and circumstances. They use hundreds of flamboyant colloquial terms to portray a tone of amiable, tolerant contempt. In this manner, they may appear to be self-assertive, brazen, overbearing, unpredictable, and obnoxious, not bothered by contradictions, which often involves themselves. Conversations do not have to be agreeable, just lively, and interesting.

Even though Australians may appear relaxed and affable at one moment, they can also express strong opinions and severe criticisms at the next. They enjoy living each day, but they can be pessimistically introspective. Although embracing of life and possessing a spirit of exuberance, Australians can impose upon themselves social policies of denial and severe restraint. This manifests in numerous ways, none more pronounced than their communal restrictions on alcohol and gambling. They tend to be unconcerned about what people think of them, and thus are not interested in influencing someone's opinions. They are most interested in a person who disagrees with them, however, since this can lead to a vibrant discussion and creates a genuine interest and respect.

One reason for this assertiveness is that Australians receive needed recognition and confirm their identity by acting against other peoples' thoughts, posturing, and beliefs. They need someone to be against them to understand and affirm who they are. Relationships are satisfying when they are challenging. Most Australians are ethnocentric, as if their beliefs and ways of doing things are cleverer than other alternatives. They do not need to speak about their approach as being better. Their silence reveals that their method is top-quality, and brusquely dismisses any challenge to these suppositions. Paradoxically, they emphatically resent assumptions of superiority, an engrained quality coming from their convict legacy of equality.

Egalitarian Collectivism

Australia's current population is approaching 26 million, and the country has assimilated large numbers of immigrants after its convict beginnings. The subcultures are homogenous since most of the early immigrants to the country were from the lower class. This has also led to the social classes being uniform, with the progression of migration reducing distinctions between classes and the Eurocentric tradition of social rank. Migration has resulted in most Australians being informal in their connections with other people and having a high degree of class-consciousness. Since the differences between the classes are small, Australians resist different treatment, especially when they believe that the action is condescending, and someone sees them as a lower classification.

Australians have a robust sense of community because of their recent frontier experience along with their lack of class, subcultural, and racial distinctiveness. They tend to be egalitarian collectivists, valuing cooperative efforts and socialist ideas through patriarchal legislation. Rugged individualism is not as respected by Australians as other societies. So highly do they value egalitarianism that they are also status-conscious, whereby, instead of working for and respecting rank and title, they tend to question and challenge it. They dislike any show of ambition that would establish someone as superior over another person. Clifton supports this analysis:

> The convict and migrant heritage gave rise to a culture that tended to avow a rigid class system. It has become almost commonplace to speak of Australia as an egalitarian nation. While the assumption of egalitarianism is no doubt mythological, yet it is true that institutions, which affirm the importance of the average person, and reject "snobbery," find resonance with the Australian psyche. (2009, 52)

Table 6.1 below shows a comparison between an Australian's perception of Christianity and Australian culture that underscores this egalitarian collectivism. People view religion as a crutch. Weak-willed individuals need a support outside themselves and their mates because they do not have the inner strength of character to persist and succeed in life. Comradeship with one's mates is a substitute for religion, demonstrated via the welfare state, allegiance to sport, climatic hardships, the pub community, Aussie barbeques, disdain of the "tall poppy," and the national celebrations of Anzac Day (April 25) and the Melbourne Cup (first Tuesday of November). Clark (1995) asserts, "Australians live in a country where neither historian, the prophets, the poets, or the priests have drawn the maps" (625).

Christianity	Australian Culture
God	Welfare state
Christ	Mateship
Holy Spirit	Sport
Devil	Climatic hardships
Sanctuary	Pub

Fellowship	Comradeship
Communion	Aussie barbeque
Sin	A "tall poppy" who forgets his mates
Easter	Anzac Day
Christmas	Melbourne Cup Day

Table 6.1: Comparison of Christianity and Australian Culture

Disrespect of Authority

Like the cultural traits of egalitarian collectivism and suspicion of religion, Australians' disrespect of authority is historically time-honored. The unofficial national anthem, "Waltzing Matilda," written by A.B. "Banjo" Paterson in 1895, demonstrates this heightened social characteristic of resentment of superiors. The song depicts a carefree, underdog swagman or itinerant outback worker, waltzing or wandering through the rural landscape with the only comfort against this harsh life being his blanket roll ("Matilda"). He steals a jumbuck (sheep) for food, and the police (troopers) and the squatter (a rich British landowner who ironically became wealthy by taking land which did not belong to him) catch him. Rather than be hung by the authorities, the free-spirited swagman commits suicide by drowning himself in the billabong or waterhole. "Waltzing Matilda" is more than a tragic song about an underdog swaggie. It embodies the rebellious spirit of Australia, reminding the singers of the punitive beginnings of white settlement, which evokes great emotion in the hearts of many contemporary Australians. For this reason, Ned Kelly, the son of poor Irish Catholics, and a bushranger, outlaw, and gang leader, is seen as a heroic anti-establishment figure who fought corrupt British colonists in the late nineteenth century.

The deep belief in democratic equality still results in a lack of respect towards authority, including religious leaders and employers. It is a challenge for an Australian to work within a controlling hierarchical structure with its constricting rules and regulations. Although the "Aussie battler" (a working-class Australian) is by nature disrespectful of superiors, he will agree to hierarchical control if those in charge put aside their badges of honor such as position, accomplishments, or networks. Australians respect sincerity, competency, and personal attributes of character. In other words, whether a person is "fair dinkum" or not. In less idiomatic terms: are people sincere in what they say and do, or are they phonies and full of pretense? Australian workers resist people who they consider are not genuine, becoming impatient with attempts to impress, fuss, or follow rigid points of decorum. They believe in people who display trustworthiness and dedication (Gallagher 1999, 10).

Table 6.2 presents a comparison between Anglicanism with its hierarchical leadership style and the anti-authoritarian Australian culture. The table illustrates that the free-spiritedness, irregularity, and informality of the Australian community is in direct contrast with the traditional formality of the ordered and constrained Church of England governance and worship. In addition, the Aussie celebration of earthiness—perpetuated within the bush mythology of being a people of the land with access to wide-open spaces and rural freedom—contradicts the stifling confines of urban-city life. This social complexity is incongruous since The World Bank (2021) estimates that the urban population of Australia has moved from 80 percent in 1980 to 89 percent in 2020.

Anglicanism	Australian Culture
God the Judge	God the Mate
"Almighty God"	"Old Hughie;" "the Boss upstairs"
Cathedral	Practical home
Formal worship	Informal, casual behavior
Traditional order	Intolerance of convention
Rules and regulations	Anti-authoritarianism
Hierarchical governance	Egalitarian collectivism
Titles and rank	Levelling tendencies
Practice and experience	Capacity for improvisation
Submission to authority	Manly independence
English gentleman	Working bushman
Loyalty to superiors	Mateship: group solidarity
Anglican Worship	Australian Worship
Composure	Freedom
Restriction	Creative energy
Sense of constraint	Wide-open spaces
Order	Irregularity
Elegance	Celebration of earthiness
Balanced beauty	Ragged beauty
Formality	Informality

Table 6.2: Comparison of Anglicanism and Australian Culture

Aussie Mateship

Several films commemorate the folklore perception of needed space and relief from conventional restrictions and dull routine. For instance, Nicholas Roeg's *Walkabout* (1971), Paul Hogan's *Crocodile Dundee* (1986), and John Curran's *Tracks* (2013). The movie Crocodile Dundee not only carries the bush mythology of an affection towards broad rural landscapes, casual informality, and free-spirited anti-authoritarianism, but is also infused with the concept of mateship, involving God himself. With boyish optimism and laconic wit, Crocodile Dundee swaggers through the Australian film in good-humored naiveté. Dundee confidently declares when questioned as to whether he is afraid of death, "Nah. I read the Bible once. You know, God and Jesus and all of them apostles. They were all fishermen, just like me. Yep. Straight to heaven for Mick Dundee. Yep. Me and God, we'd be mates." The lore of mateship implies a theological paradigm whereby Christians could present the gospel to a present-day Aussie society in spiritual decline (Gallagher 2006, 127–28).

The spirit of mateship stems from the historic and geographic conditions of an unforgiving continent where physical and emotional miseries forged mutual dependence. "Mateship" is the equal and friendly fellowship that a person receives from a companion—a mate. The convict era (over 162,000 convicts transported; 1788–1868) produced strong feelings of group solidarity and allegiance. To withstand the misery of the penal system, the Anglo-Celtic pioneers clung to egalitarian-class commonality. This fraternity was not a charitable friendship, but a necessity for survival among refugees. The practice of a collectivist mateship was vital. Most convicts settled in the farmlands of eastern Australia once they earned a pardon (ticket-of-leave). Again, the difficult conditions of the outback made mateship indispensable. Immense distances, loneliness, and climatic severity forced strangers to share money, goods, and resources. People were compelled to help and trust one another. Before the turn of the twentieth century, the legend of mateship had become a powerful convention. It was further entrenched in Australian mythology by the nation's respect of the Anzac soldiers' ("diggers'") sacrifice in the two world wars; none were more admired than Private John Simpson Kirkpatrick and his donkey at Gallipoli, Turkey (Gallagher 1997, 14–15; Gallagher 2006, 127–28).

A comparison of Anglicanism and Aussie mateship in Table 6.3 again demonstrates the cultural discontinuity between society and organized Christianity. The levelling tendencies, casualness, and worker communalism of mateship at every level is in stark contrast with the hierarchical formality and ceremonial pomp of the European belief system. Australians continue to share this authentic spirit of mateship, a sense that "we would lay down our life for a friend." They strongly believe that if they stick together as mates—hold on to friendship through the good and tough times—then they will flourish as a people despite the unrelenting ruggedness of the environment with its floods, bush fires, and droughts. This attitude that encourages cohesiveness and homogeneity, while not highlighting exceptionalism, is revealed in such films as Peter Weir's *Gallipoli* (1981), Ken Olin's *In Pursuit of Honor* (1995), and Russell Crowe's *The Water Diviner* (2014).

Anglicanism	Aussie Mateship
Church of England	Church of Australia
Hierarchical leadership	Anti-authoritarianism
Upper-middle-class leadership	Working-class leadership
British-social forms	Egalitarian-community forms
Priestly vestments	Worker uniforms
Clerical dress	Casual dress
Formal-preaching style	Informal sharing of the heart
Sacred furniture	Material collectivism
Hierarchical orders	Levelling tendencies
Liturgical chanting	"Down-to-earth" communication
Liturgical hymns	Bush folk songs
Church choirs	Communal pub singing
Intellectual language	Colloquial language

Table 6.3: Comparison of Anglicanism and Aussie Mateship

Interpersonal Relationships

Combined with the cultural characteristics of a sense of mateship, disrespect of authority, egalitarianism, and conversational manner, an Australian is often resistant to decisions that are not collaborative. Procedures for making choices are more prone towards cooperative negotiation, rather than simply obeying instructions. Approached personally, any interaction with an Australian needs to include an equal appreciation of their experience and competency to prevent the arbitration spiraling towards argument and umbrage. They consider themselves equal persons in every way to their supervisors, with commendable ideas and opinions. Australians believe that the employer understands that workers share equally in the organization's goals, and achievements provide a basis for decision-making. Consequently, the workers need to be included to reach a consensus in institutional choices. As we have witnessed, this approach is in disparity to Anglicanism with its ranked determinations.

More interested in the enjoyment of living for today, the details of future planning do not overly worry Aussies. They believe that people need to slow down, not rush, and enjoy the journey with their mates in the land of the long weekend. They are not overly ambitious, and tend to be suspicious of title, rank, and wealth. Because of their egalitarian disposition, they are disinclined to acknowledge excellence publicly, even if the person displays extraordinary qualities. Intentionally easy-going, Australians nonetheless tend to thrive on conflict. Indeed, they relish it, and even foster the opportunity to pursue it deliberately. Accustomed to disagreement and resilient to it, they seldom over-react to those who retaliate in like-mindedness. Furthermore, they give honor to people who engage in disagreement with poise and wit. This is historically evident with members of Parliament who have governmental privilege whereby no one can sue them for anything they say in Assembly about each other or about persons outside the Legislature. This privilege has produced numerous occasions where a member of Parliament has hurled inflammatory barbs at opposition members (Bryson 2001, 15–16).

Australians are critical of any affectation and suspicious of posturing. They are strongly resentful of anyone who is patronizing or attempts to unduly exercise authority over them. With their highly attuned awareness of status and abhorrence towards superiority, Australians are particularly alert to any pretensions when interacting with people, especially with perceived attitudes that exude, "We are the world's best and biggest." As a result, there are strong leveling tendencies within the Australian "knocker" culture. This plays out in numerous situations resulting from a long history of "underdog" mentality in tension with the British feudal heritage. The derogatory term used to describe this social phenomenon is the "tall poppy syndrome," in which accomplished people are cut down or criticized because their achievements raise them above their colleagues. Australians enjoy challenging people as they prod and poke to see if a person has gumption and integrity.

Communicating Christ

An Australian's interpersonal relationships once again confirm the interpretation of the preceding insights with respect to the culture's interface with Christianity. In simpler terms, the historic and geographic roots of Anglo-Celtic Australian society, with its Protestant domination by the Church of England, has forged a worldview that pushes against organized religion, and collides with most of Anglican tradition and custom. How then does today's Australian church present Christ in a way that is appropriate and understandable? In other words, how do you communicate the gospel in an Australian context? The Christian message may be 100 percent true, yet its communicators can package it in such a way that it is 100 percent irrelevant. The truth of God's Son needs to link the cultural gap between church and society to be pertinent to modern Australian people, who are well established in their own specific socio-cultural and historical context. The church needs to enter the people's worldview and allow them to embrace Jesus using their own cultural forms. The concluding section of this treatise will suggest ways to contextualize an Australian gospel by first analyzing the declining national influence of the Anglican Church before illustrating contemporary models and features of effective mateship evangelism.

Declining Influence of Christianity

This chapter employs the Anglican Church in Australia as a foil only to highlight the cultural discrepancies of any European imported religion. This focus on Anglicanism does not imply that the leaders or laity of this ecclesial body are insincere in their Christian faith, incompetent in governance, or theologically inadequate. Nor does it suggest that the writer is unappreciative of the long and animist spirituality of the indigenous nationals. The historic British-church institution as a counter measure to Australian society is relevant simply because of the denomination's duration, reputation, and supremacy. Additionallly, this limited essay can only treat the reasons for the overall waning impact of Anglicanism in preference to drawing attention to broader models and patterns of contextual success.

Immigrants bring their own forms of Christianity with them. The non-indigenous population in Australia from the First Fleet of British convicts in 1788 to the end of World War Two was primarily composed of Protestants from the British Isles. By 1901, the year of the Federation of Australia, Christianity had grown to 96 percent of the national population, but the denominational percentages had changed whereby Anglicans were 40 percent and Catholics 23 percent of the populace. It was after the Second World War that this religious scene radically changed when government-sponsored immigration from southern Europe increased the membership of the Catholic Church. The Church of England remained the largest denomination until 1986, when the Catholics surpassed it (Gallagher 2012, 171–72).

By 1970, 2 million immigrants had disembarked to work in the country's expanding industries. One year later, the proportion of Anglicans to Catholics nearly equaled one another with Anglicans 31 percent, Catholics 27 percent, and other Christians 28 percent. Twenty years later, Catholics were by far the largest Christian group with 27 percent of the population, while Anglicans and other Protestants had dropped to 24 and 23 percent, respectively. The non-religious categories had grown in twenty years from 7 to 18 percent, while the total percent of Christians decreased from 86 to 74 percent, even though the population increased by 4 million (Hutchinson 2000, 95–97). The most recent Australian census was held in 2016 and confirmed that 52 percent of Australians classified themselves as Christians. The largest denominations were Catholic (23 percent), Anglican (13 percent), and no religion (30 percent). The census found that there was a 7 percent decrease in the number of Christians since 2011.

Models of Mateship Evangelism

There is no straightforward way to explain or remedy the decreasing percentage of Australians affiliated with the Christian faith, including Anglicanism. Some church leaders have looked to society and found reasons for the decline in secular humanism, urbanization, and the increasing power of the state over the church. Few investigators have looked within the church itself to find the solution. Since World War Two, Australians have increasingly struggled to identify their national character. In this process, they have found little reason to pay attention to the church. Quite simply, they have found it easy to reject any form of Christianity that does not speak with an Aussie accent. It has been progressively difficult for ordinary persons to comprehend a message of Christ that does not address the problems of life in Australia. How then are the churches to contextualize the gospel within society's ethos? If churches seek to move beyond their existing populace, they need to consider the nature of their community and its needs. The increasingly multicultural aspect of Australian civilization requires the development of new visions that will allow new forms of ministry to emerge, which should foster a willingness to include people whom the Christian community previously excluded.

The ingredients of character discussed in the earlier part of this paper—pragmatism, informality, democratic equality, and authenticity—are what the average citizen is looking for in religious communicators. The late John Smith, one of Australia's leading evangelists, incorporated both a down-to-earth approach and a passion to reach the unchurched with the message of Christian reconciliation. He was committed to transforming the lives of youth and society's outcasts with a strong voice for social justice, coupled with a capacity for practical action. To communicate the Christian message to a society that is drifting further from it, he gave a common person's view of Christ. For Smithy, Jesus mixed with average blokes (talking to farmers and fishermen), using stories that attracted regular people who frequented the pubs, beer gardens, and clubs of Palestine. In rejecting the Christian subculture that alienates itself from those outside the church, Smith took the gospel to the people through mateship evangelism, telling passionate stories that were appealing, entertaining, and relevant in a manner that was attractive to most Australians (see Gallagher 2005a, 152–54).

> It has been progressively difficult for ordinary persons to comprehend a message of Christ that does not address the problems of life in Australia.

The mateship premise is a narrow approach to a complex subject that demands a greater nuance of expression. There are many more aspects of indigenizing the gospel within a culture than any one simple issue. Still, using an integrating factor such as mateship does enable a concentration of study that could be a helpful platform for future deliberations. That is, reflections towards a praxis of contextualized mateship that would communicate a more effectual Christian message wherein Christ speaks with an Aussie accent. Table 6.4 suggests models of mateship evangelism that effectively communicate Jesus Christ in a contextualized manner. For example, John Smith of the para church Truth and Liberation Concern in Melbourne, Robert and Julie Banks with the house-church movement in Canberra, Michael Frost and the missional church in Sydney, and Warwick and Alison Marsh with the minstrel church in rural arenas around the nation.

Model	Ministry	Method
Para Church	John Smith: Melbourne author and speaker	Smith was a practical-minded person who could talk the common language and speak from his heart. He spoke to businesspeople as well as thousands of high school and university students each year. His message concerned Christ in everyday life.
House Church	Robert and Julie Banks: People's Movement in Canberra	The central focus is a responsibility for each other in Christ. The language and style tend to the ordinary person and relates to the normal experiences of life.

Missional Church	Michael Frost: Sydney missiologist and theologian	Frost uses a missional church framework to reach postmodern society. He founded "smallboatbigsea" in Manly (a northern suburb of Sydney): a faith community reaching people using regular language about Christ. He ministers in a practical way that relates to most Australians.
Minstrel Church	Warwick and Alison Marsh: Gospel musicians in Wollongong	The Marshes tour country regions with their family of four singing Australian folk and rock with a strong Christian message. From rural high schools to indigenous encampments and town parks, they serve as types of medieval minstrels of Christ.

Table 6.4: Models of Mateship Evangelism

Features of Mateship Evangelism

This segment challenges the current communication praxis in Australia from a practical viewpoint. Preaching in Australian churches often operates within a narrow applicational hermeneutic and hence communicates the gospel ineffectually to ordinary Australians. It is not true to say that Australia was or is the most godless place under heaven. There is a need for contextualized and dialogical preaching. Aussies are seeking a national church movement enriched by a variety of cultural influences that develops a praxis of contextualized mateship incorporating human identity, justice in society, personal and family morals, and discovery of the land. In considering models of mateship evangelism, the features shown in Figure 6.1 are pertinent. Realism in everyday life, compassion for the common person, and the use of ordinary language and humor in context are significant and help in deciding how to develop contextualized styles of mission that will make connections for those uncomfortable with traditional church practices (see Clancy 2004, 31–50).

Realism in everyday life is a key component since triumphal Christianity is out of place in Australian culture. Many Australians are strong skeptics who see the idea of "the endless possibilities for life's happiness in Christ" as completely unrealistic. The irrelevance of the church to everyday life is a shared cry among the burgeoning non-religious in Australia. The church needs to remind the nation of a Christianity that has its sleeves rolled up. For instance, Catholic lay-worker Caroline Chisholm who worked towards improving the conditions of women migrants in the 1840s; Saint Mary MacKillop (1842–1909), Australia's first canonized saint of the Catholic Church who founded schools, convents, and charitable institutions throughout the country; and John Flynn of the Presbyterian Church (Flynn of the Inland) who founded the nation's first air-ambulance service in 1928 at Cloncurry, Queensland, which became the Royal Flying Doctor Service. All of the above trusted Christian leaders have defended the lowly while challenging those in power.

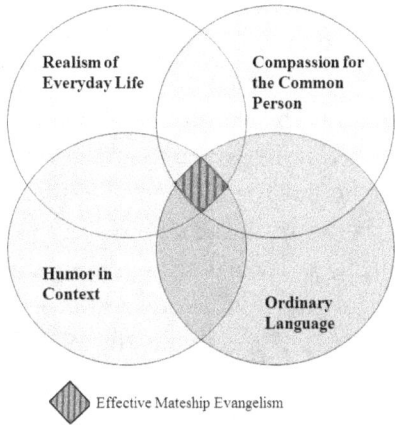

Figure 6.1 Features of Effective Mateship Evangelism

Compassion for the common person will gain respect. The Australian community will listen to those whose deeds speak louder than their words. Christians must demonstrate that they care about the concerns of ordinary people. Incarnational mission speaks most effectively to an Australian society (Gallagher 2005b, 538). The direction of this incarnation is towards public friendship, solidarity with the poor, compassion, and justice, which is demonstrated in the Salvation Army (lovingly nicknamed "Salvos"). It is difficult to convince average Australians of the truth of the Christian faith simply through argument. Because they think of themselves as a matter-of-fact people, they concentrate on issues that require practical solutions. In a society of skilled "knockers" who are sensitive to hollow pretension, clergy need to first present themselves as good blokes with the common touch if they desire to have any chance of being heard.

Another feature of mateship evangelism is the use of ordinary language. Bob Hawke, the Australian Prime Minister between 1983 and 1991, was a good bloke with the common touch who used ordinary language to communicate. Hawke saw himself as a man of the people. In this special relationship was his enthusiasm for cigars, horseracing, and all forms of sport, together with heavy drinking and women, which only made him more popular with the public. In his role as Prime Minister, he still holds the highest approval rating.

His approach to government was pragmatic, concerning himself with making improvements to workers' lives from within the traditional institutions of government. Among his social reforms were Medicare, the Family Assistance Scheme, and pensions for all workers. In addition, the Hawke government revolutionized the economy, raised awareness of the indigenous people and the environment, as well as centering foreign policy in Asia, all the while communicating in a language that all of society embraced.

The last feature important to an Aussie contextualized gospel is the use of humor in context, which is often missing in the church. Australian audiences appreciate warmth of humor and naivete. Australians celebrate Christmas in the heat of the southern hemisphere with many European traditions faithfully observed, for instance, the hot-roast dinner. Despite that, amid the annual Chrissie pilgrimage to the nearest beach, there are arising Aussie adaptations such as carols-by-candlelight. These large open-air carol services conducted on summer evenings plant Aussie musical creations firmly in the context of heat, dry winds, and red dust. For example, the 1948 Christian carol by John Wheeler and William G. James, "Three Drovers," and Rolf Harris and John D. Brown's 1960 Christmas song, "Six White Boomers," that has Santa flying around the Australian continent pulled by six white-boomer kangaroos in place of reindeer.

Conclusion

The Anglo-Celtic Australian culture is still developing its own recognizable identity, and at the same time is concerned about maintaining its distinctiveness. The nation's history, people, and land have shaped a way of life that is uniquely Australian. Hidden within this struggle for national exclusivity is a search for meaning and purpose. There is a sense of uncertainty and lack of common direction as the nation begins moving through the twenty-first century. Australians are concerned about their collective national life, and desire to be independent, self-initiating, and self-sufficient.

The church in Australia will need to change its strategy if there is any real desire to reverse the present decline in attendance. To simply go on as an institution and maintain existing structures and operations for their own sake will not erect bridges between the church and the community. Some of the reasons for the decline in church attendance may lie within Australian society, but the decline is a complex phenomenon with multiple causes. It is also possible that many churches have simply been insensitive to Australian culture, which can explain the persistent drift away from the institutionalized church. At this critical juncture, the churches should join with the Australian people, and help to shape their cultural distinctiveness. There is a need to work together to produce an authentic Christianity genuine to Australia.

This chapter has proposed that one of the Australian church's main challenges is the cultural divide between itself and the community it desires to serve. Too many churches do not include essential cultural concerns in their Christian faith. The foundation of church life, though, must be within the experiences, attitudes, and reflections of its people if they are going to change their allegiance to Christ. By bridging this divide, the church may see a reversal of present trends. Christianity in Australia needs an approach that presents a contextualized gospel in harmony with the cultural elements. Australians still respect the concepts of mateship since these urban and industrialized people have found no suitable alternative. Mateship can provide a starting point for Australian Christianity to achieve these goals by empowering Christ to communicate with an Aussie accent.

References Cited

Bryson, Bill. 2001. *In a Sunburned Country*. New York: Broadway Books.

Clancy, Laurie. 2004. *Culture and Customs of Australia*. Westport, CT: Greenwood Press.

Clark, Manning. 1995. *Manning Clark's History of Australia*. Abridged by Michael Cathcart. Ringwood, VIC: Penguin.

Clark, Manning. 2006. *A Short History of Australia*. 4th edition. Sydney, NSW: Penguin Books Australia.

Clifton, Shane. 2009. *Pentecostal Churches in Transition: Analyzing the Developing Ecclesiology of the Assemblies of God in Australia*. Leiden, The Netherlands: Koninklijke Brill NV.

Conn, Harvie. 1984. *Eternal Word and Changing Worlds*. Grand Rapids, MI: Zondervan.

Fletcher, Mal. 2007. *Five Big Ideas: Concepts That Shape Our Culture*. London: Next Wave International.

Gallagher, Robert L. 1997. "Blinky Bill Rides Again: An Australian Folk Tale's Impact." *Theology, News and Notes* 44, no. 4 (December): 14–15.

Gallagher, Robert L. 1999. "Aussie Men Don't Cry—Do They?" *Crusade Action* 2, no. 4 (Spring): 10.

Gallagher, Robert L. 2005a. "The Hebraic Covenant as a Model for Contextualization." In *Appropriate Christianity*, edited by Charles H. Kraft, 135–54. Pasadena, CA: William Carey Library.

Gallagher, Robert L. 2005b. "Review of The Word Made Flesh: Towards an Incarnational Missiology by Ross Langmead." *Evangelical Missions Quarterly* 41, no. 4 (October): 538, 540.

Gallagher, Robert L. 2006. "'Me and God, We'd Be Mates:' Towards an Aussie Contextualized Gospel." *International Bulletin of Missionary Research* 30, no. 3 (July): 127–32.

Gallagher, Robert L. 2012. "Australian Christianity." In *The Encyclopedia of Christian Civilization*, edited by George Thomas Kurian, 168–73. Volume 1. Chichester, UK: Wiley-Blackwell.

Gallagher, Robert L. 2019. "Contextualization in Context." The Great Commission edition. *International Journal of Pentecostal Mission* 6, no. 1 (Winter): 112–14.

Garvin, Mal. 1992. *Us Aussies: The Fascinating History They Didn't Tell Us at School*. Sale, VIC: Hayzon.

Gilliland, Dean S. 1989. "Contextual Theology as Incarnational Mission." In *The Word among Us: Contextualizing Theology for Mission Today*, edited by Dean S. Gilliland, 9–31. Dallas, TX: Word Publishing.

Hughes, Robert. 1986. *The Fatal Shore: The Epic of Australia's Founding*. New York: Alfred A. Knopf.

Hutchinson, Mark. 2000. "Australia." In *Evangelical Dictionary of World Missions*, edited by A. Scott Moreau, 95–97. Grand Rapids, MI: Baker Books.

Mackay, Hugh. 1993. *Reinventing Australia: The Mind and Mood of Australia*. Sydney, NSW: Angus & Robertson.

Moreau, A. Scott. 2018. *Contextualizing the Faith: A Holistic Approach*. Grand Rapids, MI: Baker Academic.

Renwick, George W. 1980. *Interact: Guidelines for Australians and North Americans*. Yarmouth, ME: Intercultural Press.

Smith, John. 1987. *On the Side of the Angels*. Oxford, UK: Lion Publishing.

Smith, John. 1992. *Advance Australia Where*? Sydney, NSW: Anzea.

The World Bank. 2021. "Urban Population" (http://data.worldbank.org/indicator). Worldbank.org.

Chapter 7

Honor/Shame Culture

Analyzing Impact on Christian Women's Social Exchanges

Kara L. Garrison

During the writing of this paper, Myanmar is again in the international news because of social chaos. The Myanmar church has the potential to be a social reconciler. However, ingrained social structures and practices prevent the Myanmar Christian church from being a place of safety. What does a missionary entering Southeast Asian culture need to grasp regarding the communication patterns and system thinking in this region?

This chapter proposes a framework for understanding the complexities of social exchange inside Myanmar. The content represents an excerpt of a two-year study and dissertation seeking to better understand how worldview and communication patterns impacted trust building and breaking among Myanmar Christian women (MCW) (Garrison 2020). In this chapter, "communication" goes beyond words, gestures, and facial expression to include ideas, behaviors, desires, and suppressed fears of both the individual and the surrounding social environment.

Cultural Context

Honor/Shame Contextualized in Eastern Worldview

Missiologist Jackson Wu describes three general aspects of an honor/shame worldview in the East Asian context: a concern for "face," deference toward vertical relationships, and collectivism as an identity (Wu 2016). These cultural aspects are also found in Southeast Asia's Myanmar. Wu writes, "In broad terms, a person's 'honor' refers to his or her perceived public worth within a relational context. ... By contrast, 'shame' is the ill repute that results when a person has an alleged deficiency or fails to meet the standards prescribed by his or her community" (Wu 2016, 376).

Face

Socio-psychologists Ho, Fu, and Ng (2004) explain the concept of face in reference to public worth and identity originates in China. The authors provide interesting insight regarding inner emotions and facial expression—or the lack of, in Eastern cultures:

> Western literature has focused primarily on the expression of emotions. We submit that concealment, non-expression and deceptive expression deserve no less research attention. In any society emotional expressions have to be regulated by external demands. To this extent, internal emotional states have to be subjugated, and spontaneous expressions circumscribed. (Ho, Fu, and Ng 2004, 70)

Confucian hierarchical teaching creates a dissonance between mind and expression. Accordingly, a social inferior who demonstrates emotion is immodest and risks displeasing a superior with his disrespectful countenance, which may result in extreme consequences. By contrast, a superior who constrains expression—an act equated with trustworthiness in the annals of Confucius—gains greater face. (Confucius, trans. Lyall 1909)

This study argues that emotional deception inhibits trust building, making vulnerability too costly. "An actor may play the game of face with emotional detachment ... this generates strain in interpersonal relationships ... and more occasions for losing face," (Ho, Fu, and Ng 2004, 70). In the Burmese context, it creates the tension of *ahnade*,[1] or the pressure to outwardly present one response while, in reality, a different constrained and disguised emotion exists.

Social Hierarchy

Hierarchy is not a new concept in Southeast Asia. Rather, it is ancient, traveling from the east (India) and from the north (China). While Myanmar did not adopt India's overt caste system, the Confucian moral code from China continues to impact the Southeast Asian region: "Respecting the superior defines ethical obligations in a hierarchy so that the relationships among the actors determine the appropriate course of action for a given situation," (Bedford and Hwang 2003, 134).

Social hierarchy (rather than one's religious convictions) determines a social actor's expected behavior, making moral responses complex and dynamic. The research of anthropologist Daniel M. T. Fessler in Indonesia (Fessler 2007) confirms hierarchal social structure with shame as a social regulator.

According to the Myanmar Christian women (MCW) who shared their personal stories, even the church sub-cultures are hierarchal. Honor is bestowed upon members of the Christian community who are rich, have a title or higher education, and/or "own" a church. One male Myanmar family sociologist confided,

---

[1] The literal translation for *ahnade* is "the strength hurts," indicating assertiveness or directness is in violation of the cultural norm of passiveness.

I think the influence (honor/shame worldview) is very deep. We are taught from a young age to differentiate between people so that people in authority receive the highest honor. In every tribal group there is an honoring of tribal chief and family. Educated people are automatically honored. This exists even in the Christian community—very much. It is everywhere. Educated, rich, clans, dignity ... even Christians may love the poor man as they do the rich man, but they cannot show them the same honor. They are not equal. (Garrison 2020, 75)

A tension exists for Myanmar Christians between the biblical code of loving the neighbor as self and the moral Asian code of submitting to the social hierarchy.

Collectivistic Culture

In East and Southeast Asian cultures, the individual's identity is dependent on who he/she is within their group, and who the group is within the larger social context. As a result, a concept of self is dynamic, relational, and perceivable only as it exists within the collective (Bedford and Hwang 2003). Concepts of self are therefore interdependent, reflecting connectedness and belonging (Markus and Kitayama 1991) as well as containing a fear of the disruption of relationships (Karasawa 2001, Creed et al 2014).

Sociologist Jack Barbalet (2013) raises concerns about collectivist communities such as Myanmar: "There is empirical evidence that community undermines rather than promotes trust within a community itself. Strong community networks tend to generate envy and envious gossip and are therefore likely sources of not trust but distrust ... and mistrust, which undermines trust when it exists" (Barbalet 2013, 59).

Barbalet explains that norm violation in collectivistic cultures yields "the necessity of third-party intervention ... typically, but not exclusively, through gossip," to threaten an individual's reputation and identity bonds (Barbalet 2013, 59). Gossip is therefore utilized as both a shaming device and a control mechanism.

Shame and a Culture of Conflict

David I. Steinberg (2000) presented a paper to the Asian World Bank titled, "The Problems with Myanmar and Myanmar's Problems." Steinberg informs this discussion of MCW making and breaking trusting relationships by highlighting the country's culture of conflict. Additionally, shame researcher Brené Brown links a culture of conflict with shame: "Shame is highly correlated with addiction, violence, aggression, depression, eating disorders, and bullying," (Brown 2012, 73).

In the shared stories of MCW in this study, gossip is a primary tool to shame others. To make sense of these communication patterns, the frequency and type of episodic shaming were analyzed. This paper explains, in part, how Confucian hierarchy within the Asian code hinders healthy communication patterns inside the Myanmar church and, by extension, Southeast Asia.

Research Results and Discussion

During the months from December 2018 through July 2019, qualitative and quantitative research methods were used with 152 MCW from nine regions of Myanmar. Focus groups were gathered in four regions for feedback. Qualitative research included both short answer questions and open-ended questions encouraged story-telling.

In one short answer question participants were asked to list trustworthy persons (TWP) in their lives not by name, but by relationship. Twenty-nine percent of the participants wrote "none" or "no one" and 58 percent listed one relationship, indicating a dearth of trusting relationships for Christian women across Myanmar.

A second short-answer question inquired: *In your opinion, what are the hindrances to close relationships among MCW?* Participants (n=91) expressed that belittling, gossip, and a sense of superiority were the biggest hindrances to MCW building trust between each other (Garrison 2020, 115). Figure 7.1 highlights the responses to the short answer questions.

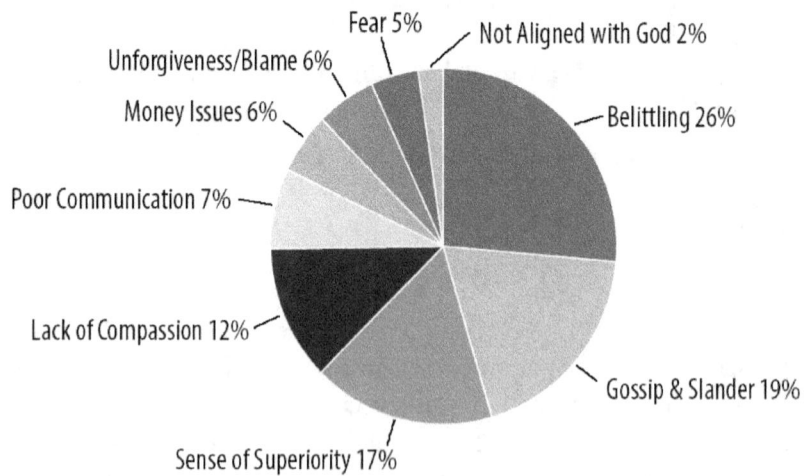

Figure 7.1 Hindrances to Trusting Relationships[2] (Garrison 2020, 114)

---

[2] Greater detail is available in the original report (Garrison 2020, 114).

In addition to the short answer questions, open-ended questions were also asked. Based on the work of sociologist Brené Brown in *Shame Resilience Theory: A Grounded Theory Study on Women and Shame* (2006), and organization theorist Karl Weick's work (1995), an open-ended approach was necessary to begin building a sensemaking framework. To capture qualitative data from MCW participants, two questions were asked:

- Q: Do you have a story from childhood when you experienced or observed shame?
- Q: Do you have a story of shame in your adult life that you could share?

Qualitative interviews revealed honor is not upheld for the spiritually devout but for those who build churches in which others can gather for worship, wealth, and status (education, title, family). Public shaming and gossip are not the primary problems for trust building as originally proposed. Instead, they are institutional tools of the dominant Buddhist culture and Christian subcultures for maintaining the social hierarchy. Therefore, shaming and gossip are not poor choices made by an individual, but rather systemic problems of hierarchy that need to be addressed by the church collective.

MCW narratives revealed *overt mechanisms* and *covert mechanisms* for maintaining existing hierarchy within the Myanmar church subcultures. Public belittling and public gossip were overt mechanism themes, while acquiescence and avoidance were covert mechanism themes that emerged during storytelling. Clear subthemes were also revealed in the stories collected.

The following chart is designed to assist understanding the complexities of social exchange patterns in Myanmar, based on the narratives collected, from MCW. (Refer to figure 7.2 on the following page.)

Overt Maintenance Mechanisms

Overt maintenance mechanisms are tools to assist "the haves" in retaining their positions in the social hierarchy according to interviews of MCW. These practices include the presence of an audience, supporting the earlier work on shame by psychologists Tracy and Robins (2004). Differences in the public audiences found in this study were three-fold: the presence of the target (person shamed), the frequency of shaming gatherings, and the intimacy of the shaming group.

Belittling was differentiated from gossip in three ways. First, in public belittling the target of criticism is present, but in gossip circles the target of gossip is infrequently present. Second, the frequency in which the participatory audience gathered (gossip circles being regular, public belittling being random) differ. Third, and worthy of further study, is the intimacy of the shaming group: gossip circles appeared closer, perhaps because they frequently shared common enemies, whether real or imagined. The MCW narratives revealed multiple

Implicit Hierarchy
Honor based on:

Building a place where others can worship; Wealth; Education; Position; Family cohesiveness

---

Overt Maintenance Mechanisms: Belittling, Gossip

Public Belittling

Speaking words to "put one in their place"...which means below the speaker. Target of criticism is present. instills fear in the minds of others present to, "remember their place."

- **Comparison:** this is perceived as a "motivational tool" by the speaker. Many mothers brag about their use of this shaming device "to help teach" their children. When comparisons are used on adults, it is very offensive to the one being compared.
- **Competing for Dignity/Honor:** "building self up by pushing others down" through public criticism.

Public Gossip

Conversations alleged to correct behaviors that deviate from group's norm. Target of criticism infrequently present.

- **Corrective & Entertaining Gossip:** Some claims alleged it "helped behaviors." Others said it was "entertaining" and chose to "just listen" even though they knew stories weren't true. Inclusion in the gossip helps to keep from being a target of gossip, a demotion in the hierarchy.
- **Gossip Currency & Fraudulent Honor:** The speaker with titillating information makes a market exchange... buying attention in exchange for details about another individual, using gossip as currency. For a brief few moments the speaker buys the honor of the group, by selling a product that wasn't theirs to sell.

Covert Maintenance Mechanisms: Acquiescence, *Ahnade*

Acquiescence: a Social Obligation

Expectation found in Confucian Teaching and Hindu/Buddhist teaching of karma. Myanmar expression: Accept (it) just as (it) is.
Di ah tine let kan lite pa ဒီအတိုင်း လက်ခံလိုက်ပါ။

- **Reconciliation Expectations Low:** Expectation for extending forgiveness, but no expectation for apologizing/repenting. Pretending no conflict occurred and accepting the new state of brokenness and mistrust to maintain a false peace.
- **Unjust Resolution Accepted:** The poor are held to the highest standards, while the wrong-doing of the rich are to be overlooked and unspoken.

Ahnade: Conflict Avoidance

I don't want you to be bothered OR offended by what I say, do, or feel so I politely practice the code of *Ahnade*.

- **White Lies:** I don't want the awkwardness of refusing your request, so I will say what you want to hear, but have no intention of following through.
- **False Peace:** I can't apologize because I have reconciliation fears (1) you may get angry all over again; (2) you may reject my apology and bring your rejection into the public arena. The perceived best course of action, is pretending nothing ever happened… a false peace.
- **Emotion Suppression:** "You especially can't show negative emotions because you make others feel bad. So it is better to change. You avoid any triggers that may reignite traumatic feelings rather than showing emotions. So it removes the idea that 'your story matters.'"

Figure 7.2 Narrative Themes Regarding Implicit Hierarchy from Myanmar Christian Women (Garrison 2020, 160)

types of publicly spoken discrimination and multiple types of gossip; however, only a few are relayed here.

Public Belittling: Comparison, Competition

Belittling by comparison and competition emerged in the narratives of MCW, and in interviews with two Myanmar Christian men, two Christian women in Thailand, a Christian woman from Malaysia, and a Christian man from Indonesia. Belittling, described by MCW, is the act of spoken words intended to "put one in one's place," meaning socially below the speaker, exercised by those who perceive themselves socially superior. For example:

> When I was twelve, mom and dad divorced, and mom left us. The people in the community would say, "You are abandoned by your mom." I was so sad. Whenever we had problems with other kids, we would always lose the fight, because their parents would say, 'abandoned.' My dad was a soldier and most of the time he was gone. We were like orphans. People looked down on us. I was discouraged and sad. (Garrison 2020, 116)

Several narratives revealed that times when people were at their lowest, when they needed the greatest help, they were more intensely attacked by fellow Christians, rather than assisted. One young woman relayed her experience when her mother became a widow with daughters:

> I realized that the way the people from the church treated me was strange. People looked at me like I was not supposed to be there. One day, a friend from the church came to me and told me that she heard unpleasant rumors ... a woman from our church (told) everyone in our church that my mom was using me to get money from [family friends]. I was so angry and sad. I wanted to disappear from the earth. I hated that woman so much and I decided not to talk to her anymore. I stopped going to that church. They were supposed to protect me and guide me when I was in need but instead, they joined the gossip and treated me as if I was not worthy to be in their community. I never went back to that church. (Garrison 2020, 87)

Shunning experiences were heard from twenty-two participants. What is not clear is whether alienating the wounded person is because of a karma mentality or a public dissociation in order to secure the shunner's own social position in the hierarchy. Both dynamics could possibly be at play.

Comparison is a perceived motivational tool which a speaker uses to inspire someone to work harder. Several mothers bragged that they compared their children to one another, and to others outside the home as well, in order to teach their children. One woman shared the destructiveness it caused in her family:

> When we were young ... my parents always compared me to my younger sister. My younger sister started to feel that our mom and dad didn't love her. My younger sister is not good with education; she is still uneducated, and I was always on top of my classes. Even now when I return home, my parents always put me first, making my sister sad ... shamed unintentionally because of my parents' comparisons, and perhaps she has felt rejected. However, my parents love her, and just wanted her to be good like me. (Garrison 2020, 117)

Comparison suggests acceptance is conditional. The brokenness that begins in homes finds its way into the church culture. When the childhood practice of comparison is brought to church, the MCW find it offensive.

Competition for dignity or honor was a problem alleged by several participants. This competition often involves public criticism and labeling, also described as "building up self by pushing others down publicly." The following is an example:

> I went to a wedding but couldn't afford a new dress. I wore my mom's old dress that was old fashioned. A lady from my church came up to me in front of other people and said that I was not supposed to wear that kind of dress to a wedding. I was so ashamed. Sad. Discouraged that I was looked down on by that group of ladies. They were looking at my dress, whispering, and smiling. I went home and cried so hard. My mom said to brace myself and move forward. (Garrison 2020, 118)

Competition and comparison are interlinked and practiced in the familial and social settings, including in the church. As an example, two individuals are compared and open criticism of the perceived inferior occurs, generating a spirit of competition.

In the various narratives of MCW, belittling appears in homes, neighborhoods, schools, and churches and is divisive in nature. The targeted individual frequently chooses to further isolate. Advocating for such an individual threatens one's own social bonds, and success is dependent upon the defender having higher social clout than the speaker of the shaming words.

Public Gossip: Corrective, Entertaining, and Fraudulent Honor

While MCW listed gossip second only to belittling in terms of destructiveness to trust building, they nonetheless justified it in practice. Some claimed it helped in teaching better behaviors, while others found it entertaining and chose to "just listen," even though they knew stories were not true. Inclusion in the gossip helps to keep a participant from being a target of gossip. Additionally, being a good storyteller can raise an individual's sense of dignity when an audience appears.

Corrective gossip is like the corrective shaming previously mentioned, but differs by frequency, and the level of intimacy of the gossip audience. The following narrative is an example of women perceiving themselves as "institutional guardians," presuming shaming brings about conformity (Creed et al 2014):

> When I became a mom, there were many other women in the church, and we were referred to as "Mothers of the Church." The older mothers always gossiped about the youth, what they are doing wrong. … One day my kids came to me and addressed me, "Do you know that the young people of our church hate you because you are like the other gossiping mothers?" (Garrison 2020, 119)

The mothers formed a cohesive bond by giving each other permission to criticize their children. However, the relational bonds were not built on trustworthiness and appeared to be more self-serving (for entertainment purposes) than instructive (for cultural correction).

Several narratives of MCW indicated that gossip was an important part of their social exchange, appearing to be of higher value than having correct information. *Gossip entertainment* is an accepted and defended form of communication:

> In our church community women gossip a lot, but men also gossip. I listen to other people's gossip. I never asked for evidence if it is true. It is still prevalent to gossip. We like each other, but we just want to have something to talk about. It is okay that we do it. It is not slander, but it is gossip. (Garrison 2020, 120)

Several narratives demonstrated that in cases of slander, lies were upheld as truth by the church community for years, and even a lifetime. One translator explained, "No one takes the time to search for the truth because they themselves have already transferred the lie to someone else" (Garrison 2020, 120).[3]

In this study, *fraudulent honor* refers to dignity obtained through a "market exchange," buying attention in exchange for provocative details about another, details which will be traded again, like currency. Thus, *currency gossip* purchases fraudulent honor. For a few moments, the speaker buys the honor of the group or individual by selling a product that is not his or hers to sell. Take the following story as an example:

> One of my friends came to gossip to me about another woman. I trusted her and listened. I thought she was saying the right news. However, it was not. Because I trusted her … I don't want to give details, but there were consequences for the victim of the problem. I had much regret. Something bad happened to her. (Garrison 2020, 120–21)

---

[3] Myanmar Translator (T1) provided both spoken and cultural interpretation as participant responses were further analyzed.

Ironically, the storyteller perceived herself a victim of inaccurate story telling rather than part of the problem of gossiping. Had she not been so quick to relay the information she would not have caused further harm to the subject of the gossip and would have protected her own dignity.

The overt public shaming mechanisms of belittling and gossip come in many forms, often intertwined. Inclusivity woos (Rosnow and Foster 2005) and blinds the participating social actors to the long-term repercussions to the victim of the gossip, his/her family, and the church community.

Covert Maintenance Mechanisms

From the narratives of MCW, two types of covert mechanisms for maintaining social hierarchy surfaced: acquiesce and *ahnade*. In the MCW narratives, acquiesce is an obligation to one's social superior, and *ahnade* is a communication construct of indirect speaking as a sign of politeness.

Social Obligation to Acquiesce

A mindset of *low reconciliation expectations* and *acceptance of unjust resolution* occurs in Confucian teachings of social hierarchy and spiritual teachings related to Hindu/Buddhist teaching of karma. Anthropologist Daniel M. T. Fessler found this mindset in his work among Indonesians (2007). Graciously accepting the status assigned does not bring honor, but prevents one from further indignity. Popular Myanmar advice to those experiencing difficulties is, "just endure." *Di ah tine let kan lite pa* means "just endure" but is sometimes translated "just accept." One Christian woman expressed,

> Most rich people look down on the poor. The poor don't want to communicate with the rich because they look down on them. Even if we try [to improve broken relationships in church] we are still poor, and we are used to it. We won't be dead from the broken relationship, so we don't try to fix it. We believe it is better to not try to fix it, it will just make us feel upset. We just accept. (Garrison 2020, 122)

This participant's response is also an example of the *low reconciliation expectations* found in the MCW narratives. A strong emphasis on forgiveness is present in the Myanmar church culture without a cultural expectation of apologizing. Face-saving pretense suggests no conflict has occurred and an acceptance of each new state of brokenness and mistrust maintains a false peace.

Moreover, the MCW narratives demonstrate *acceptance of unjust resolution*. Social actors hold the poor to the highest standards, while offenses of the rich are overlooked and unspoken. The narrative of an impoverished ethnic minority woman provides an example:

> I got married with a minister from a different tribe. ... I am Kachin and he was Bamar. My parents had rejected us, and my mother-in-law interfered in our marriage a lot. She said, "You are doing God's work, so we will take care of this child for you." They took my eldest son to their home.
>
> When our elder son was in middle school and my husband began to die, we had to go to the hospital and my mother-in-law gave the money, so she had authority. I had no say when she declared that she was going to bring up my first child. I had no energy or clout or finances, so she claimed ownership over him. ... I eventually realized things happen for a reason. (Garrison 2020, 12)

This socially ingrained acceptance of injustice immobilizes even the heart-sick mother whose child has been removed from her life. The mindset of "just endure" is a powerful maintenance mechanism for those near the bottom of the social ladder. Even amid great injustice to one's own welfare, acceptance of injustice is preferable to challenging the system of hierarchy.

Ahnade: Conflict Avoidance

The literal translation for *ahnade* is "the strength hurts," indicating that assertiveness or directness is in violation of the cultural norm of passiveness (Khaing 1984, 194). While the phrase often offers a polite apology, the mindset appears to create hindrances to direct communication and clear expression, which MCW expressed were needed for improving trusting relationships. The general mindset of *anhade* is, "I don't want to bother or offend by 1) what I say, 2) what I do, or 3) what I feel."[4] An example of each follows; the first two are paraphrased translations based on several narratives, while the third, an exact quote, was spoken in English.

> White Lies: I don't want the awkwardness of refusing your request, so I will say what you want to hear, but I have no intention of following through. In this manner I appear to be following the Burmese code of accommodation, and then when I don't follow through, I use the phrase "*ahnade*," as a weak apology for my inconvenient negligence. While on the surface it gives the appearance of politeness, it unintentionally violates integrity.
>
> False Peace: I can't apologize because I fear 1) you may get angry all over again or 2) you may reject my apology and bring our broken relationship and your rejection into the public arena. Consequently, the perceived best course of action is pretending nothing ever happened ... a false peace.

---

4 Myanmar Translator (T1), *Personal Communication,* based on repeated discussions in person, WhatsApp Conversations, emails and texts in 2019. Wording finalized November 16, 2019.

Emotion Suppression: You can't show negative emotions because you make others feel bad. So, it is better to change. You avoid any triggers that may reignite traumatic feelings rather than showing emotions. This removes the idea that your story matters, because it could affect the community. (Garrison 2020, 123)

Borrowing from Tim Sensing's *Qualitative Research,* (2011) "The Constructionist Principle" proposes "words create worlds," (Sensing 2011, 169). Mindsets, socially constructed through language and conversations, are dynamic, not fixed. Kingdom transformation is possible in every culture.

Language and Culture

Empirical evidence suggests the areas of greatest concern to a culture have the richest terminology (Bedford and Hwang 2003). Yet, several participants in the storytelling indicated that the Burmese equivalent for "I'm sorry" was either not learned in the home or restricted to children using conciliatory language with adults only.

In reflection of language and cultural shaping, MCW have great potential for improving conflict resolution. Encouraging the emergence of a new language usage with terminology of honoring all, restraining from gossip, practicing the giving/receiving of empathy, and committing to restorative conflict resolution would bring transformation in church fellowship, homes, and surrounding communities.

Summary and Contextual Implications

The Myanmar church has the potential to be a social reconciler in a nation of conflict. However, according to the views of 152 Myanmar Christian women, ingrained social structures and communication practices prevent the Myanmar Christian church from being a place of safety. This chapter explains, in part, how Confucian hierarchy within the Asian code hinders healthy communication patterns inside the Myanmar church and, by extension, Southeast Asia.

Three cultural constructs of Confucianism were found disruptive to relationship building within the Christian church of Myanmar. First, the social expectation of "face" inhibits trust building by creating pressure to outwardly present one response while a constrained and disguised emotion exists as *ahnade*. Second, social hierarchy (rather than one's religious convictions) determines a social actor's expected behavior, creating a tension for Myanmar Christians between the biblical code of loving the neighbor as self and the moral Asian code of submitting to the social hierarchy. Third, collectivistic practices help retain hierarchy norms in Myanmar through types of gossip, inhibiting trust-building among Myanmar Christian women.

The ninety-one participants of this study expressed that belittling, gossip, and a sense of superiority were the biggest hindrances to MCW building trust between each other (Garrison 2020, 115). To make sense of these communication patterns, the frequency and type of episodic shaming were analyzed and a framework was proposed. Gossip (behavior) revealed a deeper cultural problem: hierarchy (belief). Only when networks of support and openness replace walls of protection and isolation will the Myanmar church community become a safe place for its members and influential in the healing of its country's multiple conflicts.

References Cited

Barbalet, Jack. 2013. "The Structure of Guanxi: Resolving Problems of Network Assurance." *Theory and Society* 43: 51–69.

Bedford, Olwen, and Kwang-Kuo Hwang. 2003. "Guilt and Shame in Chinese Culture: A Cross-Cultural Framework from the Perspective of Morality and Identity." *Journal for the Theory of Social Behaviour* 33, no. 2: 127–44.

Brown, Brené. 2006. "Shame Resilience Theory: A Grounded Theory Study on Women and Shame." *Families in Society: The Journal of Contemporary Social Sciences* 87, no. 1 (January): 43–52.

Brown, Brené. 2012. *Daring Greatly: How the Courage to Be Vulnerable Transforms the Way We Live, Love, Parent, and Lead*. 1st ed. New York: Gotham Books.

Confucius. 1909. *The Sayings of Confucius*. Translated by Leonard A. Lyall. London: Longmans, Green and Co.

Creed, W. E. Douglas, Bryant Ashley Hudson, Gerardo A. Okhuysen, and Kristin Smith-Crowe. 2014. "Swimming in a Sea of Shame: Incorporating Emotion into Explanations of Institutional Reproduction and Change." *Academy of Management Review* 39, no. 3: 275–307.

Fessler, Daniel M. T. 2007. "From Appeasement to Conformity: Evolutionary and Cultural Perspectives on Shame, Competition, and Cooperation." In *The Self-Conscious Emotions*, edited by Jessica L. Tracy, Richard W. Robbins, and June Price Tangney, 174–93. New York, NY: Guilford Press.

Garrison, Kara L. 2020. "Sensemaking in an Honor/Shame Worldview: Investigating How Myanmar Christian Women Build and Break Trust." DTL diss., Bakke Graduate University.

Ho, D. Y., W. Fu, and S. M. Ng. 2004. "Guilt, Shame and Embarrassment: Revelations of Face and Self." *Culture and Psychology* 10, no. 1: 64–84.

Karasawa, Mayumi. 2001. "A Japanese Mode of Self-making: Self Criticism and Other Enhancement." *Japanese Journal of Psychology* 72, no. 4: 198–209.

Khaing, Mi Mi. 1984. *The World of Burmese Women*. Totowa, NJ: Zed Books; US distributor, Biblio Distribution Center.

Markus, H. R., and S. Kitayama. 1991. "Culture and the Self: Implications for Cognition, Emotion, and Motivation." *Psychological Review* 98: 224–53.

Mesquita, Batja, and Mayumi Karasawa. 2004. "Self-Conscious Emotions as Dynamic Cultural Processes." *Psychological Inquiry* 15: 161–66.

Rosnow, Ralph L., and Eric K. Foster. 2005. "Rumor and Gossip Research." *Psychological Science Agenda*, American Psychological Association. https://www.apa.org/science/about/psa/2005/04/gossip.

Sensing, Tim. 2011. *Qualitative Research: A Multi-Methods Approach to Projects for Doctor of Ministry Theses*. Eugene, OR: Wipf & Stock.

Steinberg, David I. 2000. "The Problems of Myanmar and Myanmar's Problems." Asia Regional Consultation on Social Cohesion and Conflict Prevention, Manila, March 16–17.

Tracy, J. L., and R. W. Robins. 2004. "Putting the Self into Self-Concious Emotions: A Theoretical Model." *Psychological Inquiry* 15: 103–25.

Weick, Karl E. 1995. *Sensemaking in Organizations*. Thousand Oaks, CA: Sage Publications.

Wu, Jackson. 2016. "How Christ Saves God's Face ... and Ours: A Soteriology of Honor and Shame." *Missiology: An International Review* 44, no. 4: 375–87.

Chapter 8

Conversing with Unique Identities
American Muslim Youth in a Multicultural Religiously Plural World

Matthew Henning

Today, with more people rapidly traveling around the world in search of new careers and better lives, cities are becoming multicultural and religiously plural. With a more culturally and religiously diverse environment, people are asking questions about their personal and corporate identities. Investigating identity can be a rewarding process as it leads to self-reflection and growth. While globalization has offered this benefit to many, others face it as a trial. This is especially true for young members of society as they juggle their desire to have a semblance of the old while also wanting to live in the reality of the new. Youth are forced to pick and choose from a wide range of cultures and a hybrid form of identity emerges (Hiebert 2008, 409). For missiologists, these people no longer fit perfectly into the neat boxes of "world religions."

Recognition of this struggle has made its way to film in a recent Hulu original television series *Ramy*. This series follows a first-generation American Muslim who is too spiritual for his American life but not spiritual enough for his Muslim life. Every episode explores Ramy's complex life as he seeks to find his identity as an American Muslim (*Ramy* 2019). Ramy's story is being lived out by Muslims all across America.

For Muslim youth in North America, as in other parts of the world, there is search for an identity with which they can find acceptance, live peacefully, and continue practicing Islam. These youth live within a world of conflicting ethics. As they grow up and evolve, American Muslim youth begin asking how to live rightly in this new cultural context, a process that can feel confusing and very isolating. In this chapter, I argue that the American church can come alongside Muslims as they navigate this difficult process and enable communication toward gospel witness in two ways: by recognizing who Muslims are and by building relationships both individually and corporately. If the church hopes to engage the American Muslim youth and communicate the message of Christ clearly, it must first understand the tensions they face in America as they form their identities.

Islam in America: A Brief History

Islam in North America has been consistently growing since the late nineteenth century. While many stories of Muslim slaves being brought to the new world have circulated, very little evidence exists of Muslims practicing their faith. In 1875, a large group of Muslim immigrants arrived in the United States from Syria, present-day Lebanon, Jordan, and Palestine. This was the first of four "waves" of Muslim immigration to the US. The fourth and final wave came under President Lyndon Johnson in 1967 when he instituted immigration laws. Still today migrants come as a result of similar immigration laws (Johnson 2018, 25–26).

Throughout American history, Islam has struggled to find its place because of political tensions. Many would point to the Turkish genocide in Armenia and the Iranian Revolution as events that caused fear among Americans. Today, however, many Americans remember 9/11 when they reflect on Islam's place within America. Yet, Kidd reminds us that because of the 9/11 attacks Americans simply "replayed" older, familiar themes: the attempt to convert Muslims, apologetic attacks on Islamic beliefs, the blending of political and theological opinions, and the use of biblical prophecy to reimagine Islam's place in America. The events and aftermath of 9/11 simply made these themes more "focused" and "intense" (Kidd 2009, 173).

Modern-Day Tensions

Looking at tensions Muslim youth face while growing up in American society, I recognize the fact that Islam is experienced differently by many groups. Both conservative and progressive forms of Islam are present in America. How people understand Islam is also impacted by numerous sects and different ethnic rituals.

However, almost all Muslim youth will experience these tensions for the simple reason that they live in a now globalized world. They will need to interpret law, choose who to vote for, react to progressive ideologies, and face exposure to Islamophobia.

Interpreting Law

Necessary legal judgements based on questions emerging from new societies and cultures is nothing new to the Islamic faith. In the sixteenth century, coffee houses popped up quickly across the Middle East. In Mecca, the question was raised over whether drinking coffee was legal. After assembling legal scholars and medical witnesses, Kha'ir Beg, governor of Mecca, banned the consumption and distribution of coffee. Stores were burned to the ground and those distributing the coffee were punished (Brown 2009, 336). In 2016, The Ayatollah of Iran decided that it was illegal for his Twelver Shia followers to insult Sunni companions of Muhammad (Khamenei 2016). As recently as March 2020, in the midst of the COVID-19 pandemic, the Grand Mufi of Bosnia and Herzegovina offered new guidelines for how an individual can be protected while washing and shrouding the body of someone who died of an infectious disease (Kavazović 2020).

Today, Islamic youth in America can tweet out questions to America's famous legal scholars. Following Dr. Yasir Qadhi on Twitter presents a plethora of questions and rulings. *Is it permissible to give your spouse a wedding ring? I bought something online and it was cancelled. They gave me $10 for inconvenience, is this permissible? Is it permissible to pray with a T-shirt that has an animal logo on it like Puma or Ralph Lauren? Can we read the Quran from a mobile device?* (Qadhi 2020). Youth face these types of questions daily as they are introduced to new facets of life that are not covered in historical rulings.

While local mosques still hold Islamic education, the spiritual formation of youth appears to be moving outside their local communities. Short interactive videos led by one of America's most famous Imams, Omar Suleiman, are added regularly to the Yaqeen Institute website. Whatever the burning questions are, it seems like the Yaqeen Institutes webpage has a video, podcast series, or article to help Muslims dive deep into these issues. Young Muslims from many cultures and sects follow along and subscribe to many of these platforms.

Another interesting place to look is the first undergraduate private Islamic school in America, Zaytuna College. Zaytuna College was founded in 2008 by Hamza Jusuf, a white convert and now legal scholar. The university home page describes the school's mission as "grounding students in the Islamic scholarly tradition as well as in the cultural and critical ideas shaping modern society" (Zaytuna College 2020). It boasts that students can come together to try to answer some of the difficult questions youths face in the global world today.

So, how does a young Muslim in America decide where to go if they have a question about whether something is haram or halal? Do they look to their traditional Islamic sect's authority? Do they have a local mosque with an accessible Imam who gives advice? Do they look to celebrity Imams online? One thing is clear: Muslim youth in America are forced to decide where their moral allegiance lies.

Politics

Another dilemma Muslim youth face today is how they identify politically. Many outsiders are confused by their choices to support a certain politician, especially when that politician's morals do not seem to conform to Islamic ethics. Yet, it is important to remember that there is a history behind every dilemma.

In January 2001, George Bush became the forty-third president of the United States. Bush narrowly won Florida by a few hundred votes and clinched the victory in one of the closest elections in American history. The American Muslim Alliance estimated that sixty thousand Muslims voted for George Bush in Florida. Multiple exit polls and studies showed Bush's overwhelming support amongst Muslims. It was the Muslim vote that pushed George Bush to victory. Yet after 9/11 the numbers drastically changed. In 2004, one poll found that only 7 percent of Muslim voters supported Bush. In 2008, a similar poll determined that Barack Obama drew 89 percent of the Muslim vote (Graham 2015). The Bush administration had been known to support Muslims, yet, after signing the Patriot Act, things became difficult for many Muslims in America. The Iraqi war and the rhetoric against Islamic terrorism completely changed the narrative (Hamid 2020).

Many Democrats believe Muslims are now a concrete voting block of theirs. However, even today this is rapidly changing. The Institute for Social Policy and Understanding (ISPU) released a poll that Donald Trump increased his approval rating among American Muslims from 13 percent in 2018 to 30 percent in 2020. The Muslims who supported Trump cited opposition to building coalitions with Black Lives Matter, religious liberty issues, and economic growth. These trends represent some of the political tensions found within the Muslim community. For example, as a whole, Muslims are the faith group most likely to support Black Lives Matter (65 percent) (ISPU 2020). Clearly, Muslim support in politics is not easy to analyze, and correlations are not easily made.

US foreign policy is another major issue for Muslims. Time and again Muslim youth must grapple with how the US government interacts with their brothers and sisters in other parts of the world. Many Muslims say that they love American values, but that US foreign policy does not reflect American values. They may cite the CIA overthrow of the legitimate leader of Iran in the 1950s, the unconditional support for Israel, or the war in Iraq which killed two million civilians (Johnson 2018, 25). For many Americans, these are not political issues but instead everyday business in the Middle East. However, the implications are different for Muslims. Supporting a certain political party might mean condoning actions that directly hurt their families. For this reason, the Muslim youth do not know who they should be in alliance with. Should they call themselves conservative, aligning with some who have Islamophobic rhetoric? Should they partner with liberals and champion pro-choice and

LGBTQ practices? Can they describe themselves as patriotic and support a foreign policy that hurts their brothers and sisters in the faith? Clearly, Muslim youth in America have a difficult decision to make when it comes to American politics. Their political identities are complex and, at times, full of contradictions. This is why their political support is not fixed, but it continues to evolve and change.

> Today, Muslim youth must navigate progressive ideologies that their parents and elders have not faced.

Progressive Ideology

With freedom of belief comes factions and sects. Today, Muslim youth must navigate progressive ideologies that their parents and elders have not faced. Many of these issues come to light out of the freedom found in American democracy. Other issues, however, are born out of the cultural progression of the present-day. Many of these topics are points of concern for people of other faiths as well.

Islamic feminism is a timely example of this. Proponents of this movement point out that it was always men interpreting the Quran. They do not question the validity of Islamic teaching, but instead question the interpreters' potential biases. For example, Ziba Mir-Hosseini fought for five years in an Iranian court for the right to divorce her husband. Iranian law that is based on Islamic law, interpreted by men only, would not allow for a woman to divorce her husband without his consent. After many years of study, she obtained her divorce by convincing the judge it was her right under Islamic law (Amirpur 2015, 39).

In America, Amina Wadud has emerged as a leading voice in progressive Islamic feminism. After observing the way women are positioned within Islam, Wadud began to study Islam for herself. She enrolled in an MA program in Middle Eastern studies at the University of Pennsylvania. After this she went on to study at the University of Cairo and attended lectures at al-Azhar University, the "intellectual centre of the Sunni world." At al-Azhar, Wadud approached her teacher and asked why she was not being taught to interpret the Quran for herself. She would go on to get her PhD at the University of Michigan (Amirpur 2015, 132–33). Over time she made many discoveries. One is that she did not see a rule anywhere in the Quran or Sunnah prohibiting women from leading the Friday community prayer. In 2005, she became the first Muslim woman to lead a prayer (Amirpur 2015, 142). This movement of Islamic feminism is widely spreading throughout the world (Amirpur 2015, 158). The debate continues in mosques and student associations across America.

Another issue that Muslim youth face is sexuality. Muslim youth simply do not have the black and white views on sexuality that their parents' generation has.

A survey conducted by the ISPU indicated that young Muslims, compared to the older sample, are more supportive of building coalitions with LGBTQ activists; 48 percent of Muslims aged 18–29 support these coalitions as opposed to Muslims aged 50+ at only 26 percent (ISPU 2020). On top of this, some groups are using portions of the Quran to show their approval of homosexuality. Surah 49:13 states,

> O people, we created you all from a male and female, And made you into different communities and different tribes, so that you should come to know one another, acknowledging that the most noble among you, is the one most aware of God. (Droge 2013, 49:13)

For many Muslims, the implication of this verse is that no Muslim is better than another based on social categories, "race, ethnicity, economic class, or gender" (Kugle 2010, 13). However, the Al-Fatiha Foundation uses this verse to combat "male sexism, gender injustice, and social stigmatizing of homosexuals." They cite this verse to support people of the LGBTQ community (Kugle 2010, 14).

Some Muslims desire to be accepted as progressive Americans, while others fervently oppose progressive forms of Islam. Polling continues to display a shift amongst the younger generation from the older generation when it comes to progressive ideology. Muslim youth are ultimately still undecided on where to position themselves within these groups.

Islamophobia

Islamophobia is often understood as hate crimes committed as fearful responses to terrorism. Islamophobia is a fear-based rhetoric used by people who do not fully understand their own biases. It can also be a cultural mindset implemented and promoted by society.

Mike Bleich says that Islamophobia is "indiscriminate negative attitudes or emotions directed at Islam or Muslims" (Bleich 2011, 1585). Hate crimes and the negative press afforded to Muslims are often discussed. However, we rarely talk about the culturally prejudiced pictures embedded in society or the "indiscriminate negative attitudes or emotions" within our society. It is this form of unaddressed, unnoticeable Islamophobia that inflicts some of the worst harm on the Muslim community as well as Muslim youth.

Omar Suleiman conducted a wide study on the connection between Muslim male identity and the apologetic some Christians use in representing Muhammad. These apologists claim that Muhammad was wrong for marrying his young wife Aisha; therefore, his reputation is ruined and he should not be trusted. Suleiman questions why this, throughout all of time, was never brought up before. He notes that Muhammad had many opponents in his day and this was never brought forward. Suleiman believes that it is done to give the world a picture of Muslim men:

> Vicious Muslim men that are in need of restraining. It's the same image that you get from Hollywood of angry Muslim men. Violent, old, and brutal and abusive toward young children, particularly young girls. It is a way to portray Muslim men, by extension of portrayal of the prophet, as these violent men in need of restraint. And it also goes to the women's side. Why portray Aisha as a child bride? Because it fits the portrayal of Muslim women in need of rescue. (Suleiman 2018, author's transcription)

Suleiman believes that it is a culturally embedded image that has been adopted by American culture. Muslim men are inherently in need of restraint and Muslim women are inherently in need of rescue. Suleiman believes this attack on Muhammad is by extension portraying Muslim men in a certain way. Saba Mahmood writes,

> One of the most common reactions is the supposition that women Islamist supporters are pawns in a grand patriarchal plan, who, if freed from their bondage, would naturally express their instinctual abhorrence for the traditional Islamic mores used to enchain them. (Mahmood 2005, 1–2)

Muslim men in effect have a projection upon them from birth. This form of Islamophobia confuses them and changes the way they interact with society. For Muslim women, they have a projection put upon them as well. They are constantly trying to show that they are not in need of physical rescuing from progressive elites or well-meaning Christians. Their identities, whether they like it or not, are affected by this narrative.

> As suspicion arises, Muslim youth question who they are in America, what their place is, and if they should use their voice.

Muslims recognize that there are violent and radical groups within their religion. Muslim youth are particularly aware of what is happening around the world. Yet, their experience in America is not of violence and aggression toward others. Their fathers are not violent men who need restraint while their mothers are not women in need of rescue. Yet, they know many in the United States believe this to be their reality. These youth also know that their opinions are often prematurely discredited. As suspicion arises, Muslim youth question who they are in America, what their place is, and if they should use their voice. This leads to an angst that reestablishes their feelings of being outsiders in American society.

Missiological Calls-to-Action

It is clear that the identity of an American Muslim youth is complicated and everchanging. How they identify and how they view the world changes depending on where they are and who they are with. In order to bridge a great divide between the two groups, Christians must understand the struggles that Muslim youth experience. How then can Christians communicate with clarity and reach out in love?

Let Them Be Seen: Recognize and Honor Accomplishment

It could be argued that how certain groups see the world is built around their version of history. In discussing history, the topics people choose to talk about often reveal prejudices and blind spots. For example, if someone were to ask, "who are the Muslims that have changed the world," how might someone respond? Not with athletes or performers, but with respected Muslim intellectuals who have changed the world. Many evangelicals would have a difficult time with this question.

Averroes, for example, is credited for reawakening Western Europe to Greek philosophy. He became so popular in Europe that the church was forced to condemn "Averroesians" (school of medieval philosopher based on the application of works by Averroes) in 1270 (Eshkevari 2014, 12). Yet, this awakening of Greek Philosophy in Europe led to the advancement of mathematics, astronomy, medicine, chemistry, and physics (Eshkevari 2014, 14–19). Averroes' role in the translation, preservation, and distribution of Greek thought into Europe cannot be understated.

Ibn Khaldun, born in 1332, is another name lost to many Christians in the West. However, George Ritzer calls him the first to practice sociology (Ritzer 2017, 279). A plethora of other sociologists call him the Father of Sociology. Khaldun, who is cited by Karl Marx in his works, was surely read by Engels and Comte. (Alatas 2006, 786). His works laid the groundwork for labor theory, cyclical understandings of society, and was even used by President Ronald Reagan to support "supply-side economics" (Alatas 206). Very few sociology books give Ibn Khaldun the credit he deserves for his contribution to sociology.

Finally, one of the world's first great explorers may not be a commonly known name. Many have heard of Marco Polo, but few have heard of Ibn Battuta. Ibn Battuta lived a hundred years before Marco Polo and traveled seventy-five thousand miles around the world all on his own. This record of travel would remain unbeaten until steam engines were invented in the eighteenth century (Khan 2008, 416). This scholar explorer went to the old worlds of the fourteenth century and lived to write about it. He details all of his adventures in his work entitled, *A Masterpiece to Those Who Contemplate the Wonders of Cities and the Marvels of Travelling*.

While many may only know who Marco Polo is, Muslims also know who Ibn Battuta is. Their world involves both explorers. They know of "so-called" western philosophers as well as their own. They study western sociology and are familiar with their own. They know of western scholars, adventurers, philosophers, and heroes. But does the American church know of theirs? They wonder why the only celebrated Muslims are athletes and performers.

To fully see Muslim American neighbors, the church would do well to venture into their world and influencers, both present day and historically. This would serve in showing Muslim Americans that the church is serious about understanding who they are and where they have come from. To truly "see them" is an act of kindness and reveals their worth before God.

Draw Toward Them: Individually and Corporately through Multi-Ethnic Approaches

In Matthew, Jesus' final command to his disciples is to "Go therefore and make disciples of all nations" (Matt 28:19). In the seventeenth century, clear borders between nations began to form. "Going" became less about willingness and more about allowance. Many countries today are closed to missionaries. How then should the church respond to this new hurdle in fulfilling the Great Commission? Many would point to immigration as an obvious answer to prayer concerning these new restrictions. People from all ethnicities and all walks of faith are coming to the West.

Yet, Pew research shows that local churches are not seeing it this way. Only 21 percent of evangelicals have been encouraged to reach out to immigrants. Only 50 percent have looked into what the Bible says about how Christians are to engage with immigrants. However, 75 percent of evangelicals believe that immigration will present the church with opportunities for evangelism (Fries 2018, 111).

Americans, by and large, fear Muslim influence and worry that their American way of life will change with the growth of Muslim immigration. Muslims, on the other hand, fear Western influence upon their families. A natural divide is created and the "going" part of the Great Commission ends at neighbors' doorsteps.

Accepting the Great Commission by drawing towards others is not just difficult because of lengthy travel and hefty amounts of paperwork. Accepting this commission requires steps of faith that move out of comfort zones and into places where safety is not guaranteed. Loving others means going wherever God calls and proclaiming the gospel, whether that is just across the street or across the Atlantic.

These immigrant communities along with the first- and second-generation Muslim youth are most likely the future of Islam in America. For those who believe the Great Commission is a calling for the church today, they must act as they see the nations coming to them. Not only considering the individual roles within the Great Commission, but they should consider also the church's corporate role in fulfilling the Great Commission. That is, how can the church use its resources to best fulfill the Great Commission?

One of the greatest tools the global Christian church possesses is its diversity. Christianity has spread to every continent in the world. Christianity does not only have a global presence, but it also has a contextualized presence across the globe. The tensions facing Muslims in the form of hybrid identities is nothing new to Christians, much less American minority Christians.

Sam George, in *Understanding the Coconut Generation*, clearly acknowledges the dual identities of Indian American Christians:

> Their lives seem to be bifurcated between the land of their parents and the land of birth or adoption. They are pulled in one direction at home and another direction at school. They speak their ancestral language at home and English elsewhere. Their mothers put their younger siblings to sleep singing Indian lullabies, while they heard another kind of music at college dorm. (George 2006, 67)

George notes that Indian Americans do not live in an "either-or" world but a "both-and" world (George 2006, 70). Some might see this as a "divided self" or a "cultural schizophrenia," but others see this as simply a "double consciousness" (George 2006, 87). Whatever the case, Indian American Christians know the tensions that Muslim Americans are facing. They not only have natural relationships because many Indian Americans are also Hindu and Muslim, but they have natural empathy because they have lived with similar cultural tensions and dual identities.

Another avenue the church might want to take into consideration is proximity. Who is in closest proximity to Muslim Americans? As noted above, Indian Americans have organic friendships because India is home to a large population of Hindus and Muslims. Yet, what is often overlooked is the familial ties that black Americans have with Muslims in the United States.

Kevin Brown (2020), an African American pastor, offers insight into this trouble. He questions the proximity that white evangelicals have to Muslim peoples. He explains that African Americans almost always have a Muslim family member. His church does not have to strive to develop relationships with Muslim people from the community. Usually, they have preexisting relationships.

Proximity and shared experience characterize many Muslim-Christian relationships within the African American community. Christians and Muslims who share the immigrant experience also have a sense of solidarity that bonds them. This gives an advantage to Christians who have lived the immigrant experience or come from families who already have a voice in the community. Yet, most mission organizations in America focus almost entirely on college students from European backgrounds. Support raising is geared toward a majority culture that feels little shame in asking for financial support. Missionary cultures cater toward majority culture and rarely, if ever, celebrate minority experiences (Perry 2011).

Matthew 28:19–20 commands the church to "baptize and teach." If the Great Commission is given to the church, should the church not look at the fullness of gifts within its body? Is it not the case that the church should send the people best equipped to do the work? Should evangelicals consider both shared experience, natural relationship, and proximity when sending out those to minister? The church should certainly not exclude anyone from seeking to reach the lost. However, the church would be wise to do inventory on who they are sending, where are they sending them, and who they are excluding, especially if those being excluded from the ministry are the most natural fit for it.

Drawing toward Muslims might mean drawing toward Muslims as individuals. It might also mean supporting others in the body of Christ to do the same. If the church wants to be a witness to the world, they must commit themselves to supporting one another within the body. Therefore, the corporate decision is made with the other people in mind. In this way, the church displays true fellowship and wholeness in Christ. My hope is that these approaches are helpful in beginning the conversation about ways the church might approach Muslims both individually and collectively and spark the reader to more.

Conclusion

Understanding an American Muslim youth's identity is complicated. As Hiebert suggests, hybrid cultures emerge which leads to the youth struggling to create a unique identity for themselves within competing cultures (Hiebert 2008, 249). In this chapter, I argue that part of the Great Commission calls Christians to understand these struggles that Muslim youth experience as they form complex hybridized identities. In understanding Muslims' moral dilemmas

> In understanding Muslims' moral dilemmas and offering support, the church will be able to bridge a great divide between Christians and Muslims.

and offering support, the church will be able to bridge a great divide between Christians and Muslims. In light of understanding these tensions, I suggest a commitment to knowing and seeing the other as well as engaging both individually and corporately. Through this I believe the church, by the power of the Spirit, can restore communication and clearly convey the love of Christ.

References Cited

Alatas, Syed. 2006. "Ibn Khaldun and Contemporary Sociology." *International Sociology* 21: 782–95.

Amirpur, Katajun. 2015. *New Thinking in Islam*. London: Gingko Library.

Bleich, Erik. 2011. "What Is Islamophobia and How Much Is There? Theorizing and Measuring an Emerging Comparative Concept." *American Behavioral Scientist* 55, no. 12: 1581–1600.

Brown, Daniel. 2009. *A New Introduction to Islam*. Hoboken: John Wiley & Sons.

Brown, Kevin. 2020. "Evangelicals Respond to New ISPU Data on American Muslims." Neighborly Faith website. https://he-il.facebook.com/neighborlyfaith/videos/380152226455325/.

Droge, A. J. 2013. *The Quran: A New Annotated Translation*. New York: Equinox.

Eshkevari, Mohammad. 2014. "The Impact of Islam on European Civilization." *Horizon of Thought* 1: 1–22.

Fries, Micah. 2018. "Discovering the Missional Opportunity." In *Islam and North America: Loving Our Muslim Neighbors*, edited by Micah Fries and Keith Whitfield, 107–17. Nashville: B&H Academic.

George, Sam. 2006. *Understanding the Coconut Generation*. Niles, IL: Mall Publishing.

Graham, David. 2015. "How Republicans Won and Then Lost the Muslim Vote." *The Atlantic*, https://www.theatlantic.com/politics/archive/2015/12/republicans-muslim-vote-george-w-bush-donald-trump/419481/.

Hamid, Shadi. 2020. "Holding Our Own." *Plough*. https://www.plough.com/en/articles/holding-our-own?fbclid=IwAR0TQGNltXcvM7ESGVnfgWDrXUlxb6pfbgic03XQXwbJGHxeah6MG_eVac.

Hiebert, Paul. 2008. *Transforming Worldview*. Grand Rapids, MI: Baker Academic.

Institute for Social Policy and Understanding (ISPU). 2020. *American Muslim Poll: Fifth Anniversary Collection 2016–2020*. https://www.ispu.org/public-policy/american-muslim-poll/.

Johnson, Steve. 2018. "Overview of Global Islam and Demographics of Islam in North America." In *Islam in North America*, edited by Micah Fries and Keith Whitfield, 19–33. Nashville: B&H Academic.

Kavazović, Husein. 2020. "Fatwa on Ghusl Mayyit, Shrouding and Janazah for Those Who Died of Infectious Diseases." https://english.islamskazajednica.ba/news/363-fatwa-on-ghusl-mayyit-shrouding-and-janazah-for-those-who-died-of-infectious-diseases.

Khamenei, Ali. 2016. "Ayatollah Khamenei's Fatwa: Insulting the Mother of the Faithful Aisha Is Prohibited." https://english.khamenei.ir/news/3905/Ayatollah-Khamenei-s-fatwa-Insulting-the-Mother-of-the-Faithful.

Khan, Muhammad. 2008. *The Muslim 100: The Lives, Thoughts and Achievements of the Most Influential Muslims in History.* Leicestershire: Kube Publishing.

Kidd, Thomas. 2009. *American Christians and Islam.* Princeton: Princeton University Press.

Kugle, Scott Siraj al-Haqq. 2010. *Homosexuality in Islam.* Oxford: Oneworld Publications.

Maalouf, Tony, 2003. *Arabs in the Shadow of Israel.* Grand Rapids, MI: Kregel Publications.

Mahmood, Saba. 2005. *Politics of Piety.* Princeton: Princeton University Press.

Perry, Samuel L. 2012. "Diversity, Donations, and Disadvantage: The Implications of Personal Fundraising for Racial Diversity in Evangelical Outreach Ministries." *Review of Religious Research* 53, no. 4: 397–418.

Ramy, S1, Ep 5. "Do the Ramadan." Aired April 19, 2019, on Hulu. hulu.com/series/ramy.

Ritzer, George, and Jeffrey Stepniksy. 2017. *Contemporary Sociology and Its Roots.* New York: Sage Publications.

Suleiman, Omar. 2018. "Ending the Debate on Aisha(ra)'s Age." Yaqeen Institute. https://www.youtube.com/watch?v=5gDTh-6X9vo&t=2075s.

Part 3

Communicating Well in Mission

Global missions work has always been complicated by diverse contextual, cultural, social, and lingual dynamics. The authors in this section highlight a few of the communication challenges that people within global missions face and offer some ways forward in learning to communicate well. Presented as one of the plenary sessions, in chapter 9 Theon Hill takes a deep, critical look at the ways in which Christian missions and the church continue to communicate a colonial mindset. Too often preaching and making disciples are still merged with colonization, and thus point more towards Western White culture than the kingdom of God. In his writing, Hill points to a way out of this, providing guidance for communicating the gospel that frees it from its Western moorings so that all may more clearly see Jesus as their Savior.

In a more specific context, Hannah Nation, in chapter 10, writes of the emerging work of the Center for House Church Theology (CHCT) that promotes the writings and publications of church leaders in China primarily for the benefit of the Chinese church, and secondarily for the global church. The goal is to build a "textual community" that is intentional and missiological, starting with sermon materials, so that both believers in China and around the world can listen to the movement of the Spirit in this growing church rather than just reading from the academia of the West.

In chapter 11, Linda Saunders reframes the conversation regarding the status of the Black church's involvement in global missions. Through historical examples and contemporary interviews, Saunders reveals how the Black church understands and communicates its mission theology through the lens of Black history, struggle, and socioeconomic realities. She concludes that while the Black church may need to reengage in global mission endeavors, the evangelical missionary movement also needs "to move away from a Eurocentric colonialist missions theology" by listening to and learning from past and current Black churches.

Jessica Udall, in chapter 12, challenges the reader to reflect on what we communicate when fundraising. She carefully points out problems with fundraising that stem from information overload, material overabundance, and spiritual apathy. Fundraising in this mode falls short of fostering spiritual growth for both the donor and the recipient. Instead, Udall calls the missions community to ask questions that start with God, the spiritual needs of donors, and the strengths of the recipients, rather than the financial needs of the recipients. This repositions giving as God's work more than ours.

—Marcus Dean

Chapter 9

Communicating a Decolonized Gospel

Theon E. Hill

The persistence of racial unrest and xenophobia around the globe concerns me. In the US, where I live, the names Brianna Taylor, Ahmaud Arbery, and George Floyd reverberate throughout the nation as powerful reminders of the vicious legacy of white supremacy (see, for example, Bella 2020). Of course, I recognize that the US is not alone in perpetuating forms of injustice against vulnerable populations. One need only look to the Rohingya in Myanmar, the Nuer in South Sudan, or Christians and Yazidis in Iraq and Syria for heartbreaking examples of the persistence of xenophobia and genocide (Pamuk and Latiff 2021; Chason 2021; Vohra 2021).

This historical moment confronts us with darkness and discouragement. In times like these, God calls the church to serve as light amid darkness. As Dr. King declared, "Only when it's dark enough can you see the stars" (King 2004, 317). Yet, the church often contributes to the darkness of the moment. The church has and continues to embrace forms of racism, prejudice, and xenophobia. Historically, Christians partnered with nation-states to steal indigenous lands, defend chattel slavery, and justify apartheid (Dunbar-Ortiz 2015; Raboteau 1994; Jennings 2010; and Hill 2016). This partnership means that racism, xenophobia, and injustice are not simply external forces that complicate the work of the church. Instead, they are sinful practices and attitudes that have fundamentally shaped the trajectory and perceived mission of the body of Christ.

Critics regularly point to this history when they challenge the legitimacy of the church. The prominent Black Power activist Stokely Carmichael offered a powerful example of this critique in his 1967 speech on the philosophy of Black Power. Specifically, his arguments on the legacy of Christian missionary work in Africa speak to the legacy of the church among its critics. He argued,

> The white supremacist attitude, which you have either consciously or subconsciously, is running rampant through society today. For example, missionaries were sent to Africa with the attitude that blacks were automatically inferior. As a matter of fact, the first act the missionaries did when they got to Africa was to make us cover up our bodies, because they said it got them excited. We couldn't go bare breasted anymore because they got excited! When the missionaries came to civilize us because we were uncivilized, to

educate us because we were uneducated, and to give us some literate studies because we were illiterate, they charged a price. The missionaries came with the Bible, and we had the land: When they left, they had the land, and we still have the Bible. That's been the rationalization for Western civilization as it moves across the world—stealing, plundering, and raping everybody in its path. (Carmichael 1966)

Carmichael articulates a well-documented connection between Christian missions, as practiced, and colonialism (see also Dunbar-Ortiz 2015; Said 1978; Fanon 2008). He blasts the hypocrisy of Christians in using a faith defined by justice, freedom, and holiness as a tool of imperial control and domination. Contemporary discussions of the legacy of colonialism often center on topics like the theft of indigenous lands and imposition of foreign rule on indigenous peoples. Yet, my focus lies not with colonialism's material manifestations but its discursive forms. That is, I am concerned that the legacy of colonialism endures in the Christian imagination in the ways that Christians understand and preach the gospel. Formal colonial rule in nation-states like India, Kenya, and Vietnam may have concluded in the 1950s and 60s, but it persists in the forms of ideological colonialism that surface in preaching, evangelism, and missions.

Let me illustrate this point. Recently, I stepped out of the pulpit as a guest preacher at a church in my area. A congregant rushed to introduce me to his visitor, an individual from another country who had recently migrated to the US. The congregant asked me if I could say a special word of prayer for his visitor because the individual was trapped in destructive cycles of alcoholism and addiction. I am regularly asked to pray for or counsel people facing spiritual challenges, so nothing about this encounter was uncommon. However, the conversation took an unexpected turn when the congregant decided to explain why his visitor struggled with destructive behavior. After testifying to the redemptive power of the gospel to liberate us from destructive cycles, this congregant immediately placed blame for his visitor's destructive behavior on the visitor's native culture. I will not soon forget his words as he spoke to his visitor. He said, "The problem is that in your culture the goal is to hold people back from reaching their full potential. If you want to break these cycles of destructive behavior you must reject the culture that produces this destructive behavior. In America, we desire to see people reach their potential. Unlike the people from your home country, we want to see you flourish not languish in cycles of destructive behavior."

This conversation stood out not because of the congregant's condescending attitude toward someone of a non-Western culture. Molefi Asante has written at length about the destructive power of Western imperialism and Eurocentrism (1998; 2003). Yet, the connection this congregant made between what he perceived to be dominant US values and the gospel intrigued me. For him, US values serve as an extension of the gospel. Attitudes like this alarm me. This congregant unconsciously embraced an attitude of cultural superiority that has consistently served as the foundation for colonial endeavors (Jennings 2010). His solution for his friend struggling with sin was to embrace the "gospel" of Western values. My fear lies in the way(s) that this type of colonial mindset informs our missionary endeavors. To the extent that Christians embrace colonial mindsets, we continue the colonial legacy of setting ourselves up as the marker of desire, the ideal to which everyone should aspire.

As a rhetorical scholar, I am concerned that our communication practices in sharing the gospel may reflect the legacy of colonialism. Like the congregant at the church where I was preaching, I am afraid that many of us see little difference between the gospel we preach and the culture with which we identify. I am talking especially about Christians living in the West. This threatens our evangelistic efforts and turns people off to the gospel of Christ because the content of our preaching often bears a striking similarity to Western values and priorities. We, consciously or unconsciously, preach Eurocentric Jesus, Capitalist Jesus, and/or Racist Jesus. We preach a colonized gospel not even recognizing the ways that colonialism has infiltrated our understanding of the gospel.

In his 1963 classic, *Strength to Love*, the Rev. Dr. Martin King Jr. criticized the Christian church for the ways that it served imperial and colonial powers instead of holding them accountable. He wrote,

> The church must be reminded that it is not the master or the servant of the state, but rather the conscience of the state. It must be the guide and the critic of the state, and never its tool. If the church does not recapture its prophetic zeal, it will become an irrelevant social club without moral or spiritual authority. (King 1963, 59)

My concern as a brother in Christ and a scholar of race is that the colonial legacy that has defined much of the Western church's history persists in our presentation of the gospel. We may not be actively supporting the hostile takeover of indigenous lands, but this does not mean that we have freed ourselves from the specter of colonialism. Because of this danger, contemporary Christians should interrogate their communication practices to discern whether they perpetuate the legacy of colonialism. In this chapter, I consider what it would look like to communicate a decolonized gospel, a gospel that does not serve a nation-state, but one that serves as the conscience of the state as Dr. King noted.

For me, this line of inquiry extends beyond academic interests to personal concerns. As a doctoral student, I first encountered the perspective that viewed Christianity as a tool of colonialism. My coursework on postcolonial theory exposed me to the work of brilliant scholars like Gayatri Spivak (1999; 2000), Edward Said (1978; 1994), Homi Bhabba (2004), and Frantz Fanon (2005; 2008). I wrestled to understand the perspectives that I encountered in their writings. Having been raised in a Christian home, I always viewed my faith as a force for good. Even when Christians failed, I never attributed their failures to a broader problem with the faith. Yet, as I engaged these authors and more, I came face to face with heartbreaking stories of the ways that Christianity functioned as a tool of colonial power and rule in places like India, Africa, and South America. As a descendant of slaves, I began to recognize similar uses of Christian doctrine in the unique ways that slaves' masters used Christianity in an attempt to pacify my ancestors (see, for example, Raboteau 1994). Everywhere I turned, I found new instances in which Christianity served colonial ends.

Unsurprisingly, this newly acquired knowledge triggered a crisis of faith in my life. I wondered, "Is Christianity a mere tool that the West employs to maintain power over the rest of the world?" I spent a year wrestling with this question, poring over Scripture, studying the history of Christian missionary endeavors, and engaging postcolonial scholarship. As I re-engaged the writings of famous missionaries like David Brainerd, I increasingly noticed the racist labels like "savages" that they used to describe indigenous people (Brainerd 1992, 113). This observation awakened me to the ways that colonial mindsets had infected missionary endeavors throughout the West.

Suddenly, I understood why many non-Christian friends held such strong opposition to Christianity. Stokely Carmichael's attacks on Christian missions as a colonial endeavor made sense to me. I understood why Dr. King blasted the Christian church for serving as a tool of the state. For the first time, I understood with painful clarity what Paul was trying to communicate in Romans 2:24 when he declared to the Jewish members of the church in Rome, "The name of God is blasphemed among the Gentiles because of you."

In Romans 1, Paul identifies a laundry list of sins that were common among the people of Rome. Paul anticipates the response of Jewish brothers and sisters committed to the Torah in chapter 2. His approach suggests that he believes that Jewish brothers and sisters will celebrate the condemnation of the sinful culture of Rome. However, Paul challenges his Jewish readers to recognize that they are no better than the people that they are looking to condemn. He destabilized the source of their sense of cultural superiority. He writes,

> If you call yourself a Jew and rely on the law and boast in God and know his will and approve what is excellent, because you are instructed from the law; and if you are sure that you yourself are a guide to the blind, a light to those who are in darkness, an instructor of the foolish, a teacher of children, having in the law the embodiment of knowledge and truth—you then who teach others, do you not teach yourself? While you preach against stealing, do you steal? You who say that one must not commit adultery, do you commit adultery? You who abhor idols, do you rob temples? You who boast in the law dishonor God by breaking the law. (Rom 2:17–23)

This passage revolutionized my understanding of the gospel. If Paul is correct when he says elsewhere that "all have sinned and come short of the glory of God," then there is no room for cultural imperialism in the life of the Christian. Colonialism rests on a foundation of the perceived cultural, intellectual, and even biological superiority of the West. The gospel destroys this foundation by revealing the depravity that lies at the heart of our shared humanity.

The question we face in this moment concerns how to preach a gospel that does not serve the nation-state or other colonial agents but provides a biblical counterpoint to the normalization of sin in global society. The authenticity of our gospel witness depends on our answer to this question. I believe that Old Testament prophets model a form of communication that faithfully communicates the Word of God in a manner that is not beholden to social and political mores of contemporary society. They model how to communicate a decolonized gospel.

Rhetorical scholarship, in part, considers how people craft messages for audiences. Old Testament prophets present an interesting case study because they seemingly break all of the rules of effective communication (Darsey 1999, 15–34). The prophets delivered messages that at first glance appear out-of-step with the prevailing social norms of their times. Amos referred to the women of Israel as "cows of Bashan" (Amos 4:1). Isaiah walked around naked for three years to dramatize the sinful condition of the people (Isa 20:2–4). Ezekiel compared God's people to sex workers so undesirable that they had to pay their customers (Ezek 16). The prophetic word stands in stark contrast to the conventional rhetoric that you'd be likely to hear from a politician, lawyer, or business leader. While conventional rhetoric pursues diplomacy, the prophet embraces radicalism. While conventional rhetoric adapts to social norms, the prophets acted like they "didn't have no home training." They lacked civility. While conventional rhetoric values compromise, the prophet views it as a betrayal of principle. While conventional rhetoric seeks to uphold the status quo, the prophet views the same status quo as the problem.

Prophets see society differently. At their best, their prophetic imagination frees them from the sense of normalcy that often informs colonial mindsets. As Rabbi Abraham Joshua Heschel said in his celebrated book on the prophets,

> To us a single act of injustice ... is slight; to the prophet, a disaster. To us injustice is injurious to the welfare of the people; to the prophets it is a deathblow to existence; to us, an episode, to them a catastrophe, a threat to the world. (2010, 4)

The extreme messages delivered by prophets like Amos, Isaiah, and Ezekiel reflect their perception of the severity of the crisis. As Walter Brueggemann writes, "The task of prophetic ministry is to nurture, nourish, and evoke a consciousness and perception alternative to the consciousness and perception of the dominant culture around us" (2001, 3). The prophetic word seeks to awaken people from apathy. Prophecy provides an alternative consciousness to the status quo. As Heschel went on to say, "Prophecy is the voice that God has lent to silent agony, a voice to the plundered poor, to the profaned riches of this world" (Heschel 2010, 5). Or, as rhetorical scholar James Darsey observes, "It is the prophet's task to create an emotional response to sin, a reaction to the pathos of God" (1999, 76). Ultimately, the prophet's success lies not in the reception of their message, but in fidelity to the prophetic word. God told Ezekiel, "You shall speak my words to them, whether they hear or refuse to hear, for they are a rebellious house" (Ezek 2:7).

> The prophetic tradition challenges the sense of normalcy that makes colonial endeavors possible.

At crucial moments in US history, social reformers have channeled this tradition to awaken people to the injustice of that which has become normalized. Susan B. Anthony called on it to challenge the US to treat our dear sisters with the same measure of equality afforded to men. Cesar Chavez invoked the tradition when he demanded that the US provide equitable pay and better working conditions for farm workers. Journalists like Ida B. Wells-Barnett demonstrated the prophetic potential of the written word when she courageously chronicled the devastating reality of lynching in American culture at a time when many Black people cowered in fear from the controversial subject. The prophetic tradition challenges the sense of normalcy that makes colonial endeavors possible. It disrupts the perceived harmony between the gospel and the status quo by reminding hearers of the God who stands opposed to sin. The tragedy of the twentieth century surfaces in the ways that "an atheist might take a prophetic stance more readily and faithfully than a typical twentieth-century Christian," especially in response to racism, colonialism, sexism, and xenophobia (Chappell 2005, 3).

At the heart of the prophetic tradition, Darsey writes, is a "commitment to an absolute sacred truth" (1999, 76). The challenge for Christians who have been socialized into ways of living that blind them or dull their spiritual sensibilities to the sinfulness of colonial endeavors concerns how to recognize and respond to that which has been normalized. Christian philosopher Cornel West, throughout his career, identifies three distinguishing traits that I believe help Christians to recognize and respond to the persistence of colonialism in our presentation of the gospel (1992; 2002).

First, the prophet raises critical or Socratic questions about a society's normative practices. For example, when ex-slave Frederick Douglass was invited to speak on the Fourth of July in 1852 to celebrate the nation's independence, he stepped boldly to the lectern and asked the audience, "What to the slave is the fourth of July?" (Douglass 1852; Blight 2018, 228–38). In this brief question, he highlighted the inherent hypocrisy of America's commitment to freedom and embrace of slavery. Many musicians demonstrate this capacity to raise critical questions. Consider the voice that Marvin Gaye gave to the pain of urban communities during a period of deindustrialization and division over the Vietnam War when he asked, "What's going on?" (1971). Rapper Tupac Shakur questioned America's priorities when he reflected on the fact that the country "has money for war but can't feed the poor" (1993). Critical or Socratic questioning exposes inconsistencies between a people's stated values and their actual practices. It offers vital insight into the difference between the Great Commission and the Doctrine of Discovery that fueled so much of the colonial activity in the West.

The second component of this tradition involves maintaining a prophetic witness. The prophet embraces the responsibility and burden of speaking out about crucial issues facing contemporary society. Like the prophets of the Old Testament, prophetic concern does not extend only to one issue or one group of people. The prophet bears witness wherever injustice exists. The prophet was that person who could not stay silent in the face of state-sponsored genocide against our Native American brothers and sisters. The prophet was that person who refused to accept the idea of children working in sweatshops at the turn of the twentieth century. Even today, the prophet is that person who speaks out on behalf of the women and men around the world who are subjected daily to the horrors of the sexual trafficking industry. The prophet cannot stay silent because, as a group of pastors wrote at the height of social unrest in the 1960s, "a time comes when silence is betrayal" (Branch 2006, 591).

Society rarely appreciates prophets until they are gone. While he's lionized today, few people recognize how much King suffered during his lifetime. Throughout his public career, the FBI kept him under constant surveillance and even encouraged him to kill himself on a couple of occasions. Polls in King's day revealed that a majority of Americas often viewed him more as a troublemaker than as a national hero (Branch 1986; 1999; Garrow 1986). Because prophets disrupt and threaten our way of life, society rejects them, labeling them as hateful, unpatriotic, and enemies of the state. Yet, nothing could be further from the truth. The prophet is motivated by a deep love for the people, for the least of these. This love does not allow prophetic figures like King to stand idly by while injustice persists. James Baldwin expressed this sentiment when he memorably declared, "I love America more than any other nation on earth, which is why I reserve the right to criticize her perpetually" (1998, 9).

Third, prophetic rhetoric operates with a "blues sensibility." That is, the prophet has the unique ability to stare into the face of darkness without falling prey to darkness. People often shield themselves from dark realities. We avoid eye contact with the homeless person on the street so that we do not feel bad about not supporting her or him. We justify our actions by talking about how they would only misuse whatever support we might offer. Our response to suffering betrays the fact that if we were in the story of the Good Samaritan, we would often be more likely to respond like the priest or Levite than the Samaritan. Furthermore, our attitude toward suffering blinds us to broader questions concerning the conditions that foster homelessness in society. We structure our lives to avoid social pain because it's easier to ignore suffering than to face the heartbreaking reality that, even as I speak, people around the nation and the world experience injustice, exploitation, and oppression. Whether it's gang violence in Chicago, water in Flint, Michigan, or crystal meth in Appalachia, the prophet does not run from the darkness, she pierces through it with the light of the truth. She musters up the courage to confront tragedy without losing hope.

In her classic book *Their Eyes Were Watching God*, Zora Neale Hurston captures this notion of a blues sensibility. Describing her main characters in the face of disaster, pain, and death, she writes, "They looked as though they were staring into the dark, but their eyes were watching God" (1937, 160). The power of perspective lies at the heart of a blues sensibility. Zechariah aptly describes the prophet as a "prisoner of hope" (Zech 9:12). The prophet understands, in the words of King Solomon, that "Sorrow is better than laughter, for sadness has a refining influence on us" (Eccl 7:3). Prophets reside in darkness, but the darkness does not reside in them. The prophetic tradition is more than an approach to social critique. It provides vital insight into what it means to be a Christian. Prophets embody the principle of living on earth but being citizens of heaven. The prophet serves as a moral compass, guiding the people back to God. In the face of moral compromise and hypocrisy, prophets challenge society to be faithful to its core values. As sociologist W. E. B. Du Bois said, the prophets "say ugly things to an ugly world … they cry aloud and spare not; they shout from the housetops, and they make this world so damned uncomfortable with its nasty burden of evil that it tries to get good and does get better" (1986, 1158).

We need prophets. Every day we wake up to a world in which over one hundred million children are homeless, 40 million people are in slavery, and nearly one-half of the world's population lives on less than $2.50 per day. An onlooking world wonders, in the words of theologian Howard Thurman, what is "the significance of the religion of Jesus to people who stand with their backs against the wall" (1949, 7). Prophets force us to wrestle with the institutional and systemic realities that foster these conditions. They bring us face to face with the role of colonialism, racism, sexism, and materialism in contemporary forms of oppression.

We live in some dark times. Hearing prophetic voices is difficult because they force us to question basic assumptions that govern our society and daily conduct. Adopting a prophetic voice is even harder because it requires us to be willing to say what no one wants to hear, but everyone needs to know. This explains the popularity of false prophets in ancient Israel. They made the people feel good about themselves. But when God's people adopt prophetic stances in response to injustice, we give society a small glimpse into the heart of God. We reveal a God who hates oppression, who cares for the refugee and the immigrant, who is concerned for the widow and the orphan, and who views all people as equal regardless of their ethnicity or gender because he made them in his image. We reveal a God who desires for "justice to roll down like waters and righteousness like a mighty stream" (Amos 5:24).

References Cited

Asante, Molefi Kete. 1998. *The Afrocentric Idea*. Philadelphia: Temple University Press.

Asante, Molefi Kete. 2003. *Afrocentricity: The Theory of Social Change*. Chicago: African American Images.

Baldwin, James. 1998. *James Baldwin: Collected Essays*. Edited by Toni Morrison. New York: Library of America.

Bella, Timothy. 2020. "White Men Mocked George Floyd's Death at a Protest. Now a Corrections Officer in the Group Has Been Suspended." *Washington Post*, June 10, 2020. https://www.washingtonpost.com/nation/2020/06/10/george-floyd-new-jersey-protest/.

Bhabha, Homi K. 2004. *The Location of Culture*. New York: Routledge.

Blight, David W. 2018. *Frederick Douglass: Prophet of Freedom*. New York: Simon & Schuster.

Brainerd, David. 1992. *The Life and Diary of David Brainerd*. Edited by Jonathan Edwards. Grand Rapids, MI: Baker Book House.

Branch, Taylor. 1999. *Pillar of Fire: America in the King Years 1963–65*. New York: Simon & Schuster.

Branch, Taylor. 2006. *At Canaan's Edge: America in the King Years, 1965–68*. New York: Simon & Schuster.

Brueggemann, Walter. 2001. *The Prophetic Imagination*. Minneapolis: Fortress Press.

Carmichael, Stokely. 1966. "Black Power." Transcript of speech delivered at the University of California, Berkeley. https://www.blackpast.org/african-american-history/speeches-african-american-history/1966-stokely-carmichael-black-power/.

Chappell, David L. 2005. *A Stone of Hope: Prophetic Religion and the Death of Jim Crow*. Chapel Hill, NC: University of North Carolina Press.

Chason, Rachel. 2021. "South Sudan, the World's Youngest Country, Is Deep in Crisis. But Foreign Interest Is Fading." *Washington Post*, November 14, 2021. https://www.washingtonpost.com/world/2021/11/14/south-sudan-10-year/.

Darsey, James. 1999. *The Prophetic Tradition and Radical Rhetoric in America*. New York: NYU Press.

Douglass, Frederick. 1852. "Speech at Rochester, July 5, 1852." In *Negro Orators and Their Orations*. Edited by Carter G. Woodson, 197–223. New York: Russell & Russell.

Du Bois, William E. B. 1986. "A Question of Policy–The Philosophy of Mr. Dole." In *Du Bois: Writings*. New York: Library of America, 1158.

Dunbar-Ortiz, Roxanne. 2015. *An Indigenous Peoples' History of the United States*. Boston: Beacon Press.

Fanon, Frantz. 2005. *The Wretched of the Earth*. Translated by Richard Philcox. Reprint edition. New York: Grove Press.

Fanon, Frantz. 2008. *Black Skin, White Masks*. New York: Grove Press.

Garrow, David J. 1986. *Bearing the Cross: Martin Luther King, Jr., and the Southern Christian Leadership Conference*. New York: William Morrow & Co.

Gaye, Marvin. 1971. "What's Going On." Track 1 on *What's Going On*. Detroit: Tamla.

Heschel, Abraham Joshua. 2010. *The Prophets*, 3rd ed., vol. 1. Peabody, MA: Hendrickson.

Hill, Theon E. 2016. "The Exodus: The Textual Heart of American Civil Religion." In *The Rhetoric of American Civil Religion*, edited by Jason A. Edwards and Joseph M. Valenzano III, 1–19. Lanham, MD: Lexington Books.

Hurston, Zora Neale. 1937. *Their Eyes Were Watching God*. New York: Harper.

Jennings, Willie James. 2010, *The Christian Imagination: Theology and the Origins of Race*. New Haven, CT: Yale University Press.

King, Martin Luther, Jr. 1963. *Strength to Love*. Philadelphia: Fortress Press.

King, Martin Luther, Jr. 2004. "I've Been to the Mountaintop." In *Ripples of Hope: Great American Civil Rights Speeches*, edited by Josh Gottheimer. New York: Basic Civitas Books.

Pamuk, Humeyra and Rozanna Latiff. 2021. "Blinken Says U.S. to Look at More Myanmar Measures, Plans ASEAN Summit." *Reuters*, December 15, 2021. https://www.reuters.com/world/china/us-looking-whether-myanmar-treatment-rohingya-is-genocide-blinken-2021-12-15/.

Raboteau, Albert J. 1994. "African-Americans, Exodus, and the American Israel." In *African-American Christianity: Essays in History*, edited by Paul E. Johnson, 1–17. Berkeley: University of California Press.

Said, Edward W. 1978. *Orientalism*. New York: Vintage.

Said, Edward W. 1994. *Culture and Imperialism*, 1st edition. New York: Vintage.

Shakur, TuPac. 1993. "Keep Ya Head Up." Track 11 on *Strictly 4 My N.I.G.G.A.Z.* New York: Interscope and Jive Records.

Spivak, Gayatri Chakravorty. 1999. A Critique of Postcolonial Reason: Toward a History of the Vanishing Present. Cambridge, MA: Harvard University Press

Spivak, Gayatri Chakravorty. 2000. "The New Subaltern: A Silent Interview." In *Mapping Subaltern Studies and the Postcolonial*, edited by V. Chaturvedi, 324–40. London: Verso.

Thurman, Howard. 1949. *Jesus and the Disinherited*. Boston: Beacon Press.

Vohra, Anchal. 2021. "'Constant Fear': Iraq and Syria Face ISIL Resurgence." *Al Jazeera*. https://www.aljazeera.com/news/2021/3/2/we-liv-in-constant-fear-iraq-and-syria-face-isil-resurgence.

West, Cornel. 1993. *Prophetic Fragments: Illuminations of the Crisis in American Religion and Culture*. Grand Rapids, MI: Eerdmans.

West, Cornel. 2002. *Prophesy Deliverance*! Louisville, KY: Westminster John Knox Press.

Chapter 10

Pursuing Textual Community with a Chinese House Church Movement

Hannah Nation

Beginning in February 2020, as the pandemic swept across China and city after city locked down to confine hundreds of millions of people to their apartments, a group of pastors made a bold decision. Deciding to "let the light shine in the darkness," they began hosting public evangelistic Zoom meetings open to anyone with the link across China. Though the organizers have so far been unable to count just how many attendees have participated over the past year, they believe the number is well in the thousands.

Given the increased levels of religious persecution in China since 2018, participating in these meetings has not been without risk for those involved. The speakers undertake a series of precautions in order to try to mitigate the risks, but, nonetheless, they keep their cameras on to reveal their full identity and location in one of the world's most restricted internet communities. They believe that the past year of pandemic has been no time to hide; this has been the most important time in recent history for the church to prophetically preach the gospel to a society with no answers to the problem of death.

As soon as these preaching events began, it was clear to those involved that the growing collection of sermons being produced would be important. They are richly emblematic of the house church movement called Grace to the City (恩典城市), one of the fastest growing and largest house church movements in urban China today. This movement is comprised of roughly one-third nondenominational churches, one-third Presbyterian churches, and one-third Baptist churches, and all of these churches are committed to the historic theology of the gospel of grace. They are also distinct in their commitment to China's growing cities, seeking to be salt in a society they perceive to be without social and moral order. When China's cities began to suffer from the outbreak of COVID-19, these two core commitments were central to Grace to the City's response to the death and suffering surrounding their churches.

In this chapter, I will posit that there is a need for other global churches (especially the Western church) to glean from the teaching of the Chinese house church. While I believe it is vital for Chinese churches to develop

> While I believe it is vital for Chinese churches to develop their own theological writing and resources ... I also believe that now is the time for global Christians to begin hearing and learning from the urban Chinese house church.

their own theological writing and resources, and a good portion of my time goes to encouraging such work, I also believe that now is the time for global Christians to begin hearing and learning from the urban Chinese house church.

Western Christianity is struggling to comprehend and understand its increasing social marginalization in a secular, digital, and competitive society that often feels morally fractured and disintegrated. Who better to learn from regarding the gospel's role in such a society than from a church that was birthed in the fires of persecution, and that struggles to love its city not from a position of power, but from positions of weakness and marginalization? Furthermore, as we face the reality of ever-increasing numbers of younger generations of Christians in the West deconstructing their faith, might it not be beneficial for us to take seriously the teaching and writings of a community that is currently actively constructing its faith?

I would argue that now is an important time for us to seek to establish textual community with the urban Chinese house church. Furthermore, I hope that as we seek to do so, it may inspire the building of similar textual community with other global churches. To support this endeavor missiologically, I first try to build upon Andrew Walls' analogy of the human auditorium and then look at the term "evangelical textual community" as used by historian Candy Gunther Brown, imagining how it might be applied today. Finally, I will share about my own efforts to establish such textual community through the establishment of the new Center for House Church Theology, and offer my observations and suggestions for others who might wish to pursue similar initiatives.

Revisiting Andrew Walls' Human Auditorium

In his essay titled "Culture and Conversion in Christian History," Walls paints a picture of what he calls the human auditorium. He describes a theater with a huge stage, upon which an elaborate story is enacted. Everyone in the audience is able to see the stage and story, but no one group of seats is able to see the entire stage, thereby leaving the audience unable to understand the story in its fullness. Walls writes:

> As a result, though everyone in the audience sees the same play and hears the same words, they have different views of the conjunction of word and action, according to their seat in the theatre. Those on one side get a sharply

focused view of certain scenes which those placed elsewhere do not have to the same degree, and people in the balcony are puzzled to hear laughter in the stalls when they themselves have seen nothing to cause it. But the position is reversed when the scene changes, and the main action is on another part of the stage. (Walls 1996, 43)

Of course, there are many factors which might mitigate the confusion of someone sitting in the audience. Those in the audience may change their seats and they may also confer with those sitting in other sections to compare notes. Nevertheless, the main point Walls intends to press upon the reader is that "it is a condition of being in the audience that what we see most clearly is governed by where we are sitting in the theater" (Walls 1996, 44).

For Walls, this is an important defense of contextualized local theology, for of course the play being enacted on the stage is the drama of life and the greatest act which occurs upon the stage and may be witnessed by those in the audience is the Jesus Act. Even accounting for revelation through the Scriptures, Walls writes of the Jesus Act, "The conditions are the same as for all the others; everyone sees the stage, but no one sees the whole stage. People in the auditorium view the Jesus Act on the part of the stage most open to them where they are sitting" (Walls 1996, 44).

And this is where Walls raises a very important question, which in my opinion, he does not satisfactorily answer. Why was such a theater, with its balconies and pillars that obstruct the view, chosen for this play? Why wasn't a theater chosen which could provide an unlimited and unobstructed view of the Jesus Act? For Walls, the answer is that it simply wouldn't do. The Jesus Act is a part of the drama of life, and therefore we must accept these limitations. I agree. Divine revelation gives us the Jesus Act in the midst of a fallen, as yet unredeemed creation that divides and obstructs Christians from a full understanding. But while Walls skillfully and beautifully defends the important uniqueness of localized, contextualized theologies, what he does not do is push us to bring these theologies into conversation with each other. In defending the local, his analogy does not suggest that those in the audience might have an obligation to seek out other sections of the audience to discover what they see. What if Walls' image had said that comparing notes might not be optional, but rather required of those trying to see and understand the Jesus Act?

Reading Walls closely, I do think he tacitly assumes some level of such conversation taking place, for he writes:

> Once again what we see or hear in the process will be affected by where we are sitting in the auditorium. People seated in another part of the house will see some things we cannot, and be unable to see some things that to us seem

important. They cannot see them, not through blindness or willfulness, but because they have been sitting in another place. From that place they may well be seeing that the Jesus Act is fitting exactly into an earlier development that escaped our notice because of that overhanging balcony that interrupts our view so constantly that we have forgotten its existence. (Walls 1996, 44)

However, this is where I would suggest that Paul's language of the body in 1 Corinthians 12 must be introduced to flesh out Walls' very helpful image (pun intended!). Walls' image of the theater encourages us to allow for and celebrate local perspectives, yet Scripture itself pushes us to consider how interaction between local perspectives is not an option for certain inquisitive members of the audience, but rather, necessary for the life and existence of the body. As a community, the various members of the global church are obligated to communicate among themselves what aspects of the play they see and understand.

If there has ever been a time in living memory for such a moment, surely it is now when the entire world has been watching the same event of the COVID-19 pandemic play out on the stage of life. We are experiencing a global event and, unlike the last truly global events, which took place in the early twentieth century before the dismantling of Europe's imperial powers and before the rise and empowerment of indigenous church leadership, we now profess to be part of a global church where the majority of Christians live outside of the Western context and are pastored by their own leaders rather than white European and American missionaries. If this is true, we must ask ourselves: as witnesses of the Jesus Act on the stage of life, are we comparing notes with other members of the audience? Are we listening to each other? Or are we all remaining in our seats, focused on the minute differences from what the person seated next to us sees on the stage?

The Evangelical Textual Community

In my work, I have found the term "evangelical textual community," as used by Candy Gunther Brown, a nineteenth century literary historian, to be particularly helpful for imagining an answer to these questions. In her book *The Word in the World: Evangelical Writing, Publishing, and Reading in America*, 1789-1880, Brown examines the print culture created by American evangelicals of the early nineteenth century. She argues powerfully that from 1789 to 1880 evangelicalism developed "a distinctive set of writing, publishing, and reading practices centered on the power of the Word to transform the world" (2004, 1). She demonstrates that early evangelicals believed the Holy Spirit worked through the Word to sanctify readers across time and space; that an informal canon of evangelical texts aided Christians on their pilgrimage through the world; and that shared narratives structures in these texts were important for their spiritual and religious goals (2004, 1-2).

Of course, it's a given that twenty-first century evangelical reading, writing, and publishing has changed since the nineteenth century; however, I would posture that much of what our forefathers created remains intact today. Brown argues that the evangelical textual community of the nineteenth century helped to create evangelicalism's distinctive culture as books, magazines, and journals played a vital role for the spiritual formation and identity of American Christians. Texts were important for both their converting power and also for sustaining and transmitting evangelical culture among the converted, or what we might call their perceived sanctifying power. They created webs of relationships, mediated through texts, which connected local believers with larger social processes and influenced the entire community's sanctification (2004, 9-10). Brown writes:

> Readers and writers made progress in a spiritual journey through textual practices, giving and receiving encouragement from other readers and writers, by placing themselves within the story of the church's communal pilgrimage. In performing shared narrative frameworks, such as a Christian pilgrimage, participants reenacted a story of redemption history and intensified that story's authority to structure their lives. Texts acquired ritual significance as evangelicals used words, in the context of relationship with other members of their textual community, to order experiences and formulate connections between embedded patterns and the details of everyday life. (2004, 11-12)

Let us consider the evangelical textual communities we participate in today. *Christianity Today*, *The Gospel Coalition*, *World Magazine*, *Christ and Pop Culture*, and *Relevant* would be some of the most important textual communities in which twenty-first century American Christians participate. Directly connected to these are the various affiliated publishing houses such as Zondervan, Baker, InterVarsity, Crossway, and many more. And both the publishers and magazines are now embedded in and sustained by the textual communities of social media and the influencers which dominate such platforms as Twitter, Instagram, and Facebook. It is hard not to see Gunther's description of the nineteenth century evangelical textual community as still relevant to today when she writes:

> The meanings of evangelical print culture emerged at the moving intersection of what Paul Ricoeur terms the 'world of the text' and the 'world of the reader.' Conventions embedded in the evangelical canon partially determined the choices available to nineteenth century writers, publishers, and readers, while

interactions among print market participants contributed to the development of larger patterns of meaning. A dialectical process of textual 'sedimentation' and 'innovation,' to again quote Ricoeur, alternately stabilized narrative structures and provided the rules that guided legitimate experimentation. Familiarity with previous texts affected authors' and publishers' organization of experiences and oriented readers to receive new texts in partially prescribed ways. Socialization into evangelical print culture involved learning conventionalized ways of writing, publishing, and reading, the practices of which continually re-created the evangelical canon as members chose from among interpretive options. (2004, 11)

To my mind the question is not whether we continue to live and exist within the evangelical textual community created for American Christians two centuries ago. Rather, the question I ask is whether Walls' human auditorium has become for us a textual echo chamber? Has the evangelical textual community allowed us to listen only to the audience members seated directly before, behind, and next to us? The question we must ask is not whether this textual community exists. And it is not whether it should be dismantled. The correct question is how to get to the other side of the auditorium to hear what the audience observes over there. How do we grow our textual community?

The Center for House Church Theology (CHCT)

The very first thing I must say is that I do not believe there is any simple answer to this question. I am still trying to answer the question myself and I anticipate it will look differently according to the various communities involved. But I would like to use a project I am involved with as a case study.

For the past seven years, I have been working to bring the theology of the urban Chinese house church to Western audiences. It has not been easy. Especially when I started seven years ago, very few people within the Western evangelical textual community were seeking to bring global theology to the Western world on a popular level. Western evangelicalism has generally had two objectives when it comes to theological publishing and the global church. The first might be exemplified by the *Gospel Coalition's* "theological famine" campaign, which declared that majority world churches suffered from a lack of access to theological books and therefore sought to translate and disseminate Western theology to majority world churches for free (Walsh 2013; 2016a; 2016b). The second example can be found in Langham Partnership which is working to foster the publication of global theology for local contexts. Along with their focus on theological training for global pastors, they are making a concentrated effort at fostering the writing and publication of contextualized theology for majority world local contexts, which I applaud. They state, "We distribute biblical resources to churches, pastors, Bible colleges and seminaries. We help develop groundbreaking commentaries written in and for the local context. We support writers and publishers who translate and write books for the local context" (Langham 2021). But so far, I have come across very few who are interested in and committed to publishing global theology for Western contexts.

I first began growing support for this idea with a blog for China Partnership which weekly features translations of Chinese pastors' sermons and writings. Additionally, China Partnership self-published a collection of sermons I edited for Western audiences called *Grace to the City*. With the success of these two projects, the question became how to continue pushing for a recalibration of the evangelical textual community?

To continue working toward this goal, last year I became involved in launching the new CHCT. The center aims "to foster and further the international publishing of pastors, church leaders, and teachers committed to the historic gospel of grace in China's urban house churches. In promoting the theological leadership of China's urban house churches, we believe dialogue between Christians in China and those from other cultural contexts will lead to mutual edification and sanctification" (CHCT 2021). As Brown astutely observed in her study of nineteenth century American evangelicalism, we give books converting and sanctifying power. The question I frequently raise when discussing the Center for House Church Theology is, if we want to see revival in the Western church, shouldn't we be reading those currently experiencing revival? If the Western church fears marginalization, shouldn't we be reading those currently marginalized? If we see our friends and children deconstructing their faith, shouldn't we be reading those constructing their faith?

> In promoting the theological leadership of China's urban house churches, we believe dialogue between Christians in China and those from other cultural contexts will lead to mutual edification and sanctification.

Already, CHCT is involved in a host of projects to this end. First, we are publishing the collection of pandemic sermons mentioned in my introduction. Second, we are publishing the house church manifesto of Wang Yi, a pastor currently serving a nine-year jail sentence. Both of these books are being published with large, gatekeeping publishers in the evangelical textual community. We do not yet know how they will be received, but I am hopeful that there is evidence of growing support for publishing global voices for Western readers struggling to understand our changing world.

Closing Observations

There is, of course, so much I could share regarding the technical details of launching and maintaining such a center, but there is not space to do so here. But I would like to end with a few things that I have believed to be crucial for pursuing textual community with a Chinese house church movement as an American evangelical organization. I imagine these points would be relevant for any other Western institution seeking to do the same with global churches.

First, whereas Brown lists literacy as a prerequisite for participation in the evangelical textual community of the nineteenth century, I would suggest that translation is a prerequisite for a twenty-first century evangelical textual community. Accordingly, twenty-first century evangelicalism must learn to see translation as just as spiritually important as nineteenth century evangelicals understood basic literacy. It is normal for us to discuss reading and writing as integral to the Christian experience; we must learn to see translation in a similar light. We will need to bring the gifts of Pentecost to not only our missionary activity, but to our textual community as well.

This has been an important shift in my own perspective. When I first took up this work almost seven years ago, we almost exclusively sought volunteer translators. And while I do not think that volunteer translation should be dismissed or discounted, and I believe it is wonderful when attainable, we had to start conceiving of translation as a spiritual gift and take to heart Paul's admonition that "the laborer deserves his wages" (1 Tim 5:18). Committing ourselves to building textual community has meant years of building a robust budget that sustains a translation manager and translation team, encouraging their gifts and skills in the kingdom of God not only with our praise and appreciation, but with adequate compensation for their labor.

Intimately connected to the issue of translation, I suggest that it is important to find cultural interlocutors *who can write*. In our work, we rely mostly on Chinese-Americans, as well as on a few Anglo-Americans who were former missionaries. These are gifted and winsome writers, people with feet in two worlds, who are able to help build the bridge between two cultural contexts. The work cannot be done without interpreters who not only interpret linguistically, but culturally and spiritually. Similarly, the work cannot be done without smooth writing. Cultural interlocuters are often the most able to see where the Chinese church has wisdom that speaks to the Western context and are able to act as popularizers in the receptive culture, winsomely persuading local audiences that they are missing something that others might be able to provide.

Second, I have found that we must be willing and able to move away from our Western expectations surrounding the production of theological texts. In the West, theologians are those capable of sitting down and writing systematically for a year in order to produce a book. If we want to build textual community with global churches, we must anticipate this tradition of textual production may not always apply. In my opinion it is likely helpful at times to teach such systematic writing in global contexts, but not always. Often, focusing on such methods blinds us to what is already available.

Specifically, we ought to be quick and willing to go to the preaching of the global church to understand local theological distinctives. I have met resistance by various Western content developers to developing books from sermons or other spoken material, and I believe this is a significant oversight. After all, some of Western Christianity's most beloved texts were produced from preachers' sermons. Edwards, Spurgeon, Tozer, and even much of Timothy Keller's content were developed from spoken contexts for print.

Recently, I proposed something new to a house church pastor I communicate with. He is a brilliant and literary thinker and I have personally been enthralled by everything of his we have translated. I believe he should be authoring books, both for China and for the global church, but instead of proposing that he write a book from scratch—a daunting task for any pastor not already in the habit—I asked him about some of his recent sermon series and if he has a favorite series he has preached. As it turns out, several of his sermon series from the past couple of years are extremely relevant to the questions we are currently asking about suffering and the meaning of the church in society. And not only that, but he writes full manuscripts for each sermon he preaches and keeps meticulous notes and files. This is not one, but several latent books! We discussed his ideas and now he is in the process of turning his own, favorite sermon series into a book. The primary audience for it will be the Chinese house church, but I am eagerly waiting in the wings to receive his manuscript so that we might translate it, and glean from it in the English-speaking world as well.

Missiologically, I believe it is important for writers such as this pastor to write for their own context, *while also understanding that their voice has value for global Christianity.* China's house churches have long articulated a desire to be connected to the global church and they view their forced disconnectedness as a hardship to bear. Many of China's house church pastors are seeking to locate themselves within global church history and tradition, desiring to be recognized as full members of the universal body of Christ. Writing is a way for China's house church to form its own identity not only within and for China, but within global Christianity as well. For churches that are marginalized and persecuted, participating in a global evangelical textual community pushes back against the isolation they experience. By reading what they write, we tell them that we see and hear them and value their contributions to understanding Jesus.

In summary, the Western church is struggling. Referencing Andrew Walls' image of the human auditorium, the Western evangelical church is struggling to understand how the Jesus Act connects to the play of life. Our view is obstructed. We need to seek out other members in the audience to compare notes. It is time for us to get out of our seats and make the effort to grow the evangelical textual community which influences and mediates so much of what it means to be a Christian in the twenty-first century. To do so takes a significant investment and much risk. But true community rarely happens spontaneously. It requires commitment to the vision, patience, and persistence.

Theology is specific to local contexts. But global interaction with local theology is also vital for growing a unified understanding of and vision for Jesus' work in this world. We have only begun to scratch the surface of what pursuing textual community with Chinese house churches looks like, but I am hopeful that in time the Western evangelical textual community will come to understand its need to grow.

References Cited

Brown, Candy Gunther. 2004. *The Word in the World: Evangelical Writing, Publishing, and Reading in America, 1789–1880.* Chapel Hill, NC: University of North Carolina Press.

Center for House Church Theology (CHCT). 2021. "Mission Statement." www.housechurchtheology.org.

Langham Partnership. 2021. "Develop Books." us.langham.org/develop-books/.

Walls, Andrew F. 1996. *The Missionary Movement in Christian History: Studies in the Transmission of Faith.* Maryknoll, NY: Orbis Books.

Walsh, Bill. 2013. "Books as Powerful Tools for Theological Famine Relief." *The Gospel Coalition.* www.thegospelcoalition.org/article/books-as-powerful-tools-for-theological-famine-relief/.

Walsh, Bill. 2016a. "Celebrating 10 Years of Theological Famine Relief." *The Gospel Coalition.* www.thegospelcoalition.org/article/celebrating-10-years-of-theological-famine-relief/.

Walsh, Bill. 2016b. "A Global Update on Theological Famine Relief." *The Gospel Coalition.* www.thegospelcoalition.org/article/theological-famine-relief-remains-strong-after-10-years/.

Chapter 11

Communicating a Missions Theology through the Prism of the Black Church
A Case Study

Linda P. Saunders

The African American missionary is an anomaly; however, the particulars surrounding the absence of the Black church in the global missions enterprise remains an obscurity enmeshed in both historical and contemporary complexities. For the traditional Black church in America, it is either "backyard missions" or global missions, but rarely both. Moreover, for the majority of Black churches, the option is to remain in the fight for racial equality on the home front. Vaughn Walston contends, "They [the Black church] cannot see the needs of the world because they are focused on the needs right next door" (2002, 189). This is a contemporary challenge within the modern evangelical missionary movement—born out of the Black church's missional world view—and is worthy of a thorough examination. In this chapter, I argue that the Black church's missions theology has an insular focus on backyard missions at the expense of global missions; and point out the way in which the juxtaposition of Black church theology against missions theology communicates the nature of the missions praxis of the Black church.

Three points must be made to fully understand the nature of this chapter. Firstly, the Black church's missions theology is complex. Secondly, the Black pastor is the lifeblood of the traditional Black church; therefore, his or her voice must be included in this discussion. Thirdly, closely examined, the Black church's insular focus is a manifestation of her continual need to engage in a fight for survival at home. To completely appreciate this case study, it is imperative to keep in mind the above points—they provide both a sense of clarity and comfort.

While the perception persists that the Black church has neglected her global missionary duty for a more insular worldview and church theology, another perspective that must be considered involves the contemporary crises within the Black community (oppression in urban centers, inequality at the ballot, inequality in the ability to earn a living, inequality in education, and homelessness rates, to list a few), crises that induce a paralysis in the context of global missions.

One of the best ways to begin to tackle these issues is by allowing the Black pastor to cast his or her vision for the twenty-first century missionary movement in the context of the Black church's participation in the global missions endeavor. Thus, this chapter is based upon a case study involving three African American pastors to allow the Black pastor to give voice to perhaps the most perplexing and complex issue for the twenty-first century African American church: her global missions theology and how Black church theology—juxtaposed against missions theology—communicates the missions praxis of the Black church. Also, it is crucial to acknowledge and understand the Black pastor's missions ideology because the Black pastor still establishes the culture and tone of the Black church. Therefore, without the voice of the Black pastor, the role of the Black church in the twenty-first century missionary movement will be limited at best.

The individuals who participated in this study include an African Methodist Episcopal Zion, a Baptist, a Pentecostal, and a Presbyterian pastor[1] who interacted with the biographies of five Black missionary figures—Rebekka Protten, George Liele, Lott Cary, William Sheppard, and Amanda Berry Smith—to articulate the Black church's missional theology in a contemporary era. In contemporary times, how do Black pastors express the urgency to engage in backyard missions without feeling compelled to engage in the global missions endeavors? How do they respond to the missionary heroism of their predecessors?

First, each pastor was asked to respond to Vaughn Walston's assertion: "They [the Black church] cannot see the needs of the world because they are focused on the needs right next door" (2002, 189). They were then asked to interact with the Black missionaries previously mentioned, who helped shape the modern Protestant missionary movement. I read the biographies of these historical figures and asked the pastors to engage with their predecessors by responding to contemporary issues faced by each historical figure. For the sake of time, I will provide an abbreviated biographical sketch of each Black missionary chosen to be part of this study.

---

1 The pastors will remain anonymous; however, it is important to note all pastors interviewed for this case study have earned an MDiv, and a couple of the pastors have earned a DMin or PhD. Therefore, they are prominent scholars in this discussion and their voices bring a much needed and well-deserved perspective to this topic. Also, the fourth pastor mentioned in this chapter was not interviewed as part of this study but took part in a previous study; however, the information is germane to this discussion.

Question Prompt

In the twenty-first century Walston contends, the Black church is too focused on their own needs to recognize the needs of others around the globe.

Question: *What is your assessment of Walston's summation? Is Walston's statement accurate or off base? And why?*

The Pastors' Response

The pastors did not embrace Vaughn Walston's summation regarding the Black church's lack of desire to evangelize globally because she—the Black church—is short-sighted regarding the world's needs. Initially, the pastors reacted with strong disagreement and disapproval of Walston's assumption about the Black church's lack of vision and empathy toward global others. However, when allowed to contemplate Walston's assertion, while they did not embrace his accusation, they understood how he arrived at his conclusion. One pastor contended, to say the Black church does not "see," implying they do not care to see, or they lack spiritual vision, is to view the Black church as a dead organism whose efficacy has waned (Pastor 1, interviewed by author February 6, 2021). The pastor also contended the world is "here" in the United States, therefore it is not necessary to physically "go" (Pastor 1). Every pastor agreed the Black church is still in survival mode, trying to survive centuries of systemic injustices endured in the United States, which makes it nearly impossible to focus on global evangelization.

To say the Black church is so enmeshed with her own dilemma as to lack empathy for cultural others is to miss the historical implications for what happened to the Black church during the early days of the modern missionary movement. Moreover, it would be extremely difficult to find a Black pastor who does not endorse Matthew 28:18–20 as God's mandate to the church; however, making disciples and "going" into the world means going into one's own community, which is part of this world, whether near or far (Pastor 3, interviewed by author February 18, 2021).

Historically, the Black church was created as a missions-training and missions-sending organization, proven by her integration of the Lord's mandate (Matt 28:18–20), which she placed at the very apex of her worship. To make disciples and send them out to make disciples for the purpose of winning souls for Christ was the model Rebekka Protten implemented. Rebekka Protten, a woman of African descent, envisioned a place of worship where the Negro slave would have the freedom to worship God in their cultural context—free of syncretism. What was born out of these worship services was a desire not just to express jubilation for spiritual freedom, but a desire to take the gospel to those who would be considered "unreachable" in today's context. To be clear, the slaves on the island of St. Thomas were the unreached people group during the eighteenth century.

Missionary Vignette and Question Prompt

Rebekka Protten was born on the island of Antigua circa 1718 and given the name Shelly. While it is not known whether Shelly was born free or enslaved, according to her own account, she was abducted and sold into slavery as a young child. It was in the home of her slave master, Lucas Van Beverhout, where she was given opportunities rarely afforded slaves. She learned to read, she learned basic math skills, and she was a linguist. Arguably, her linguistic abilities were God-given talents more so than learned skills as Shelly fluently spoke several languages. Another gift she received was her emancipation from slavery. Most importantly, in the Beverhout house, Shelly was introduced to the precepts of Christianity. When a priest baptized Shelly, he christened her Rebekka, and Rebekka embraced both Christianity and her new name from that day until her death. It was Rebekka who transformed the island of St. Thomas into a missions post reaching lost slaves for the cause of Christ. Rebekka was a Moravian missionary and the Moravians are credited with preserving her legacy.

Rebekka Protten contextualized the gospel and the delivery of the gospel centuries before Shoki Coe coined the term in 1970 (Coe 1968, 127–28; Coe 1993, 270–75). She discipled the slave population on the island of St. Thomas and taught them to become disciple makers and she instituted a three-self-governing system before Henry Venn and Rufus Anderson coined this term.

Question: *Should you, as a pastor, be concerned with the uttermost parts of the world when you are being oppressed in your corner of the world? Explain your position.*

The Pastors' Response

While the pastors applauded Rebekka Protten's zeal and courage for her missionary strategy and genius, they emphasized the fact that Rebekka did what they are doing, reaching the "unreachable" people groups which are a stone's throw from the Black church's doorstep. When a Black pastor thinks about unreachable people groups, he or she imagines those who live in environmentally, socially, and economically impoverished communities who are forgotten by most churches—unfortunately most White churches. Moreover, many of these churches do not know these communities exist—

communities replete with "unreached" people groups—and perhaps White churches do not care. Furthermore, the pastors emphasized, this lackadaisical attitude is the same accusation railed against the Black church regarding her participation in global missions (Pastor 1).

This crisis raises another question: Is the Black church forever the mission field and never the missionary? The answer is a resounding no. The answer is no because the Black church recognizes and ministers to those in her community: those who are in need, those who are hurting, those who do not know Jesus as their Savior. In this context the Black church is a missionary to her own people, which is what Rebekka Protten accomplished. The Black church is a caring, empathic, visionary, missionary leader—reaching people who are "unreachable." Within this context, the query is posed, how does the Black church engage in backyard missions without neglecting global missions? Another question posed by the Black pastor: Can the White church embrace the "both and" approach in the missions endeavor? This case study does not answer the multiplicity of questions posed by the Black pastor; this case study serves to elucidate the far-reaching complexities of this dilemma.

Regarding oppression, the African American community and the African American church are intimately familiar with oppression. To be clear, the traditional Black church exists because historically Blacks embraced spirituality as a coping mechanism to deal with their temporal trauma—another pressing issue which is outside the scope of this chapter. Also, Blacks were not allowed to worship together with Whites (there were rare times when interracial worship gatherings occurred—Reconstruction Era is one example—however, segregation of the races during worship is a centuries-old custom), thus Blacks were forced to create their own spaces and traditions for worship. It is from this vantage point the Black pastor empathizes with his or her predecessors.

Missionary Vignette and Question Prompt

George Liele was born into slavery in 1750 and thanks to the Baptist Church of Jamaica, his legacy is preserved. Liele co-founded the First Bryan Baptist Church and the First African Baptist Church, in Savannah, Georgia. After purchasing emancipation for himself and his family, Liele joined the British Army. After the Revolutionary war and fearing re-enslavement, he purchased passage to Jamaica for himself and his family (Lawson 2012, 116–17).

Liele was a pioneer in the early missionary movement, arriving in Jamaica nearly a decade before William Carey penned *An Enquiry into the Obligations of Christians*. Liele was an educator, an agriculturalist (he owned his own farm), a pastor, and a spiritual leader. Letters written by Liele evince his keen sense of awareness and acceptance of his African identity and his Christian identity. He referred to himself as an "Ethiopian" in the context of Scripture—a reference to Psalm 68:31 (Russell 2012, 9).

Question: *Would the Black church re-engage in global missions if she knew her rich history regarding the movement? Would African Americans Christians re-engage if they knew their people were responsible for pioneering the movement?*

The Pastors' Response

Knowing that Blacks pioneered the modern missionary movement is encouraging, and perhaps if African Americans understood the history behind the missionary movement, there would be greater appreciation for global missions, but changing the Black church's outlook concerning global missions is a more complex issue, and one that will not change based upon historical knowledge regarding the missionary movement. While the Black church would welcome the opportunity to learn about Black missionaries who pioneered a missionary movement, this may not necessarily be the impetus to move them toward global missions activation. There is a chasm that must be bridged, a chasm induced by racism and racial inequality. As one pastor asserted, it is difficult to engage in the global missionary movement of the twenty-first century because it is a movement entrenched in "a Eurocentric theology and white evangelicalism tied to racism" (Pastor 3). The pastors reflected that if more Blacks understood the historical footprint the Afro American missionary left on the movement, they would be comforted and proud, but there would still be a chasm that must be bridged (Pastor 2, interviewed by author February 8, 2021). Analyzing the Black pastors' reflection will lead toward the discovery of the Black church's missions theology.

Missionary Vignette and Question Prompt

Lott Cary—born into slavery circa 1780—was able to purchase his freedom several years after becoming a believer. Soon a zeal for taking the gospel to distant lands, especially his people in Africa, was all Cary could talk about. In 1815, he cofounded a mission organization to raise funds for missions work in Africa. Soon Cary was asking brethren to join him in taking the gospel to Africa. Carey was earning $800 annually and when his boss found out Cary's intentions were to leave the job and travel to Africa as a missionary, he raised Cary's annual salary to $1,000! This did not persuade Cary to stay in his job though. Cary even confused Christian brothers and sisters, as evidenced by their queries. One brother asked Cary how he (Cary) could leave his comfortable lifestyle to encounter the dangers of Africa. Cary responded,

"I am an African, and in this country [United States], however meritorious my conduct, and respectable my character, I cannot receive the credit due to either. I wish to go to a country where I shall be estimated by my merits, not my complexion" (Taylor 1909, 16).

Question: *Would you encourage one of your members to pursue their call to participate in global missions?*

The Pastors' Response

The pastors were in agreement: if God had called Cary, they would not become a stumbling block. While the pastors embraced the idea that if God had called a person to global missions, they would not become a hindrance, the pastors also emphasized "it is not every individual's responsibility to go" (Pastor 1). Another pastor contended, "it is a matter of prioritizing … Global missions will take a realignment of the Black church's theology. Yet, the onus of global missions is not on every person individually" (Pastor 1 and Pastor 3).

For the Black church to reengage in global missions there must be a paradigm shift in how missions is perceived. Today, many African American pastors believe the modern missionary movement is still soaked with the stench of colonialism and imperialism. Reengaging the Black church in global missions means uncovering the sins of the past to create room for repentance, healing, and reconciliation. For this to take place in the twenty-first century's racial climate, a "walking on water" type miracle will have to occur in the context of racial healing and reconciliation.

> Reengaging the Black church in global missions means uncovering the sins of the past to create room for repentance, healing, and reconciliation.

The other piece to this puzzle is the realignment or adjustment in Black church theology that must take place. How do Black pastors realign their deeply held beliefs concerning global missions—a worldview that has fossilized in their collective consciences for more than a century? Examining these issues illustrates how deeply intertwined the Black church's theology is with her need for survival. While the pastors were not inclined to become a stumbling block to one of their parishioners, they were sensitive to and wary about modern-day realities.

Missionary Vignette and Question Prompt

Known by some historians as the "Black Livingstone," William Henry Sheppard was ordained by the Presbyterian Church. Thanks to Sheppard's meticulous personal diary, which documents his time among the Kuba tribe, his legacy is preserved. Born a free Black in Alabama shortly after the civil war, March 8, 1865; when most Blacks were still enslaved. His mother, Fannie, was a free woman of mixed race. He was afforded an education at a time when earning a university degree was not common, and among Blacks was nearly non-existent (Sheppard 1917, 12).

As a young man, Sheppard remembers a woman praying for him to go to Africa as a missionary. Although he had never heard the word Africa prior to the woman's prayer, God planted a seed in Sheppard's heart—a seed that germinated and blossomed into full fruition. Completing his degree and seminary work he petitioned the Presbyterian Church to allow him to go to Africa as a missionary. Sheppard was denied repeatedly, until the Presbyterian missions board found a White missionary (Samuel Lapsley) to accompany Sheppard as his supervisor. Lapsley died less than a year after their arrival to the Congo. Sheppard continued to live in Africa's interior and established a missions presence among the Kuba tribe. Sheppard learned the language of the Kuba tribe (Baluba-Lulua language), reduced it to a written form, and translated portions of Scriptures and hymns into Baluba-Lulua (Sheppard 1917, 136–39).

Sheppard worked among the tribes of the Congo for nearly two decades before returning to the States permanently. His adventures allowed him an audience with the president of the United States, and kings in Africa, but mostly his journeys took him to the Congo, to tell the tribal people about Jesus. He died at the age of sixty-one, leaving behind a legacy for the world of missiology to emulate.

Question: *What are your thoughts about Sheppard's contribution to the missionary movement? If one of your parishioners told you that they were called to missions in (XYZ location) because someone prayed for them to go to XYZ, and they prepared themselves to go, how would you respond?*

The Pastors' Response

From a Black pastor's perspective, William Sheppard taught us how to approach missions praxis, which could be a great point for the Black church to emulate. He found his identity in the Belgian Congo. These missionaries (referring to the vignettes they just heard) were attracted to global missions because they were drawn to their people, a people with whom they felt connected. While African Americans feel a certain connection to people of Africa, the connection is not the same as it was when they were newly/more recently arrived and Africa was "home."

Also, African Americans do not prepare themselves for missionary work. Instead, they seek degrees to better their lives in the United States. Sheppard should be applauded, said one pastor, but his calling seems like that of a distant era in a bygone day. One parishioner out of thousands might have such an encounter, but the Black pastors were not convinced that Sheppard's experience is comparable to their twenty-first century African American congregants. Once again, they would not become a stumbling block, but two of the Black pastors said this is not anything they would openly endorse. In other words, if one of their members approached them, they would not discourage them from going, but global missions is still not the Black church's priority. The fight remains at home.

Missionary Vignette and Question Prompt

Amanda Berry Smith was born a slave in 1837; however, apart from a few incidents with runaway slaves, Amanda did not have memories about the horrors of slavery. Her father bought the family's freedom when Amanda was a young child and since the family lived in Maryland, she was not familiar with the horrors of slavery in the south. She was familiar, though, with Christianity through her grandmother and father, but it was not until her early teen years when she gave her life to the Lord (Smith 1921, 17, 22, 32–36).

As was the norm during that era, education for Negroes was extremely rare; however, prior to her brief opportunity for formal schooling, Smith taught herself to read with the assistance of her mother. Smith was thirteen years old when she moved to Pennsylvania and accepted a job as a domestic (Smith, iv, 25–26).[2] Pennsylvania is where her affiliation with the AME Church began. Smith proudly admits she appointed herself to the role of missionary. She served in Liberia, Africa from 1882 until 1890, then Smith returned to the United States and settled near the Chicagoland area where she opened a home in 1899—The Amanda Smith Orphanage—located in Harvey, Illinois. Smith operated the home for girls from its inception until her health began to fail.

Smith's biography is important because it reveals a key characteristics about the African-American church's relationship to global missions during the latter half of the nineteenth century. When Blacks accepted Christ they held a deep conviction to serve globally (Sensbach 2005, 239; Frey 2008, 84-85; Wilmore 1986, 98). However, as the Black church's ministry focus turned inward, the urgency to participate in global missions died. It is imperative to note the Black church did not voluntarily turn away from global missions. Rather, a travesty of outside forces drove the Black church away from the global missionary endeavor (Saunders 2020, 32, 86).

---

2 Smith's parents were literate; however, Smith never knew how or where her parents acquired their literacy.

Missionaries such as David George and Amanda Smith served as global missionaries without neglecting their pull toward "backyard" missions and the quest for equality in the Black community. Amanda represents the missions dichotomy which began to afflict the Black church toward the end of the nineteenth century. According to Michelle Raven's research dissertation, Amanda was torn between her duty to backyard missions and the call to serve globally (Ravens 2019, 104–05). Amanda's pull between two missions worlds—backyard missions versus global missions—arguably coincides with the decline of the Black church's global missions endeavor.

Question: *What is your response to Amanda Berry Smith's "both/and" approach to missions work? Both backyard missions and global missions.*

The Pastors' Response

Amanda Berry Smith engaged in both backyard missions and global missions because the call was to do both, and was organic. Smith was raised in an era where the pull to fight for civil rights in the US was as strong as the pull to evangelize the world. This created the capacity for her to effectively engage in both (Pastor 2). The pastors also contended that the Black church does not possess the organizational structure or the socio-economic status to leave all to evangelize around the world. One pastor suggested the work of global missions is a privilege not afforded to most African Americans. By "privilege" she meant the socio-economic privilege to spend two years or two months or even two weeks away from one's job (Pastor 4, interviewed by author December 2, 2019).

Black pastors perceive the world of global missions as an unreachable attainment for most Black churches because of several factors, real or imagined. As just highlighted, many Black pastors believe the Black church does not have the financial capacity to participate in global missions. However, as one pastor suggested, if the Black church shared resources with one another, they would have the financial ability to engage in global missions. Another factor that persists within the African American community, which directly affects the African American church's global missions engagement, is the fight for racial equality. Black pastors are the vanguards for the Black community; therefore, the fight for racial equality and social justice is their fight too. Perhaps Amanda Smith's intense desire to evangelize the world created the capacity to do "both and" in the context of global missions. This is just another piece of this complex puzzle with which Black pastors grapple.

Analysis

How did these three Black pastors respond to the missionary heroism of their predecessors? The pastors' response: they are comforted, they are encouraged, and they are amazed to learn about the Black church's rich history in the missionary movement. Nonetheless, they believe evangelizing the world is best accomplished by evangelizing the community next door, which is their world. When challenged to consider the historical context of Matthew 28:19, one of the pastor's responded, "When Jesus spoke that command, he meant go into all the world, but now the world has come to us" (Pastor 1).

In contemporary times, how do Black pastors express the urgency to engage in backyard missions without feeling compelled to engage in the global missions endeavors? The pastors' response: the twenty-first century missionary movement does not fit into the Black church paradigm because it is based upon a Eurocentric theology. While the Black church will have to realign her theology to include global missions, it is also imperative for the evangelical missionary movement to move away from a Eurocentric colonialist missions theology.

It is worth noting most Black pastors are not opposed to global missions. They understand the urgency for winning the world for Christ. Their capacity to engage in world evangelization has less to do with an inability to empathize with global others—as Walston contends—and more to do with surviving the realities of life in the United States of America.

Conclusion

Arguably, the Black church's missions theology is rooted in Matthew 28:19. One pastor was convinced that while this passage applies to the church in general, it does not mean every individual is responsible to go. If we are to fully understand the Black church's missions theology—which will illuminate their missions praxis—a serious reckoning must take place. Such a reckoning must include a thorough evaluation concerning the psychological impact of historical oppression, the economic impact of historical oppression, the physiological impact of historical oppression, and the emotional impact of historical oppression. The three Black pastors who took part in this case study communicated that the Black church's missions praxis is birthed from the depths of her historical pain and fight for survival and inclusion in these United States of America.

> While the Black church will have to realign her theology to include global missions, it is also imperative for the evangelical missionary movement to move away from a Eurocentric colonialist missions theology.

References Cited

Coe, Shoki. 1968. "Text and Context: Keynote Address at NEAATS Inauguration." *Northeast Asia Journal of Theology* 1, no. 1 (February): 126–31.

Coe, Shoki. 2003. *Recollections and Reflections*. 2nd ed. Lanham, MD: Rowman & Littlefield.

Frey, Sylvia R. 2008. "The Visible Church: Historiography of African American Religion since Raboteau." *Slavery and Abolition* 29, no. 1 (March): 83–111.

Lawson, Winston A. 2012. "Pioneer George Liele in Jamaica, the British Colony." In *George Liele's Life and Legacy: An Unsung Hero*, edited by David T. Shannon, 115–28. Macon, GA: Mercer University Press.

Raven, Michelle L. K. 2019. "Serve in Your Own Backyard: An African-American Mission Dilemma." PhD diss., Columbia International University.

Russell, Horace O. 2012. "Prologue." In *George Liele's Life and Legacy: An Unsung Hero*, edited by David T. Shannon, 7–12. Macon, GA: Mercer University Press.

Saunders, P. Linda. 2020. "Laying an Historical Foundation to Examine the African-American Church's Relationship to 21st Century Global Missions to Create a Contextualized Missions Training Model for Future Generations of African-American Missionaries." PhD diss., Columbia International University. ProQuest.

Sensbach, Jon F. 2005. *Rebecca's Revival: Creating Black Christianity in the Atlantic World*. Cambridge: Harvard University Press.

Sheppard, William H. 1917. *Presbyterian Pioneers in the Congo*. Richmond: Presbyterian Committee of Publication.

Smith, Amanda. 1921. *An Autobiography: The Story of the Lord's Dealings with Mrs. Amanda Smith, the Colored Evangelist: Containing an Account of Her Life Work of Faith, and Her Travels in America, England, Ireland, Scotland, India, and Africa as an Independent Missionary*. 1893. Chicago: Meyer & Brother Publishers.

Taylor, James B. 1837. *Biography of Elder Lott Cary, Late Missionary to Africa*. Reprint, Baltimore: Armstrong & Berry J. W. Woods, 1909.

Walston, Vaughn J. 2002. "Mobilizing the African-American Church for Global Evangelization." In *African-American Experience in World Missions: A Call Beyond Community*, edited by Vaughn J. Walston and Robert J. Stevens, 187–92. Pasadena: William Carey Library.

Wilmore, Gayraud S. 1986. "Black Americans in Missions: Setting the Record Straight." *International Bulletin of Missionary Research* 10, no. 3 (July): 98–102.

Chapter 12

Faithful Fundraising
Communicating Needs without Sacrificing Dignity or Short-Circuiting Discipleship

Jessica Udall

In 1984, pop stars Bob Geldof and Midge Ure wrote the song "Do They Know It's Christmas?" in response to watching the news regarding the well-known 1983–85 famine in northeastern Ethiopia. They assembled a supergroup of musicians and recording artists from Western countries under the name Band Aid and were delighted to watch the song become a chart-topping success. The lyrics of this song encourage people to give money to help alleviate the sufferings of Ethiopia. The first lines set the tone for the song:

> It's Christmas time, there's no need to be afraid
>
> At Christmas time, we let in light and we banish shade
>
> And in our world of plenty we can spread a smile of joy
>
> Throw your arms around the world at Christmas time (Band Aid, 1984)

While the problematic nature of this song might at first glance be explained away by the fact that it was written decades ago, it has been re-recorded multiple times, most recently in 2014 (Band Aid, 2014), and was also recently featured in an episode of the TV show *Glee*. And it explains and encapsulates a Western perspective on giving to fix the non-Western world's problems in a way that is both disturbing and helpfully illustrative for our purposes in this chapter. In the song, a particular crisis was generalized. A severe regional food shortage was parlayed into a broad-brush portrayal of "the world" (meaning "the world" that is removed from the hearers in some way, whether those in a homeless shelter as portrayed in the *Glee* episode, or in the non-Western world in general) as a place with nothing.

The specific case of Ethiopia was publicized as being a place "where nothing ever grows/No rain nor rivers flow" and where, ostensibly, no one knows it is Christmastime. In reality, the famine was brutal but was confined to a specific region which was indeed devastated by severe food shortages, while my Ethiopian husband (who was born during this time) and his family, friends, and neighbors in the capital city were relatively unaffected. And in other years, before and since, plenty of food has grown and plenty of rain and rivers have flowed in Ethiopia. In addition to this, Ethiopia was one of the first nations to declare itself to be a "Christian nation" (in the fourth century AD), with biblical accounts such as Philip's encounter with the Ethiopian eunuch in Acts 8 suggesting that the Christian message reached Ethiopia far earlier than that ("Religion of Ethiopia," 2021), meaning that the ancestors of the Ethiopians affected by the famine have likely known about the incarnation of Christ for longer than the ancestors of the European-background writers and singers of the song. Christmas celebrations in Ethiopia center around church attendance, with merrymaking and feasting taking a secondary role, but even during the famine, Ethiopians absolutely knew that it was Christmastime. Unfortunately, however, the stereotypical view of Ethiopia as a land of perpetual famine, drought, ignorance, and misery has persisted, to the point that when many well-meaning but stereotypically informed people hear where my husband is from, their first and only follow-up question is about the famine that happened there over thirty-five years ago, which they assume still persists today. The purpose of belaboring this point is not to heap criticism upon the pop stars who wanted and continue to want to do something useful with their fame, penning songs and singing words that they hope will inspire people to give. Instead, this song is dissected in order to show a real-life example of well-meaning communication having negative long-term stereotypical effects.

Though one would hope that the *imago Dei* consciousness of Christians would curtail the unintentional denigration of others for the purpose of raising money to help them, this has largely not been the case. In fact, the communication style that seems to be employed by many Christian individuals and organizations seeking to rapidly raise money could be described as functionally anthropological in nature. The desperate plight of the needy and the potential power of the donors loom large, while God is unwittingly reduced to a background character in the drama of the philanthropic process.

An example of well-meaning Christian fundraising trending unfortunately into "Do They Know It's Christmas?" territory is *The Gospel Coalition's* Theological Famine Relief Fund. On their website, they state that "the problem" is that "85% of the world's evangelical churches are led by pastors with insufficient training … who don't have access to adequate theological education or resources." The "solution" is for these pastors to be "fed gospel-centered, theologically sound 'solid food'" (*The Gospel Coalition*, Inc., 2021). Consider the implications of this statement of problem and solution: majority world pastors and their flocks are wasting away on a milky diet of immature and faulty theology, and they will only grow strong if translated resources are imported and given to them free of charge. While it certainly may be helpful for pastors around the world to have access to affordable theological literature, the extreme nature of this fundraising communication—especially the deliberate choice of the words "famine relief"—is actually harmful to these pastors as well as those helping them. It portrays majority world pastors as helpless, starving, not having what is needed for survival unless relief is brought in from outside.

But what about God's Word, available to most Christians who are not part of so-called "Bible-less" unreached people groups? What about the Holy Spirit, who is living within them to "guide [them] into all truth" (John 16:13)? What about the local body of Christ, who are capable of encouraging one another with psalms, hymns, spiritual songs, encouragement, and instruction—in writing, but also likely in spoken and sung formats which may be even more useful and contextual? Who decides what is "sufficient training" or "adequate theological ... resources"? Who is choosing which theological resources to send and why? Why is the vitality of Western churches—whose pastors are extensively trained and have bulging shelves filled with theological resources—in decline, and why do Western Christians spending time in the majority world consistently comment on the zeal, power, and joy of believers there compared to more jaded American Christians? Is it possible that being theologically overfed and complacent is as much of a danger as not having enough theological resources? "For the kingdom of God does not consist in talk but in power" (1 Cor 4:20).

At this point, it would be wise to reiterate the likelihood that the creators of the Theological Famine Relief fund are well-intentioned. Years ago, before Majority World believers kindly showed me my blind spot in this area, I myself have written fundraising copy that did not respect the dignity of people in the Majority World and that may have short-circuited the discipleship process for potential donors. In this chapter, I am not claiming to be sinless and throwing the first stone. Rather, I am seeking to share the correction I have received in the hopes that others will also benefit and that future fundraising communication will be more faithful to God, humble in estimation of donors' power, and dignifying of the *imago Dei* he has placed within each person regardless of where they live or how many resources they have.

> Fundraising communication may be some of the only information that American Christians regularly receive about the world outside of America.

Some may say that these critiques are overly concerned with political correctness and hair-splitting semantics, but as the introductory example about the "Do They Know It's Christmas?" song affecting my husband's conversations with Americans today over thirty years later, these critiques are based on the fact that words paint pictures that stick in people's minds. Fundraising communication may be some of the only information that American Christians regularly receive about the world outside of America. The stories and images and general impression that they get from this communication will necessarily shape their perceptions about other countries, people who come from those countries, and even about themselves in relation to the world.

Fundraising communication that paints an unhelpfully bleak and desperate picture of the Majority World did not arise in a vacuum. Several factors contributed to fundraisers believing that status quo fundraising strategies are the only way to get the money they need for their causes.

Information Overload Leads to "Emergency Mode" Fundraising

The current information age has led to information overload on an individual level. It is impossible to keep up with everything happening in the world, so in a quest for relevance and traction, each piece of information has to claw and elbow its way into a person's attention if it hopes to stand out from the crowd. While this sense of overwhelm has crept up on humans almost imperceptibly—like a rolling boil creeps up on a frog swimming in a pot—it can be flatly explained by data units alone: "The amount of scientific information we've discovered in the last twenty years is more than all the discoveries up to that point, from the beginning of language" (Levitin 2015, 15). This hits home more practically through an example: "In 1976, the average supermarket stocked 9,000 unique products; today that number has ballooned to 40,000 of them, yet the average person gets 80%–85% of their needs in only 150 different supermarket items. That means that we need to ignore 39,850 items in the store" (Levitin 2015, 5).

It is admittedly incredibly difficult to get the attention of a potential donor who is forced to contend with tens of thousands of distractions every time they so much as seek to buy some hamburger buns. Creating a sense of emergency is one effective way to get people to take notice, and so this valid method of fundraising during a true emergency becomes twisted in order to not lose the attention of people and therefore the dollars. Overusing emergency mode in order to cope with feeling invisible due to information overload is what causes inflation of numbers and dramatization of stories in fundraising. It may seem that the end justifies the means because the dollars end up in-hand, but this method ends up reinforcing a Pavlovian cycle in which donors need extreme stimulation in order to open their wallets, eventually working against the still, small voice of the Holy Spirit and unhelpfully competing with more quiet, honest, but earnest invitations to give.

Over-Abundance Leads to Quick, Feel-Good Solutions (for the Givers)

In Western cultures where a certain supra-subsistence level of prosperity is the norm, materialism has become entrenched. It can exist unchallenged if people live only among others who enjoy the same level of prosperity as themselves, but when the stark divide between haves and have-nots is pointedly presented to those who are materially prosperous, guilt sets in and people begin to look for ways to relieve it. Quickly giving something away is the easiest option and alleviates any uncomfortable feelings that may have arisen. This may be in the form of donations to Goodwill (whose billboards, according to an informal Google search, have been known to read: "For that warm fuzzy feeling … Donate today"), clothes or shoes sent somewhere in Africa (often negatively affecting the local economy) (de Freytas-Tamura 2017), or money given to the poor at home or abroad. While such donations may in certain cases be put to good use and give "that warm fuzzy feeling" of guilt relief to the one donating, this method of fundraising is short-sighted and ultimately damaging to all involved, particularly the givers.

When given an easy "out," people are not likely to do additional work or soul-searching to figure out why they feel guilt or a sense of unease when confronted with their affluence compared to the rest of the world. Indeed, research done by the Science of Philanthropy Initiative suggests that when organizations promised potential donors that if they gave today, the organization would never contact them again, initial giving went up exponentially, but obviously, "the shelf life of that reciprocity [that is, giving and then not being contacted again] doesn't extend beyond the first donation." Providing exclusively quick-giving opportunities is essentially a lucrative but short-sighted burning of bridges. It short-circuits the discipleship process for Western believers who must, if they are to be mature, gradually confront their own materialistic culture and instead figure out how to make choices that cultivate a lifestyle of generosity that overflows from the love of God poured out in their hearts rather than making a knee-jerk donation to squelch a momentary pang of guilt and get the fundraiser to go away and stop bothering them. In quick-giving situations, donors are also not likely to consider the down-the-line results of their giving—whether it truly benefits those who receive it or whether it harms more than it helps—because their conscience has been prematurely cleared and they have likely moved on to other distractions in the information-overloaded world described above.

Spiritual Apathy Leads to a Search for Measurable Benchmarks of Maturity

In the West, church leaders are often frustrated by the spiritual apathy that they see in their congregations. In efforts to remedy this, it can be easy to look for concrete benchmarks of spiritual growth that can be quantified and recorded. I have written elsewhere about getting people into small groups possibly being a benchmark that—when myopically focused on—actually has the effect of vaccinating people against true community that goes beyond set times and settings (Udall 2020).

The financial equivalent to counting noses in the church or in small groups is counting dollars given or givers recruited. But simply giving something is not an accurate measure of spiritual growth. Giving some dollars out of one's abundance or out of a desire to relieve guilt and discomfort does not indicate any spiritual growth in the area of sacrificial generosity and actually may impede spiritual growth, because it quickly staples an apple onto a tree rather than letting many apples gradually and organically grow by nourishing the roots of the tree.

In order to cultivate joyfully generous givers in the Western church, we must refrain from fundraising in emergency mode. We must refuse to use guilt as a strong-arm tactic that short-circuits genuine generosity. We must not fall prey to assuming that any and all giving is a measure of spiritual growth. What does faithful fundraising look like in an atmosphere that faces the challenges of information overload, material overabundance, and spiritual apathy? To fundraise faithfully, I suggest that fundraisers ask the following questions:

Does my fundraising communication …

1. *Stand in awe of and rejoice in God's present and active work in the world (and invite potential donors to do the same)?*

Starting with a personal consciousness of God and amazement at his work happening around the world at this very moment is the starting place for faithful fundraising. It will also center fundraisers in the sovereign and organically-growing purposes of God which have been unfolding for millennia and will continue after we are gone. It will enable fundraisers to follow in the footsteps of Jesus who, though he was active and energetic in ministry, was never described as hurrying or becoming stressed over material things. Pausing before speaking or writing any fundraising communication to remember God's presence, example, and activity will orient the communicator and set a tone that makes possible the faithful communication of needs without sacrificing the dignity of recipients and without short-circuiting the discipleship process of donors.

2. *Stir potential donors up to love and good works flowing from that love (Heb 10:24)?*

Fundraising in emergency mode and stirring up guilt regarding overabundance or spiritual apathy creates fear in the brain: fear of having too much or not enough of something, or of someone else not having enough. It motivates the potential donor to give just enough to re-establish equilibrium, and then to avoid getting triggered by those kinds of fears again. Essentially, it makes the fundraising process harder the next time around, meaning fundraising communication needs to sound the emergency siren even louder and strong-arm people into feelings of guilt even harder in order to squeeze out more donations. This is not good for anyone.

The fact that suggesting a change to status-quo fundraising sounds naïvely idealistic simply shows how far current practices have strayed from the example of Jesus, who told his stressed-out followers: "Therefore do not be anxious, saying, 'What shall we eat?' or 'What shall we drink?' or 'What shall we wear?' For the Gentiles seek after all these things, and your heavenly Father knows that you need them all. But seek first the kingdom of God and his righteousness, and all these things will be added to you" (Matt 6:31–33).

If fundraisers consider themselves to be encouragers and disciplers, they will approach fundraising in a positive way, motivating people through love. The love and generosity of God with humankind can encourage giving as a natural, uncoerced response to that love. Cultivating a sense of awe when witnessing the image of God in all of humankind, including those who may have less resources, can create a sense of commonality that leads to a partnership of equals before God who share their varied gifts, since the materially poor are certainly included when Paul explains: "Now there are varieties of gifts, but the same Spirit; and there are varieties of service, but the same Lord; and there are varieties of activities, but it is the same God who empowers them all in everyone. To each is given the manifestation of the Spirit for the common good" (1 Cor 12:4–7).

Fundraising motivated by common humanity and divinely-fueled love refuses to sacrifice the dignity of those with less resources, and it leads to a fuller discipleship process for those who give, in the spirit of 1 John 3:16–18, which acknowledges that true giving is not simply putting cash in an offering plate: "By this we know love, that he laid down his life for us, and we ought to lay down our lives for the brothers. But if anyone has the world's goods and sees his brother in need, yet closes his heart against him, how does God's love abide in him? Little children, let us not love in word or talk but in deed and in truth."

3. *Portray other cultures in such a way that if someone from that culture read what I wrote, they would feel respected and accurately represented?*

It would be helpful and paradigm-shifting for fundraisers to imagine someone from the group who will receive the funds sitting in the second row of the church where she is speaking, or receiving the email he is writing. How would this person feel about what and how their need is being communicated? When this happens literally, it should be viewed by the fundraiser as a litmus test of the fundraising methods he or she is using. Feedback from sources "on the inside" of the group who will be receiving the funds is invaluable and should be prioritized and prayerfully incorporated in order to communicate accurately and respectfully while playing the role of a bridge between people from different backgrounds.

4. Portray those who will receive donations as the heroes of their own stories?

It is easier to motivate someone to give if they get to be the hero of the story that is playing out, but this is akin to giving the lead part of a play to the person who donates the most money to the theater after another person has learned all the lines and is ready to perform. People who come alongside a group to help them financially should view themselves as a guide (someone who comes alongside the hero to provide something needed) but not the hero of the story (Miller 2017), thus doing the hard work of truly helping in the long-term, rather than helping in a way that is ultimately short-sighted and self-serving to the people giving rather than empowering to the people doing the work.[1]

This does not mean that the stories of people from within the group receiving the funds should be told without permission, however. Though they are the heroes, not every hero wants their journey to be made public or used for fundraising purposes. If and when stories are told, they should be with the permission of the hero and/or with identifying details changed, or perhaps written in the first person by the hero himself or herself, since fundraisers are not, as the common expression goes, a voice for the voiceless. Instead, the people who are receiving the funds have perfectly functional voices that would benefit the donors to hear, both for the purposes of education as well as for mutual edification, since partnership is a two-way street.

5. Portray the places where donations are going as fully-orbed locations where much beauty resides and much good is happening?

To take Ethiopia as an example, it is easier to raise money for a project in Ethiopia if the country is portrayed as famine-addled, desperately poor, and devoid of infrastructure. But this is not a fully orbed or accurate picture of Ethiopia, which is also full of exciting potential and initiatives to grow various

---

[1] I am indebted to Donald Miller for the terms "hero" and "guide." He uses this framework in business, teaching business owners to market themselves as guides and to view their clients in the role of heroes, but I have borrowed this language and adapted the ideas to be used in a ministry context.

sectors of the economy, and whose people are generally characterized by a deep reverence for God, hospitality toward others, and a fierce love for their homeland. And even these descriptors are not nuanced enough or descriptive enough to fully express what Ethiopia is like. How do you describe a country? A people group? Ultimately, words fall short, but fundraisers should choose their words carefully and even with humble trembling and prayer, with the knowledge that what they say may well be the only or the most memorable description a potential donor has of another country or people group. The words of a fundraiser can serve to make or break stereotypes. And once formed or reinforced, stereotypes make relationships harder by building boxes for rather than creating links between two different groups.

A helpful exercise for fundraisers to do in the midst of trying to describe a different culture would be to describe their own culture from the perspective of an outsider. What descriptions would feel accurate? Which would feel stereotypical and unfair? What nuances would be helpful? These same-culture insights will create a helpful frame of reference for any other cultural descriptions fundraisers are called upon to communicate.

6. *Invite potential donors to be a part of what God is already doing (in a cosmic sense) and what local people are already doing (in a human sense) in a place?*

God does not arrive in a place when a donation arrives there. He has already been working and will continue to do so, using the donation but not limited by it. In the same way, local people are already working in an area where a donation is sent, and they may well be resourced and helped by a donation, but they are not activated by it as if they did not exist before its arrival. If donations are portrayed by fundraisers as investments in what God and people are already doing, it will help donors to see their money accurately as a tool, not a panacea. And it will also help them to resist the urge to play God by imagining themselves to be creating something out of nothing on the blank slate of an unknown land.

7. *Invite potential donors to sustained partnership which involves two-way benefits with those already working in a place (with a brother-sister, not father-son or mother-daughter understanding of the relationship)?*

If giving is motivated by love (which gives to draw near) rather than fear (which gives to get away), then relationship will always result. Whether this means personal connection with people from the group who receives the donation or simply sustained engagement and interest in who the group is and what they are doing, this loving relationship should be encouraged and cultivated by the fundraiser in terms of a brother-sister type of relationship (implying equality) rather than a paternalistic father-son or mother-daughter type of relationship, which would be inappropriate since having more money does not necessarily confer more maturity but is simply one more gift to be used for the glory of the/our Heavenly Father.

Conclusion

I conclude with four questions for further research:

1. What are some examples of organizations that have shifted their fundraising communications toward messaging that refuses to sacrifice dignity and short-circuit discipleship?

2. How should the *imago Dei* consciousness of Christians influence their fundraising communications?

3. What are healthy ways to deal with information overload other than revving up into emergency mode with fundraising communications? Investigate the psychology of information overload and the unhealthy limbic activation inherent in emergency mode fundraising.

4. Examine the psychology of over-abundance and the reality of spiritual apathy and how to healthily deal with them in the American church in a long-term way. How could healthily engaging these issues in a deeper, discipleship-oriented way actually promote sustained and intrinsically motivated generosity? Why is this preferable to guilt-motivated, surface-level giving?

References Cited

Band Aid. 1984. "Do They Know It's Christmas?" New York: Columbia Records. Audio CD.

Band Aid. 2014. "Do They Know It's Christmas?" Virgin EMI—Island. Audio CD.

de Freytas-Tamura, Kimiko. 2017. "For Dignity and Development, East Africa Curbs Used Clothes Imports." *New York Times*. https://www.nytimes.com/2017/10/12/world/africa/east-africa-rwanda-used-clothing.html.

Glee. 2013. "Extraordinary Merry Christmas." Season 3, episode 9. Directed by Matthew Morrison. Aired December 13, 2011. Fox Network.

Levitin, Daniel. 2015. *The Organized Mind: Thinking Straight in an Age of Information Overload*. New York: Dutton Penguin Random House.

Miller, Donald. 2017. *Building a Storybrand: Clarify Your Message So Customers Will Listen*. Nashville: HarperCollins Leadership.

"Religion of Ethiopia," 2021 Britannica. https://www.britannica.com/place/Ethiopia/Religion.

"Theological Famine Relief Fund." 2021. *The Gospel Coalition*. https://www.thegospelcoalition.org/sponsorable-project/theological-famine-relief-fund/.

Udall, Jessica. 2020. "Lives That Welcome: How a Non-Western Understanding of Hospitality Can Revitalize the American Church's Fellowship and Outreach." Paper presented at the national conference of the Evangelical Missiological Society, virtual, October 9, 2020.

Part 4
Communicating Mission through Social Media

The concluding section focuses on the ever-present reality of social media. The authors discuss the nature of social media, the dangers inherent in social media, and a model for using social media content to communicate the gospel in missions.

Michael Lee enlightens us with a broad perspective of social media. He looks at the nature of the medium and how it does more than add content to our lives. Utilizing McLuhan's "the medium is the message," Lee walks us through an understanding that social media not only entertains us, but more importantly changes us. He then challenges the church and those who are in missions to think carefully about the proper use of social media in God's work.

Also looking broadly at the widespread use of social media, J. T. Matthews shares the challenges of wisely and carefully using social media and technology in "restricted-access" countries. It is important to recognize that social media is part of the corporate "attention economy" and thrives on knowing much about its users. Matthews calls the missions community to heightened caution and action when serving in "restricted-access contexts" where authoritarian governments are increasingly using surveillance based on artificial intelligence that can easily identify individuals as belonging to "Digital Christianity."

Finally, Song (Joseph) Cho explores using Korean pop culture as a tool for communicating the Good News of Jesus Christ. He presents the reader with an in-depth exploration of the highly successful—among Japanese adult women—K-drama *Winter Sonata*. Cho demonstrates why the drama built an extensive following because of its portrayal of pure love. The missional challenge is to use the message of true love as a bridge to communicate the only true, pure love that is found in Jesus Christ.

—MARCUS DEAN

Chapter 13

The Medium Is the Message
Reflections on Disciple-Making in the Age of Social Media

Michael Hamkin Lee

In 2017 the South Florida Water Management District announced that they were taking "aggressive action to protect Florida's Everglades" (Python Elimination Program, n.d.) by eliminating non-native Burmese pythons, which were likely introduced by pet owners, accidentally or intentionally, into the wild. District officials described the threat that this alien species posed to the existing ecosystem: "Burmese pythons possess an insatiable appetite. They can not only kill Florida native prey species and pose a threat to humans, but also rob panthers, birds of prey, alligators and bobcats of a primary food source" (Python Elimination Program, n.d.).

Note that the Burmese python was not just a neutral player or nondisruptive addition to the existing ecosystem; over time, the pythons' presence and normal activities dramatically affected change within the ecosystem. According to media theorists, like Marshall McLuhan, a similar principle of inevitable change and disruption occurs with the introduction of new technology and innovations. McLuhan's pioneering work in the 1950s and 1960s essentially launched media ecology, a new field which explores how media and technology reciprocally impact the people and the societies who create, use, and are shaped by what they have created.

Consider the technological "Burmese pythons" of today. It is not just the pythons that have insatiable appetites; as numerous studies have shown, people, especially our young digital natives, have become increasingly addicted to their smartphones and the constant access to digital technologies, like social media, which tech insiders have testified are designed to keep our attention as long as possible. This over-dependency has only accelerated during the COVID-19 pandemic.

Furthermore, various studies from Pew Research (Auxier et al. 2020), the Barna Group (Crouch 2017), and others confirm the prevalence of serious concerns and struggles that parents and children alike have with the amount of time they spend on their phones and social media. Especially in a time when many are looking for and need guidance in their relationship with technology, we are failing in our discipleship if we are not helping people cultivate wisdom in this area.

While some simply lack the will and courage to address their unhealthy habits, I believe that a significant barrier in moving towards a healthy relationship to technology is that most do not have an adequately developed conceptual framework to think critically about and understand what is happening to them and their communities.

Marshall McLuhan is a helpful guide in this journey towards better understanding the place and impact of technology. In what follows, we will consider some key insights from McLuhan that help us build a basic conceptual foundation for what technology is, what it does, and how we can assess its impact on individuals and societies. We will then apply McLuhan's insights into assessing the social impact of social media use and consider recent social research in this area. We will conclude with reflections and recommendations.

Medium Is the Message: What Is Media and What Does It Do?

First, we will unpack the meaning of McLuhan's often quoted and often misunderstood aphorism, "the medium is the message," from his seminal book, *Understanding Media: The Extensions of Man*, first published in 1964:

> In a culture like ours, long accustomed to splitting and dividing all things as a means of control, it is sometimes a bit of a shock to be reminded that, in operational and practical fact, the medium is the message. This is merely to say that the personal and social consequences of any medium—that is, of any extension of ourselves—result from the new scale that is introduced into our affairs by each extension of ourselves, or by any new technology (McLuhan 1994, 7).

McLuhan saw any medium or technology as an extension of our bodies or minds. Clothing is an extension of our skin, a hammer is an extension of our hand, and so forth. McLuhan often uses medium and technology synonymously, though perhaps technology can be understood as a type of medium, namely a physical tool. So, whereas a spoken word is a medium that extends human thought, radio is a technology or a medium that enhances or amplifies the spoken word, which in turn is a medium that extends the mind. Also "media" is just the plural form of medium and should not be perceived as narrowly referring to products like film and songs, or as shorthand for journalists. For McLuhan, the term more expansively refers to anything that extends the human body or activity.

For McLuhan the "message" of any media or technology is not just the content of a discrete unit of communication, but rather the changes that it affects and introduces into human affairs. The changes and effects may take the form of shifts in assumptions, values, and behaviors; and they are often gradual and imperceptible. McLuhan contended that we largely miss or ignore these structural changes until we pause to notice how far things have shifted. So, by "the medium is the message," he meant that the nature or character of the medium we create and use (what it is) are revealed by the changes that they affect within individuals and communities. McLuhan's larger point is that the transformative power and social impact of any technological medium is often more significant and consequential in shaping societies and individuals than what we do or extend through that medium. For example, to understand text messaging, we must not only look at the content of what we send and receive, but more consequently, how this very technology is affecting how we communicate and relate with one other and how the very existence and usage of text messaging is changing our society. We create a medium, which in turn changes us.

> The transformative power and social impact of any technological medium is often more significant and consequential in shaping societies and individuals than what we do or extend through that medium.

In describing what technology does or what effect it has on the human environment, McLuhan (1994) asserted:

> Any invention or technology is an extension or self-amputation of our physical bodies, and such extension also demands new ratios or new equilibriums among the other organs and extensions of the body. There is, for example, no way of refusing to comply with the new sense ratios or sense "closure" evoked by the TV image. But the effect of the entry of the TV image will vary from culture to culture in accordance with the existing sense ratio in each culture (45).

Technology, as extensions of the human body and mind, can project, amplify, or augment our thoughts and activities. Cars can be thought of as extensions of our feet, which allow us, among other things, to travel distances quickly and efficiently. But with every extension there is an accompanying amputation, whereby something becomes diminished, lost, or neglected; technology both extends and amputates. Habitually using calculators to compute basic arithmetic problems, or asking Alexa to do so, while efficient, comes at the cost of eroding mental capacities to perform mental calculations. When it comes to technology, McLuhan observed that most of us see and understand extensions much more than amputations, which we tend to miss or ignore. We do so at our peril, gradually descending into idolatry and reenacting the technological hubris of the Tower of Babel. Aptly citing Psalm 115, McLuhan warned that we become what we behold: "Those who make them will be like them, and so will all who trust in them" (Ps 115:8 NIV).

As McLuhan's theories and reflections on media ecology matured, he crystalized some of his key theories in a hermeneutical framework or "tetrad" for analyzing how cultures and societies are impacted by media and technology (McLuhan and Powers 1989, 8–11). The tetrad (see figure 13.1), which consists of four laws of media framed as questions, points to McLuhan's contention that whether we are aware of it or not, all media or technology does the following: 1) enhancement, 2) obsolescence, 3) retrieval, and 4) reversal. The tetrad can be useful to help us think systematically about the effects of media that we might otherwise not notice or anticipate.

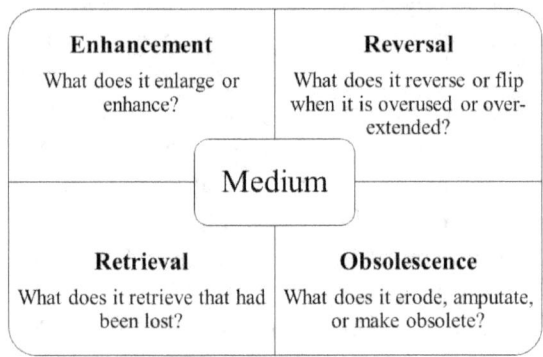

Figure 13.1 McLuhan's Tetrad: A Framework to Assess the Impact of Media (author's rendering of the tetrad)

First, as noted earlier, a medium extends or enhances natural human functions or in turn other media. What does it enlarge or enhance? For example, Zoom extends our ability to speak and see one another across distance almost instantaneously. Second, what does it erode, amputate, or make obsolete? Zoom decreases the frequency of travel, the demand for physical, centralized workspaces, and access to social and behavioral cues, and minimizes senses like touch, taste, and smell. Third, what does it retrieve that had been lost? Zoom allows us to revive neglected relationships with those whom we have lost touch with due to various restrictions. And compared to other means of communication like audio-only phone conversations, text messaging, and email, it retrieves the concern for physical appearance. Fourth, what does it reverse or flip when it is overused or over-extended? In what some are calling "Zoom fatigue," many are feeling especially drained after multiple Zoom calls, more so than face-to-face conversations (Oliver 2020).

Some point to the visual and cognitive overload of constantly seeing your own face and that of many others on one screen. Also, the barrier of being virtual, disembodied, and behind a screen may loosen our inhibition to multi-task, which can lead to practices of not being fully present with people.

Sherry Turkle (2020), helpfully points out that relationships are not meant to be efficient; technology gave us the false promise of improving our relationships through efficiency. As she argues in her helpful book *Reclaiming Conversation* (2015), we miss out on the formative experiences that hone our capacity to have real, vulnerable, messy human conversations as we increasingly rely on technology to mediate our disembodied, carefully curated mediated "connections." Turkle points out in some ways, a phone call may actually be better than Zoom because it allows you to focus on the voice rather than be distracted by the bombardment of images of others and yourself.

The Social Impact of Social Media

By social media, I am referring to online digital platforms that allow users to create an online presence or a curated projection of their identity and interact with other users through the sharing of content like messages, photos, songs, and video. These include services like Instagram, Twitter, Pinterest, TikTok, Reddit, WhatsApp, Facebook, and YouTube. In terms of McLuhan's tetrad, we can point to ways that social media has allowed millions to extend their voices and thoughts to a global audience, like facilitating the organization of social change movements like the Arab Spring and empowering us to keep connected in some way with distant friends and acquaintances and forge new relationships. Beyond what the power of social media enhances and retrieves, the focus of this section is on what it amputates and reverses, which we tend to ignore or not notice.

Much research and advocacy has emerged in response to the social media phenomenon and the increasing power and influence that large tech firms wield within our society. Advocacy groups like The Center for Humane Technology (CHT) are led by former tech insiders, who are seeking to advance "thoughtful solutions to change the culture, business incentives, design techniques, and organizational structures driving how technology hijacks our brains" (Center for Humane Technology n.d.). The CHT also supported the production of *The Social Dilemma*, the highest-ranking documentary on Netflix in 2020. In an informative 2019 US Senate Commerce subcommittee hearing titled, "Optimizing for Engagement: Understanding the Use of Persuasive Technology on Internet Platforms," Tristan Harris testified to the increasing asymmetry of power between tech companies and users. He noted that companies like Facebook (now Meta) and Google are becoming increasingly aggressive in their race to garner our attention and their products are socially engineered to be as addictive as possible. In the book *The Attention Merchants* (2016), Tim Wu also details the ways in which tech companies purposefully sought to make their products addictive regardless of the psychological and social consequences. Social media addiction, which some psychologists define as "the excessive use and habitual monitoring of social media, manifested in compulsive usage that comes at the expense of other activities" (Zivnuska et al. 2019, 747), has become prevalent enough to be an identifiable disorder with treatment protocols.

On a societal level, Harris and others have pointed to how the powerful predictive algorithms that tech companies use to keep us engaged are dangerously leading us to a more polarized society. During the 2019 Senate hearing, Harris observed:

> There's a tendency to think here that this is just human nature. Now that's just, people are polarized and this is just playing out, it's a mirror, it's holding up a mirror to society. But what it's really doing is it's an amplifier for the worst parts of us. So in the race to the bottom of the brain stem to get attention … let's take an example like Twitter … it's calculating what is the thing that I can show you that will get the most engagement and it turns out that outrage, moral outrage gets the most engagement so it was found in the study that for every word of moral outrage that you add to a tweet increases your retweet rate by 17% so in other words you know the polarization of our society is actually part of the business model … . (U.S. Congress Senate 2019)

In addition to concerns about societal discord and the rapid spread of misinformation (which recently led Twitter and Facebook to put a warning label on posts that they deem to be misleading), there is a long list of other research-based concerns correlated to digital technology use which includes mental health impact, the alarming rise of self-harm (especially with young females), impaired brain development and cognitive functions, difficulty with attention and concentration, declining school and job productivity/performance, and reduced physical health due to an increasing sedentary lifestyle (Truth About Tech 2018).

We should avoid the twin error of, on the one hand, seeing technology merely as a neutral instrument that we have ultimate control over, and on the other hand, viewing technology deterministically as having ultimate control over us and our society (which some falsely accused McLuhan of doing). Just as we are profoundly shaped by the cultures in which we inhabit, we are profoundly shaped by the technology we help create. And yet, as rational, creative, and volitional creatures we can reflexively critique, withdraw from, embrace, and refashion our social environments and the complex web of influences that subtly shape us.

An approach that views technology simply as a neutral tool that is good or desirable if it seems to serve my personal or ministry objectives is flawed, inadequate, and even ultimately perilous to individual, interpersonal, and societal well-being. Human language is not merely a neutral, arbitrary system of symbols; rather it is a powerful medium with embedded assumptions, schemas, and values that inform how we perceive and interpret reality.

> When technologies are uncritically treated as neutral tools and given free reign, it may lead to technological over-dependency whereby we increasingly look to technology to solve our problems and meet our needs.

Technology similarly both reflects and shapes our ambitions and desires. For example, Netflix may meet our desires to be entertained but having access to such a copious library of digital content and an interface that promotes binge watching can shape our habits and expectations and expand our appetite for immediate consumption. So, a medium like Netflix can not only serve our wants but also demand something from us. When technologies are uncritically treated as neutral tools and given free reign, it may lead to technological over-dependency whereby we increasingly look to technology to solve our problems and meet our needs. From a Christian perspective, it can be said that such addictions and over-dependency are expressions of idolatry, which Timothy Keller described as "anything more important to you than God, anything that absorbs your heart and imagination more than God, anything you seek to give you what only God can give" (Keller 2009, xvii). Seeking to meet our desires and needs through misplaced means can eventually erode our connection to God and human relationships.

Evangelical Posture towards Technology

Addressing evangelicals, Lawrence Terlizzese (2009) observed that,

> Technological development is the most well embraced social reality and the greatest intellectually and theologically neglected subject in Evangelicalism today. Evangelicals need to reevaluate their understanding toward modern technology, seek to renew the Evangelical mind by creating a critical dialogue with technical modernity, and discover technology's limits as opposed to the easy acceptance of technological progress (54).

On the whole, evangelicals seem quite utilitarian when it comes to technology and innovation. That is, evangelicals tend to readily embrace innovations and perceive them as good as long as the medium has the potential to serve their pursuits of ministry and evangelization. One of the most notable shifts in the US religious landscape in the last century was the dramatic decline of mainline churches and the rise of nondenominational evangelical churches, or what Donald E. Miller (1999) called "New Paradigm Churches" (e.g., Calvary Chapel), which refashioned the local church experience by lowering the barrier of entry for the unchurched and adopting new forms, like contemporary worship music. In recounting the remarkable rise of evangelicalism in the 1970s and 1980s, Robert Putnam and David Campbell (2010) attributed the evangelical ascent in part due to their inventiveness: "American evangelicals have always been innovative entrepreneurs as they reach out to save souls, and that was surely true in this period" (112).

In short, evangelicals share in the heritage, and therefore the values, of a long line of innovative and entrepreneurial leaders like Robert Schuller and his drive-in church and Billy Graham, who excelled at leveraging emerging technologies like radio and TV for mass gospel proclamation. And in the American evangelical stream, many ministry innovations have been diffused through large teaching churches like Willow Creek and Saddleback Church. Adopting and leveraging new means of communications appears to have been an important part of Rick Warren and Saddleback's early success and growth—from door-to-door surveys of people in their community to discern needs and preferences of unchurched people to mass direct mail advertising—which many other churches subsequently adopted based on Saddleback's mentoring.

In recent years, social media has emerged as the latest technological fad and communication medium that according to one influential evangelical parachurch ministry, churches cannot or should not do without. In promoting their Facebook Ad Campaign service, Outreach ministries (Outreach 2019) claims:

> Social media isn't just a choice for churches anymore, it's a necessity. The question isn't whether or not you *should* be doing it, the question is *how well* you do it! While it can seem intimidating at first, you don't have to be an expert to win at social … Be a digital missionary! Any church, any size can use social media effectively.

While it is understandable from a business perspective why this particular advertisement only highlights what utilizing media can enhance and retrieve for ministries, a search of their archives indicates that they publish significantly more material on how to cultivate a digital media strategy to expand your reach (utilitarian approach) than they do on cultivating wisdom and discernment about its use and hidden impact.

While the evangelical posture toward new forms, innovations, and technology is generally positive and open, we often seem curiously quick to censure and censor content and ideas that we find objectionable, while the medium or technologies that grant access to the content are largely uncritically accepted. That is, we tend to see the medium as a neutral tool or vehicle for what is of real consequence—content that convey ideas, beliefs, and values. While of course beliefs and ideas are consequential, McLuhan warns us that, "it is only too typical that the 'content' of any medium blinds us to the character of the medium" (1994, 9). The concern is not so much what we are watching on Netflix or TikTok but, more significantly and consequentially, how we are being shaped in the very act of using these tools. Perhaps just like that hypothetical pet owner who released the Burmese python as a convenient solution without regard to the unintended consequences, I suspect that, most users of technology have not seriously considered the personal and societal impact of their frequent use. Equipping those we have been entrusted to disciple and lead to develop wisdom in this area is imperative and it must go beyond imposing global rules and censoring the media content.

However, there seem to be limits to evangelical accommodations of technology. Recently, the Ethics and Religious Liberty Commission (ERLC) of the Southern Baptist Convention, proactively crafted an "Evangelical Statement of Principles on Artificial Intelligence" (Artificial Intelligence 2019). Then ERLC President Russell Moore remarked, "No issues keep me awake at night like those surrounding technology and artificial intelligence … The implications artificial intelligence will have for our future are vast" (Jackson 2019). Perhaps movies like the *Terminator* franchise, which imagines a world dominated by sentient machines gone rogue, have sensitized us to the dangers of overextended artificial intelligence. And while I am glad some are attentive to this area of technological development, I hope to see greater critical engagement with existing technologies like personal wireless devices and digital media platforms which may seem to be relatively innocuous.

Concluding Missiological Reflections

Would you give a young child a chainsaw? The protective parents among us might instinctively ask, why would a young child need a chainsaw? And that would be a good starting question to ask but, we should step back and also ask, what is this technology designed to do? How does it extend the body? What amputations, in the McLuhan sense, might it lead to? What can it retrieve and what might happen when pushed to its limits? If your church or ministry uses social media or livestreams services, you are in a sense encouraging people to use them and so are complicit in their adoption and use. And just like I would want to train my boys on how to properly use a chainsaw, and how not to use it, should not the church likewise equip people to engage with technologies wisely? Failing to do so would leave major gaps in our discipleship.

To develop much needed discernment and wisdom, I suggest that Christians engage in critical reflection about technology through the lens of Christian assumptions and our God-given mission of seeing God's rule being increasingly manifested in our lives, in our communities, and in our world. The social sciences have offered helpful evidence of social, psychological, and physiological impact that certain kinds of technological tools and media are having on people. While such studies can suppose a subjective baseline from which changes can be measured, objective notions of human ideals bleed into the realm of metaphysics as measures of health and well-being intersect with ultimate questions of identity and purpose. Harris (2019) astutely suggests the kinds of questions we need to address to make peace with technology:

> To create humane technology we need to think deeply about human nature, and that means more than just talking about privacy. This is a profound spiritual moment. We need to understand our natural strengths—our capacity for self-awareness and critical thinking, for reasoned debate and reflection—as well as our weaknesses and vulnerabilities, and the parts of ourselves that we've lost control over. The only way to make peace with technology is to make peace with ourselves.

In seeking to understand who we are as human beings, I have been convinced that the Christian metanarrative offers the most compelling explanation for all that I see and experience in the world—including our identity, purpose, the brokenness in the world, and God's remedy for healing the world. To make peace with technology, or to put it in its rightful place, I believe Christians must see technology through the lens of the grand biblical story; it is a script that rightly orients us to our true identity and purpose and rightly orders our ambitions and hopes. This story reminds us that everything God created was *tov* (well-formed, beautiful, good), and the first humans worked to cultivate and build upon what God had initiated, exercising divine authority in expanding the reflections of God's glory and goodness throughout the world. Their vocation was to reflect and replicate the Creator's wise stewardship in a garden of unfettered potential for the flourishing of all within the created order. So, while we can and should appreciate the works of human ingenuity as arising from our identity as God's image bearers, bestowed with remarkable intellectual, affective, and creative capacities, we should also inquire how the mediums we create and use relate to our divinely mandated vocation to be fruitful and multiply.

This story also reminds us that our proclivity towards placing ourselves instead of God at the center of it all characterizes the heart of human rebellion. When it comes to technology, our rebellion can take on various forms.

The Medium Is the Message

We are prone to misusing technology in ways that harm others and ourselves. Simultaneously, while humans have developed medicines and other medical interventions to prolong life and fight against the mortal consequence of the Fall, we also find new, inventive, and more efficient ways to kill and exploit each other. While technology can amplify and extend in constructive, redemptive ways, it can also amplify and extend the desires of the flesh, which if left unchecked, will only enable us to harm and destroy ourselves and each other more efficiently. So, we should ask what values embedded in the technology are in conflict with God's vision for humanity and the world. What harmful or destructive tendencies might using this technology elicit societally and personally, given my particular weaknesses and habits of the heart?

This story also prompts me to praise God that grace and mercy follows on the heels of human failures and that what God has always desired from us is trust and mutual love. As we see in the *protoevangelium* and thereafter throughout the biblical story, divine judgment is coupled with divine promise, climactically in the greater exodus that Jesus secured through his life, death, and resurrection. Technological rebellion can also take the form of misplaced trust such as in the idolatry of technicism, whereby we look to technology to deliver us from all that ails us and our world rather than trusting in and following God's unfolding redemptive work. God invites us to join his reclamation project of renewing all things under Christ rather than repeating the folly of the residents of Shinar who sought to use technological ingenuity in a futile attempt to return back to Eden and secure for themselves that which God promised to supply.

> We should ask how the tools we create and use are shaping our affections, aspirations, and hopes.

Our encounters with pain, suffering, disappointment, and unmet desires in our broken dysfunctional world serve as perpetual reminders that things are not as they should be or how we want them to be. The question is what or who we look to and trust in to meet our deep longings for seemingly fleeting ideals like love, belonging, justice, and peace. So, we should ask how the tools we create and use are shaping our affections, aspirations, and hopes. Do they erode or reinforce our love for and trust in our Savior? Do they point our longings in the right direction?

Electronic technology is becoming increasingly ubiquitous and inseparably integrated into our lives—perhaps quite literally. Futurists like Ray Kurzweil (2006) foresee an impending technological singularity whereby the exponential growth in technologies like computing capacity and artificial intelligence will usher in a new era of human history where the boundary between machine and human will be blurred as people seek to transcend their biological limitations through technological adaptation. Signs point to technological dependency accelerating and manifesting in new ways and as such, there is need for much greater missiological engagement in this area. The computing and internet revolution has brought an endless supply of information; wisdom and discernment about our relationship with technology is in much shorter supply.

References Cited

"Artificial Intelligence: An Evangelical Statement of Principles." 2019. *The Ethics and Religious Liberty Commission.* April 11, 2019.

Auxier, Brooke, Monica Anderson, Andrew Perrin, and Turner Erica. 2020. "Parenting Children in the Age of Screens." Pew Research Center, July.

Center for Humane Technology. n.d. "Who We Are." Accessed March 31, 2021. https://www.humanetech.com/who-we-are.

Crouch, Andy. 2017. *The Tech-Wise Family: Everyday Steps for Putting Technology in Its Proper Place.* Grand Rapids, MI: Baker.

Harris, Tristan. 2019. "Our Brains Are No Match for Our Technology." *The New York Times*, December 5, 2019, sec. Opinion.

Jackson, Griffin Paul. 2019. "The Gospel of AI: Evangelicals Want Tech to Remain Good News." *Christianity Today*.

Kaplan, Abraham. 1964. *The Conduct of Inquiry: Methodology for Behavioural Science.* San Francisco, CA: Chandler Publishing Company.

Keller, Tim. 2009. *Counterfeit Gods: The Empty Promises of Money, Sex, and Power, and the Only Hope That Matters.* New York: Penguin Books.

Kurzweil, Ray. 2006. *The Singularity Is Near: When Humans Transcend Biology.* New York: Penguin Books.

McLuhan, Marshall. 1994. *Understanding Media: The Extensions of Man.* First MIT Press edition. Cambridge, MA: MIT Press.

McLuhan, Marshall, and Bruce R. Powers. 1989. *The Global Village: Transformations in World Life and Media in the 21st Century.* New York: Oxford University Press.

Miller, Donald. E. 1999. *Reinventing American Protestantism.* Berkeley, CA: University of California Press.

Oliver, Kendra. 2020. "Are You Feeling Zoom-Ed Out? You Are Not Alone." Vanderbilt University School of Medicine (blog). https://medschool.vanderbilt.edu/basic-sciences/2020/10/01/are-you-feeling-zoom-ed-out-you-are-not-alone/.

Outreach. 2019. "Creating a Powerful Social Media Strategy for Your Church—Part 1." Outreach Blog. https://outreach.com/blog/creating-a-powerful-social-media-strategy-for-your-church-part-1/.

Putnam, Robert D., and David E. Campbell. 2010. *American Grace: How Religion Divides and Unites Us.* New York: Simon & Schuster.

South Florida Water Management District. n.d. "Python Elimination Program." Accessed March 31, 2021. https://www.sfwmd.gov/our-work/python-program.

"Truth About Tech: A Road Map for Kids' Digital Well-Being." 2018. Common Sense Media.

Turkle, Sherry. 2015. *Reclaiming Conversation: The Power of Talk in a Digital* Age. New York: Penguin Books.

Turkle, Sherry. 2020. "Staying Connected, Virtually: What We Lose Online." https://www.wbur.org/onpoint/2020/04/01/connected-physical-distancing-coronavirus.

U.S. Congress Senate. 2019. "Optimizing for Engagement: Understanding the Use of Persuasive Technology on Internet Platforms." Senate, 116th Cong., 1st sess., June 25, 2019.

Wu, Tim. 2016. *The Attention Merchants: The Epic Scramble to Get Inside Our Heads.* New York: Alfred A. Knopf.

Zivnuska, Suzanne, John R. Carlson, Dawn S. Carlson, Ranida B. Harris, and Kenneth J. Harris. 2019. "Social Media Addiction and Social Media Reactions: The Implications for Job Performance." *The Journal of Social Psychology* 159, no. 6: 746–60.

Chapter 14

Communicating for the Frontiers

How Communication in the Twenty-First Century Impacts Mission in Restricted-Access Contexts

J. T. Matthews

This chapter is premised on two ideas. The first is that the theological imperative to spread the gospel applies to all peoples of the world. The second is that the missiological considerations of how to share the gospel with the peoples of the world is significantly different in an open-access context in which the gospel can be proclaimed freely and a restricted-access context[1] in which the dominant power, whether political, tribal, or religious, restricts or prohibits the proclamation of the gospel.

The Roman Empire was relatively tolerant of religious diversity. The province of Judaea was not. Jesus lived and ministered in a relatively restricted-access context, where the dominant power intended to kill him. As a result, Jesus took actions to control the spread of information about his ministry and its public size in order to avoid premature conflict. He commanded people not to report about his work, he frequently avoided cities and crowds, he evaded tough questions, and he left places when necessary. While none of these measures worked perfectly, Jesus was not forced to the cross. He chose the perfect symbolic moment for his death (Luke 18:31–33 *inter alia*). After his death and resurrection, his followers, by the power of the Holy Spirit, began to minister in the same context, taking the same kinds of actions. The book of Acts is the story of how the church developed while ministering in a context that grew increasingly hostile to the proclamation of the gospel.

Now imagine that Jesus arrived in a restricted-access context in 2022. Imagine that all Jesus' followers became his "followers" on social media. Imagine that Peter's cell phone held the contact information of every believer on earth. Imagine that news of the riots in Ephesus went viral and Paul's photograph was available all over the internet. Now imagine that the hostile

---

1 It is very tempting to replace "context" with "nation" here because the differences that we will be examining in this chapter require a level of political power and resources that are not typically found in the pockets of unreached people that exist inside majority Christian countries, e.g., the Lamo Muslims in Kenya. However the costs of analyzing communication using AI are dropping drastically, as are the costs of coordination among anti-Christian groups. So I have retained the term "context."

Roman Empire had access to all of this information. The church would not have survived unless it adapted.

The global church of the twenty-first century has adapted to thrive in Christendom. Like a plant grown in a hothouse, the church in the majority Christian world cannot survive in its current incarnation without government protections of the freedom of religion, assembly, and free speech. This chapter is about the consequences of the intersection of twenty-first century communication technology with the theological imperative to reach people in restricted-access contexts. My conclusion is that the two cannot coexist. Jesus and the first-century church had to adapt their ministry; in the twenty-first century, we must either change our ministry *globally* or change our environment.

The complexities engendered by our ever-shrinking "global village" combined with the almost unlimited surveillance capabilities of artificial intelligence make identifying Christians easier and more accurate in 2021 than it was in 2016. It is possible *right now* to map the global church in most of the world because of the modes and methods of communication that Christians have adopted. That includes the underground church and brings us back to our opening question: Can the church survive in restricted-access contexts if a hostile power knows who they are? Where they are? And who their friends are? Communication technologies and practices in the twenty-first century have endangered the mission of God in restricted-access contexts. This chapter shows how this has happened and enumerates steps that we, as believers, can take to change the way we live and communicate in our digital world.

> It is possible *right now* to map the global church in most of the world because of the modes and methods of communication that Christians have adopted.

This chapter was written for missiologists, not computer scientists. As such, I attempt to use everyday language to present views that enjoy broad expert consensus. The first section of this chapter fills a gap in the literature by bringing applied missiology into the technological realities of the twenty-first century. It is more detailed than is strictly necessary in the hope that it will inspire thoughtful reflection in the many areas that are impacted by these technological and sociological changes. The second section explains how these new realities have given birth to a digital Christendom in which one can be identified as Christian by one's digital footprint. The final section examines principles and actions for undermining our new digital reality.

The Global Village

The rise of the internet formed a "global village" (Friedman 2005). In the aftermath of the Arab Spring of 2010, the rapid rise in internet usage, smartphone adoption, and those tools and platforms classified as "social media" seemed to have obvious positive and pro-democratic effects. Christian organizations invested significant resources into adopting and adapting these new tools to increase their ability to fund and distribute their message. All our communication became global communication.

Concerned researchers and activists quickly noticed that these new technologies were not just being used for the betterment of mankind. They were also being used for repression, suppression, and surveillance, by both governmental and non-governmental actors (Gunitsky 2015; Kyriakopoulou 2011). When the Egyptian government began to force dissidents to provide their social media passwords so that they could use their accounts to identify and arrest other dissidents, the Arab Spring became the Arab Winter.

The global village created by new communication technologies is characterized by a vast reduction in the money, time, and effort required to communicate with people at a distance. This drove many sociological changes, not least of which is the rise in broadcast (one to many) communication. The implication is that there was also a concomitant reduction in the time and effort required to observe others—which has been the interest of authoritarian governments.

Many people need to avoid revealing their identity to hostile governments—political dissidents, activists, journalists, and Christians in a restricted-access context. This chapter refers to believers whose identity and way of being allows them to live in a restricted-access context and share the gospel as *contextual workers*. Jesus was a contextual worker, as was Peter. Billy Graham and Pope John Paul II were not. This term is not restricted to foreign missionaries. The contextual worker *par excellence* is the local believer.

The "global village" endangers contextual workers by threatening to publicly expose them as Christians without their consent or even awareness, which, in these contexts, leads to persecution, imprisonment, and death. This new environment requires contextual workers to be wise in the way they (and their social groups) communicate. Creating distinct online identities by using different social media profiles and email addresses and phone numbers effectively stopped human-powered surveillance because humans have limited time, patience, attention, and memory. Mistakes were still made, and once a connection was made between the distinct identities, people were exposed. But these kinds of mistakes were relatively rare and avoidable with preparation, foresight, and a little caution.

Artificial Intelligence and Mission

The dramatic rise of artificial intelligence (AI) is an existential threat to the mission of God in restricted-access contexts.

> Technological advancements mean that … effectiveness in conducting surveillance is no longer limited by scale or duration. Declining costs of technology and data storage have eradicated financial or practical disincentives to conducting surveillance. As such, the State now has a greater capability to conduct simultaneous, invasive, targeted and broad-scale surveillance than ever before. (Feldstein 2019, 13)

In other words, observation is no longer human-powered and is essentially unlimited. In the last five years, artificial intelligence has undergone unprecedented growth in its capacity and scope of use. The mission community must come to grips with this issue quickly while there is still time to adapt.

Capabilities of Artificial Intelligence

There is still no widely accepted definition of AI, but it is sufficient to define it as "computer software that performs activities which require human-like intelligence" (Wang 2019; Bhatnagar et al. 2017; Lewis and Monett 2018). I will focus on three activities that are particularly relevant to mission in restricted-access contexts: 1) identifying humans, 2) mapping relationships between humans, and 3) extrapolating human beliefs and behaviors.

Identifying Humans

Identifying humans refers to connecting a person's digital footprint to their real-world identity. Every social media platform can accurately recognize faces in a photograph and connect those photographs to a user account. Smartphones use facial recognition in lieu of a password. AI is capable of recognizing individuals based on real-time video, even in a large crowd or a busy intersection (Wang 2018). Identification by DNA, fingerprint, biometrics, and voiceprint are also within the capabilities of AI.

Mapping Human Connections

It is trivial for a program to create a "network graph" that maps all connections on a particular social media network. See the network connections of a single Facebook user in the image on the following page (see figure 14.1).

Communicating for the Frontiers

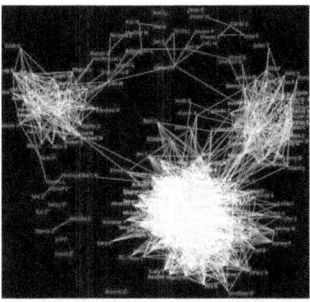

Figure 14.1 Data Visualization of Facebook Relationships (by the third-party app MyFnetwork, December 30, 2011, Kenneth Freeman/ Kencf0618, Courtesy of Wikimedia Commons)

AI can identify humans across a variety of datasets, creating a much richer set of interactions and connections. This includes mapping human connection based on real-world activities using surveillance cameras, GPS, Bluetooth data, phone calls, emails, etc. The more data the AI has access to, the more complete its map of human connections. Notice that people's connections naturally fall into disparate communities. This means that once a few underground believers or contextual workers are identified, their entire community is compromised.

Extrapolate Human Beliefs and Behaviors

The final key capability of AI is to extrapolate human beliefs, emotions, and activities based on one's digital footprint. Sentiment analysis, a subfield of natural language processing, determines a person's mood, opinions, and attitudes based on their online activities, particularly speech. With the right data, AI can extrapolate political leanings, religious identity, gender, sexual orientation, interests, hobbies, and a variety of other things (Martin 2019). This particular capability is far from perfect, but it is developing quickly.

All Together Now

These abilities are synergistic. By identifying humans and mapping their connections, it is possible to extrapolate their commonly held beliefs and behaviors. AI does not understand, it finds patterns. According to Freedom House's report on Internet Freedom,

> Advances in artificial intelligence (AI) have opened up new possibilities for automated mass surveillance. Sophisticated monitoring systems can quickly map users' relationships through link analysis; assign a meaning or attitude to their social media posts using natural-language processing and sentiment analysis; and infer their past, present, or future locations. Machine learning enables these systems to find patterns that may be invisible to humans, while deep neural networks can identify and suggest whole new categories of patterns for further investigation. *Whether accurate or inaccurate, the conclusions made*

about … one's political views, social interactions, sexual orientation, or religious faith can lead to closer scrutiny and outright punishment. (emphasis added) (Shahbaz and Funk 2020, 45)

The infamous Chinese social score is a helpful case study in what was possible in 2019. Facial recognition, geo-tracking, financial and credit scoring, emotion rating, social media analysis, and ideological analysis are all part of an overarching scheme to engineer social behavior (Campbell and Chengdu 2019). But this social score underestimates the potential impact of AI on the mission of God because its scope is so large—China has almost 1.5 billion citizens. The subset of people who are possible contextual workers is much smaller and have much less political power. As such, the use of AI to control the Uighur people group is a more relevant case study. (Andersen 2020)

Extent of Artificial Intelligence

To understand AI's capabilities is meaningless without knowing the extent to which those capabilities are being used in the real world.[2] There are two important groups using AI to analyze people: the companies profiting from the attention economy (corporate AI) and state surveillance (national AI).

Attention Economy

No human being is capable of digesting all of the available data in the Age of Information. Nobel Laureate Herbert A. Simon posited that, given the overabundance of information, attention has become the scarce commodity, the currency. This leads to a new economy, which he called the attention economy, because people are literally "paying attention" (Simon 1994). The attention economy is based on capturing human attention and focusing it on a certain object. Sean Parker (2017), former CEO of Facebook explained: "Facebook … was all about *how do we consume as much of your time and conscious* attention as possible?"

The financial success of Big Tech (Google, Amazon, Facebook, et al.) is based entirely on the use of AI to understand, manipulate, and monetize human attention, particularly through the use of social network effects and online trackers. The Cambridge Analytica political scandal in 2016 showed that Facebook has over four thousand data points on the average user, and it uses this information to model (understand) and manipulate consumers through advertising (Lanier 2018). The reason that the attention economy is relevant for

---

[2] The coronavirus pandemic that started in 2020 led to another major leap forward in the extent of AI, both by state and corporate actors (Shahbaz and Funk 2020). Cooperation between Big Tech, the telecom industry, and governments for contact tracing has created incredibly large databases of personal information.

Communicating for the Frontiers

our discussion is that state actors can access corporate data. Big Tech companies regularly comply with legal requests for data from authoritarian governments. Massive amounts of data have been stolen through hacking by state actors, particularly China (Collier 2021). Moreover, it is possible to use undetectable AI "bots" to create fake social media accounts and "scrape" valuable information off the social web without asking permission or committing a felony. Facebook estimates that at least 5 percent of social media accounts are fake (Nicas 2020).

State Surveillance

The surveillance capabilities of the nations of the world were extensively documented by Steven Feldstein with the Carnegie Endowment for International Peace in 2019.[3] State level surveillance consists not only of AI software to analyze the digital world, but surveillance cameras, GPS devices, DNA tests, etc. that allow AI to perceive and analyze the real world. Feldstein (2019, 8) writes, "At least 75 out of 176 countries globally are actively using AI technologies for surveillance purposes … *countries with authoritarian systems and low levels of political rights are investing heavily in AI surveillance techniques*" (see figure 14.2 below).

Percentage of Countries Adopting AI Surveillance by Region

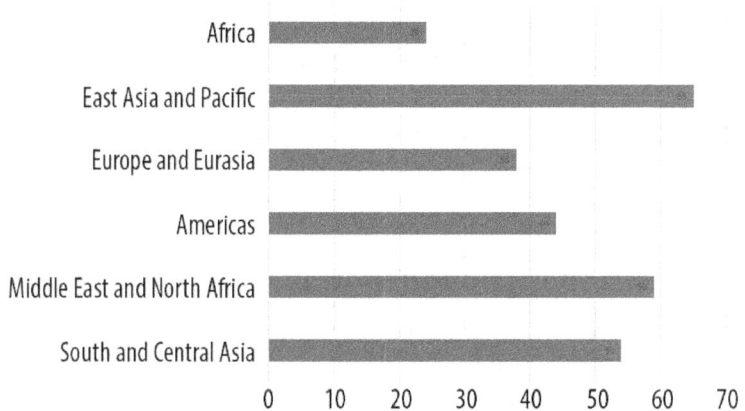

Figure 14.2 Adoption of AI Surveillance Practices by Global Regions
(based on statistics in Feldstein 2019, page 9).

"Governments are increasingly purchasing sophisticated technology to monitor their citizens' behavior on social media … from major authoritarian powers to smaller or poorer states that nevertheless hope to track dissidents

---

3 More than 1300 journal articles, technical papers, and media articles describing the extent and capability of AI surveillance are available at the following link: https://www.zotero.org/groups/2347403/global_ai_surveillance/items/QMA4RMDG/library.

and persecuted minorities" (Shahbaz and Funk 2020, 45). Authoritarian countries have always invested in surveillance in order to maintain their political and social control.[4]

The Rise of Digital Christendom

The combination of modern communication, surveillance, and AI is creating a digital Christendom, in which the world's Christians are unwillingly identified by their digital footprint, communications, and social networks. Changes in behavior, social connections and relationships, and digital communications are all data points. Digital surveillance can be performed anywhere in the world without our awareness.[5] The problem this presents for contextual workers is obvious. The problem of uncontrolled exposure that the "global village" presented has increased exponentially because AI lacks human limitations. It can search through all social networks looking for similar photos, mapping friend groups, and watching online behaviors. Digital Christendom will become more sharply defined as the capacities of AI continue to grow. We know that data storage will get cheaper, processors will get faster, cameras will get better, and everything will get smaller. We can be sure that authoritarian regimes will invest in more surveillance technology. Thus, the influence of AI will grow in both capability and extent (Ahmed and Nasir 2020; Armstrong and Sotala 2015). Unlike the early church, we find ourselves unable to control the flow of information and unable to run away from unwanted attention. As a result, we may find that some of the unreached places of the world become unreachable because their governments isolate national believers and exclude foreign believers.

Tentative Thoughts on How to Proceed

So what are we to do? Should openly Christian organizations abandon their aspiration to reach the lost in restricted-access contexts? Should contextual workers refrain from any involvement with church or Christian organizations? Should underground believers flee? In any case, there is a price to be paid by all believers. As I stated in the opening there are only two options: change our

---

4 There is an important caveat to this discussion. There are still wide variances on the capacity for physical surveillance within a country, especially between urban and rural areas. Even China, with an estimated 400 million surveillance cameras, cannot watch everyone in the physical world all the time.

5 This is not limited to authoritarian countries. According to US law, any communication company can be required to store communications on a given individual and are forbidden by the same law from informing them of the surveillance (US DOJ 9-7.000 Electronic Surveillance).

ministry or change our environment. I think that both need to happen! I focus here on the technological and not the ecclesiological.[6]

These actions center around two principles of AI surveillance. The first principle is that AI is only effective when it has enormous amounts of data to analyze. This means that every piece of information about ourselves, our network, and our work that is stored in a centralized dataset jeopardizes the ability of Christians who are similar to us or connected to us to work in restricted-access contexts. If there are no large collections of data on human interactions and communication, then there can be no digital Christendom. The second principle is that AI can only identify people who are similar to already identified Christians. AI is pattern recognition. The fewer visible, publicly identified Christians in the world, and the fewer digital connections between them, the less powerful is AI's pattern matching ability. It should be noted that these principles apply to all persecuted groups—to Uigyurs and political dissidents as much as Christians. What follows are five simple steps based on these two principles.

Pay for Secure Communication Technology

Free digital communication does not exist. The formidable costs of data centers, fiber optic cable, cell towers, programmers, and tech support are either paid for 1) by the user of the service, 2) by a third-party, or 3) both.[7] The second and third option entail creating value by collecting and analyzing data from the user, including: the contents of the communication, the recipients, address book information, and any additional browsing or other activity which the app or website can capture. This clearly violates our first principle, and these "treasure troves" of data invite legal subpoenas, cyber-attack, or outright purchase. The best, and only, secure alternative for organizations and individuals is to pay for communication services from a provider that is privacy-focused. The provider should not: 1) track your activity online or in the real world, 2) have access to your contacts, or 3) have access to the contents of your message[8]. Some notable providers are Signal and Threema for chat and Protonmail or Privatemail for email. While many platforms have free options, remember that free digital communication does not exist. There are some who cannot (impoverished believers) and must not (underground Christians) pay for such services, but everyone else who supports missions should.

---

6 The ecclesiological involves moving to an "underground" church modality that is not reliant on freedom of religion and association for survival.

7 Cell phone companies fall under the "both" category, as does Microsoft O365, and they should never be used for secure communication.

8 In technical terms, this is called zero-access, end-to-end encrypted communication.

Carefully Consider Centralized Communication Strategies

Although broadcast communication by individuals was unheard of twenty-five years ago, social media has become a mainstay of our culture and our organizational strategies. Centralized communication violates both principles because the message and its audience are exposed to data collection and analysis. Decentralized alternatives that avoid these pitfalls are still being developed, but we cannot afford to wait for those tools to mature. This means opting out of the attention economy, especially sites that collect photos and personalized data: Facebook, LinkedIn, Instagram, and Twitter. AI can match photos from different sources, including passport and social media, no matter what identities, names, or emails are used. We need to become early adopters of decentralized social media and non-invasive search providers.

Organizations which use social media for fundraising or preaching, should avoid mentioning or showcasing the work, the people, and the partners in restricted-access contexts. If possible, they should either abandon social media entirely or develop a plan to move themselves and their constituents to decentralized, safe forms in the next six to twelve months.[9] To whatever extent the organization is using the cloud or cloud-based services, it needs to investigate who "owns" their data and whether that data is being mined for information.

Build Organizational and Personal Firewalls

A "firewall" was originally a physical barrier or wall used to prevent the spread of fire in a structure. We need to carefully construct firewalls that prevent information from leaking from digital Christendom to the restricted-access context. This applies to Christian organizations wishing to work in a restricted-access context and to former contextual workers that wish to work for a Christian organization. In both cases, people are digitally connected to their networks, and making a public connection to digital Christendom potentially exposes everyone. One approach that works for both issues is to *utilize intermediate organizations unburdened with a Christian identity or reputation.* As long as the organizations are careful, this allows the work to continue while providing a level of indirection and distance that mitigates the spread of identifying information by providing separable structures and avenues of communication.

---

9 This is different from switching from Twitter to Parler or Locals. Parler has a different ideological bias than Twitter, but it is just as centralized. They are both ripe for abuse by authoritarian governments with AI.

Support the Development of the Decentralized, Privacy-Centered Internet

The decentralized, privacy-focused internet is known as the Dark Web. It has a bad reputation and is often used for nefarious purposes like human trafficking and arms deals. It is worth considering that, from the Roman Empire's perspective, *Christians* are bad people with a nefarious purpose. *The decentralized internet is the only possible solution to the AI problem in the long term.* Supporting the development of the decentralized internet by donating time, staff, or money or by paying for services contributes to that solution. Decentralized alternatives face an uphill battle against the wealthiest and most powerful organizations in the history of the world as well as the technocratic governments who benefit from the increased power that comes from more information. These initiatives will need broad support and that is a role that the Christian community can play as we discover (or develop) decentralized alternatives.

Be Cautious in Country

This seems obvious, but you should assume that you are under relatively constant digital surveillance when in a restricted-access context (Wang 2020). If your cell phone is on, assume that your location is being tracked and your conversations are being recorded. Consider the risk that your computer will be seized. Assume that every person you meet in a public place is part of your permanent social network.

Conclusion

This issue has much larger ramifications than I originally thought, and the situation will only get worse. Computers never forget. Your digital footprint will only grow. AI is real, and its capabilities are already sufficient to identify the vast majority of the world's Christians, regardless of nation, language, or public identity. These effects cannot be ignored, but they can be mitigated. But it means changing where, when, and how we communicate, both online and offline. Christians must take the lead in pursuing a privacy-first, decentralized internet. The Christian community with a passion for reaching the lost must extract itself from the attention economy. The alternative is to give up on reaching, at the very least, the unreached countries of central Asia and the Middle East.

AI is dangerous because it can create a digital Christendom by searching for patterns across a broad variety of data sets. Every stride Christians can make in the sphere of privacy benefits mission in restricted-access contexts. It is a matter of life and death for our brothers and sisters.

> Every stride Christians can make in the sphere of privacy benefits mission in restricted-access contexts.

The Christian community is at the beginning of a long and difficult journey. We must move past our first instinct: "How can I use social media to enhance the spread of my ministry?" and move to a more communal one: "How can we communicate and live in a way that the kingdom of God can spread to the hardest places?"

References Cited

Ahmed, Shahbaz, and Rida Nasir. 2020. "Evaluating the Accuracy of AI Trends Predictions by Top Tech Leaders—Then and Now." *ThinkML*. https://thinkml.ai/ai-trends-predictions-by-enterprise-tech-leaders-then-and-now/.

Andersen, Ross. 2020. "The Panopticon Is Already Here." *The Atlantic*. https://www.theatlantic.com/magazine/archive/2020/09/china-ai-surveillance/614197/.

Armstrong, Stuart, and Kaj Sotala. 2015. "How We're Predicting AI—or Failing To." In *Beyond Artificial Intelligence*, edited by Jan Romportl, Eva Zackova, and Jozef Kelemen. Cham, Switzerland: Springer International Publishing.

Bhatnagar, Sankalp, Anna Alexandrova, Shahar Avin, Stephen Cave, Lucy Cheke, Matthew Crosby, Jan Feyereisl, et al. 2017. "Mapping Intelligence: Requirements and Possibilities." In 3rd Conference on Philosophy and Theory of Artificial Intelligence, 117–35. Springer.

Campbell, Charlie, and Chengdu. 2019. "How China Is Using Big Data to Create a Social Credit Score." *Time*. https://time.com/collection/davos-2019/5502592/china-social-credit-score/.

Collier, Kevin. 2021. "U.S. Issues Warning after Microsoft Says China Hacked Its Mail Server Program." NBC News. https://www.nbcnews.com/tech/security/u-s-issues-warning-after-microsoft-says-china-hacked-its-n1259522.

Feldstein, Steven. 2019. "The Global Expansion of AI Surveillance." Working Paper. Washington, DC: Carnegie Endowment for International Peace. https://carnegieendowment.org/files/WP-Feldstein-AISurveillance_final1.pdf.

Friedman, Thomas L. 2005. *The World Is Flat: A Brief History of the Twenty-First Century*. New York: Farrar, Straus, and Giroux.

Gunitsky, Seva. 2015. "Corrupting the Cyber-Commons: Social Media as a Tool of Autocratic Stability." *Perspectives on Politics* 13, no. 1: 42–54. https://doi.org/10.1017/S1537592714003120.

Kyriakopoulou, Kalliopi. 2011. "Authoritarian States and Internet Social Media: Instruments of Democratisation or Instruments of Control?" *Human Affairs* 21, no. 1: 18–26. https://doi.org/10.2478/s13374-011-0003-y.

Lanier, Jaron. 2018. *Ten Arguments for Deleting Your Social Media Accounts Right Now*. Vol. 1. New York: Henry Holt & Co.

Lewis, Colin, and Dagmar Monett. 2018. "Text Analysis of Unstructured Data on Definitions of Intelligence." In Proceedings of the 2018 Meeting of the International Association for Computing and Philosophy, IACAP.

Martin, Nicole. 2019. "How Much Does Google Really Know About You? A Lot." *Forbes*. https://www.forbes.com/sites/nicolemartin1/2019/03/11/how-much-does-google-really-know-about-you-a-lot/.

McKinzie, Greg. 2011. "Glocalization: The New Context of the Missio Dei." *Missio Dei: A Journal of Missional Theology and Praxis* 2, no. 2. http://missiodeijournal.com/issues/md-2-2/authors/md-2-2-preface#footnote-546-8-backlink.

Myers, Bryant L. 2017. *Engaging Globalization: The Poor, Christian Mission, and Our Hyperconnected World. Mission in Global Community*. Grand Rapids, MI: Baker Academic.

Nicas, Jack. 2020. "Why Can't the Social Networks Stop Fake Accounts?" *The New York Times*, sec. Technology. https://www.nytimes.com/2020/12/08/technology/why-cant-the-social-networks-stop-fake-accounts.html.

Parker, Sean. 2017. "Sean Parker: Facebook Takes Advantage of 'Vulnerability in Human Psychology.'" https://www.cbsnews.com/news/sean-parker-facebook-takes-advantage-of-vulnerability-in-human-psychology/.

Shahbaz, Adrian, and Allie Funk. 2020. "Freedom on the Net 2020—The Pandemic's Digital Shadow." *Freedom on the Net*. Washington, DC: Freedom House. https://freedomhouse.org/sites/default/files/2020-10/10122020_FOTN2020_Complete_Report_FINAL.pdf.

Simon, H. 1994. "The Bottleneck of Attention: Connecting Thought with Motivation." Nebraska Symposium on Motivation.

Wang, Amy B. 2018. "A Suspect Tried to Blend in with 60,000 Concertgoers. China's Facial-Recognition Cameras Caught Him." *Washington Post*. https://www.washingtonpost.com/news/worldviews/wp/2018/04/13/china-crime-facial-recognition-cameras-catch-suspect-at-concert-with-60000-people/.

Wang, Pei. 2019. "On Defining Artificial Intelligence." *Journal of Artificial General Intelligence* 10, no. 2: 1–37.

Wang, Yaqiu. 2020. "In China, the 'Great Firewall' Is Changing a Generation." *POLITICO*. https://www.politico.com/news/magazine/2020/09/01/china-great-firewall-generation-405385.

Chapter 15

Understanding the Written Word through Popular Culture in Japan

Song Joseph Cho

In any casual conversation of Korea, the terms K-Pop and K-Drama rarely fail to make an entrance. The remarkable upsurge of interest in Korean popular culture is commonly known as Hallyu, or the Korean Wave. It has an undeniable allure for countless fans across the globe, propelling the study of the Korean language and culture. Consider, for example, Korean boy band BTS, whose popularity shows no sign of slowing down. Billboard officially named their song "Butter" Song of the Summer for 2021. *Parasite* was the first non-English film to win best picture Oscar in 2020. As of today, *Squid Game* is the most watched Netflix series of all time. While there has been a large body of scholarly work examining the rise of the Korean Wave, to the best of my knowledge, no substantial study has been done on how it can be used as an evangelistic tool.

> The Korean Wave has, in a curious fashion, provided a fertile ground to use Korean popular culture products such as K-Dramas as a springboard to introduce the gospel message.

For Korean missionaries, there has probably never been a more propitious time for evangelism than the present. The Korean Wave has, in a curious fashion, provided a fertile ground to use Korean popular culture products such as K-Dramas as a springboard to introduce the gospel message. They would do well to remember what founding religion editor for Publishers Weekly Phyllis Tickle once said concerning television: "More theology is conveyed in, and retained from, one hour of popular television than from all the sermons that are also delivered on any given weekend in America's synagogues, churches, and mosques" (1997, 216). With this in mind, it behooves Korean missionaries to take a fresh look at Hallyu as an evangelistic tool, taking a cue from their American counterparts who do not hesitate to use Hollywood materials. K-Dramas can serve as a cultural bridge between Korean missionaries and the people they serve by providing an ideal forum to introduce the gospel.

Understanding Korean Drama: *Winter Sonata*

Every once in a while, a television drama comes along that perfectly captures the zeitgeist of a particular social group. *Winter Sonata* was just such a series. This critically acclaimed K-Drama (known as Fuyu no sonata in Japan) holds the distinction of being the melodrama that triggered the Korean Wave, proving to be the breakthrough the Korean entertainment world needed. It sent shockwaves across the Asian entertainment industry as Korean pop culture began to exercise an irresistible fascination for many young people throughout the continent. Moreover, its success did not go unnoticed among scholars. The *Winter Sonata* phenomenon served as a catalyst for Hallyu studies in many universities. Now the question arises: Can missionaries gain something valuable from the appeal of this drama? By understanding its reception, missionaries can identify some of the key ingredients in the drama that have profoundly resonated with television audiences, particularly female viewers. Understanding these ingredients can help missionaries envision other ways of presenting the gospel message.

The stellar acting coupled with the beautiful melodies of *Winter Sonata* proved to be a magical alchemy, tapping into deep-seated nostalgia among fans in Japan. The starring actor Bae Yong-joon is affectionately known as Yon-sama. It is worth stressing that the word "sama" is an honorific title reserved for royalty and aristocrats. What warrants immediate attention is that most of his fans are middle-aged women, living in a society where they are expected to maintain a respectable public image. Transfixed by the visual storytelling of this melodrama, five thousand fans gathered expectantly at Narita Airport to greet Bae Yong-joon in 2004, some even suffering injuries in the midst of the frenzy. In contrast, five hundred fans came to see international soccer sensation David Beckham at the airport (Mori 2008, 130). The drama was so popular in Japan that then-Prime Minister Junichiro Koizumi said, "I will make great efforts so that I will be as popular as Yon-sama and be called Jun-sama" (Onishi 2004). As it happens, "2004 was the year of jun-ai (pure love), epitomized by the huge popularity of Yon-sama" (Shoji 2004). Fans looked back nostalgically as they remembered the very first time they experienced such love.

Several factors led to the success and enduring appeal of the television program. Primarily, the series managed to tap into a spectrum of emotions. A brief skim through newspaper articles reveals that fans long to experience the kind of romantic love displayed in *Winter Sonata*. The unrelenting desire to be reunited with one's first love drives the plot. Capturing every facet of emotion, this is "a tale of rekindled puppy love that has left many Japanese women hankering for an age when their own men were as sensitive and attentive as the Korean actor" (McCurry 2004). The series pulls at their nostalgic heartstrings as they take a trip down memory lane and reminisce about their first love, immersing themselves in romantic reveries. Putting themselves into the shoes of the protagonists, the women build an emotional connection with the characters. Joon-sang, the main character, radiates gentleness and tenderness—qualities that have captivated the spectators. Many of Bae's fans describe the love in *Winter Sonata* as pure and innocent. Companies were quick to jump on the *Winter Sonata* bandwagon, capitalizing on the public's fascination with Yon-sama. *The New York Times* called Bae Yong-Joon the "$2.3 Billion Man" (Onishi 2004).

The twenty-episode drama was broadcast four times in Japan. It debuted in 2003 on NHK's (Japan's national public broadcasting organization) satellite channel BS. When the leading actor arrived at Narita Airport on April 3, 2004, the drama was aired at 11:30 p.m. and was a ratings success (Mori 2008, 130). Also of note is the fact that this time slot was usually reserved for popular American TV series like *The West Wing* and *Ally McBeal* (Kamiya 2004). Late in 2004, NHK broadcast the original version in Korean with Japanese subtitles.

Korean dramas "ushered in a period of more balanced media and entertainment exchange in East Asia" (Korean Culture and Information Service 2011, 27). They helped to change the general perception of Korean men among Japanese women. According to Chikayo Tashiro, an expert on the Korean Wave in Japan, one appealing aspect of Korean drama actors is their ability to "express love straightforwardly," unlike their Japanese counterparts (Prideaux 2005). According to Professor Kinko Ito—an eloquent commentator on Japanese popular culture—Japanese men tend not to express their emotions, partly influenced by the traditional samurai principle that "silence is golden" (2006, 64). In a *Washington Post* article titled "Japanese Women catch the 'Korean Wave,'" one Japanese woman responded: "South Koreans are so sweet and romantic—not at all like Japanese guys, who never say 'I love you' … Maybe I'm living in a fantasy world. Maybe I'm looking for the TV stars I can't really have. But we are all allowed to dream, aren't we?" (Faiola 2006)

Against this background, it is easy to see why people in academia have paid considerable attention to this group of women. In the past, they were largely relegated to the periphery in Japanese popular culture studies. Women ranging in age from thirty to sixty began participating in fan meetings, many of them going on a *Winter Sonata* tour in Korea. Such activities allowed them to freely exchange their feelings without fear of being ridiculed in an honor-shame society. Particularly, for many reserved Japanese housewives, such opportunities provided a social outlet where like-minded fans were able to express their interest in Hallyu (Lee 2010).

It is hardly news to see young teenagers waiting excitedly at airports in anticipation of catching a glimpse of their favorite celebrities; however, middle-aged women responding in a similar fashion is something of a surprise. Especially as it upended social expectations. Rare is the celebrity who can evoke such a pronounced reaction. Such was Bae's influence that when he donated money in the aftermath of the tsunami that hit Southeast Asia in 2004, many did the same by donating to World Vision Japan (*Japan Times* 2005).

While it appeared from the start to be just another run-of-the-mill television series, *Winter Sonata* proved to have an appeal that endured far beyond the expectations of the production team—leaving a spellbinding effect on viewers. Nothing deterred these middle-aged fans from publicly expressing their admiration for Bae Yong-joon. One should recall that Japan is a strongly shame-based culture. To lose face is shameful in Japan (Norbury 2011, 43). Regarding shame, Paul Hiebert writes:

> Shame is a reaction to other people's criticism, an acute personal chagrin at our failure to live up to our obligations and the expectations others have for us. In true shame-oriented cultures, every person has a place and a duty in the society. Self-respect is maintained not by choosing what is good rather than what is evil, but by choosing what is expected of one. Personal desires are to be sunk in the collective expectation. (Hiebert 1985, 212)

The above invites a series of questions: What led the fans to break free from societal expectations? What drove them to transgress the bounds of social conventionality? What inspired these women, who bonded with one another over their common interest, to go outside the parameters of acceptable behavior and abandon social constraints? The Korean Culture and Information Service says about the phenomenon:

> The Yon-sama Syndrome was virtually unprecedented in Japanese society, and social critics, sociologists, and psychologists began offering their analysis. *Winter Sonata* pulled at the heartstrings of highly educated, middle-class women in their late 30s and older, and even the wives of prime ministers. The pure and noble love shown by Bae in the show evoked long-lost feelings of girlish sensitivity and nostalgia in the hearts of middle-aged women, providing them with an escape from Japan's etiquette-conscious and emotionally restrained social atmosphere. A Japanese entertainment magazine analyzed the Yon-sama Syndrome as showing that Korean male actors possess a 'romantic charisma' rare on Japanese TV: they are polite, yet know how to make a woman feel good. (2011, 24)

In examining the success of *Winter Sonata*, it is important to consider Bae's demeanor. Simply put, his fans liked everything about him. In a sense, Yon-sama became the quintessential Prince Charming as he entranced fans with his innocent smile. It is difficult to separate him from his screen persona. His name is most readily associated with kindness, gentleness, and sensitivity. Bae's fans were captivated by "his soft good looks, killer smile, the sensitivity with which he plays his roles, and his polite demeanor. No other Japanese or Western actor even comes close, admirers say" (Crowell 2005).

The drama breathes authenticity as It takes the viewers on a journey into their past. Reduced to tears, many watch it with a mixture of delight and sadness as they revisit their first love. For instance, fans look longingly to one memorable scene in which the leading characters, as young playful high school students, have fun gleefully building a snowman and snowwoman against a gorgeous scenic backdrop of trees blanketed with snow. A melody puts a sentimental gloss on this picturesque scene, achieving stylistic harmony as the pair's movements are synced with the rhythm of the music. It is a moment of pure, unfiltered joy as all of these parts cohere into a satisfying aesthetic whole. Fans see the male protagonist show flashes of affection and tenderness, provoking memories of a distant past when they, too, once experienced the loving care of a sensitive man setting their heart aflutter. Moved by awakened memories of their first love, the scene hits them at a visceral level, exerting a nostalgic tug.

The drama struck a deep chord with viewers, which led many to wait anxiously for Bae's arrival at Narita airport—leaving a visible reminder of the incontrovertible power of nostalgic love. For Professor Kinko Ito, the reaction of *Winter Sonata* viewers is akin to that of the young teenage girl fans of the movie Titanic (starring Leonardo DiCaprio) back in 1998, adding: "The avid fans of Fuyu no sonata watch the TV program on TV, videotape it, and view it again and again … and they cry" (2006, 61). Despite enjoying the series, their pain is brought on by the realization that something has eluded them in the real world.

Several creative forces are behind the success of *Winter Sonata*. With uncanny insight, the series explores the deepest recesses of the human heart. Norimitsu Onishi explains its popularity as follows:

> Fads come and go in Japan, but this one touches upon several deep issues in Japanese society and its relationship with South Korea. In a society gripped by a pervasive malaise, where uncertainty and pessimism fill magazines with headlines about men and women who don't marry, don't have children, don't have sex, Yon-sama seems to touch upon middle-aged women's yearning for

an emotional connection that they lack and perhaps believe they cannot find in Japan. (Onishi 2004)

The *Winter Sonata* phenomenon led scholars to embark on research, helping the public gain better insight into the reasons why many middle-aged fans felt emotionally attached to the melodrama. A woman in her thirties made the following comment concerning the leading male actor: "There is no man like him in Japan. Have you ever met a man like him? He is like a prince. But he might not be. We might not be able to meet him somewhere. I feel very close to him" (Hirata 2008, 149). Though the viewers are mindful that Bae is playing a fictional character, they suspend a natural inclination to disbelief. Deep within their innermost selves is a yearning that such a man embodying pure love does indeed exist.

As to the theme of love, a woman in her forties said: "In contemporary Japan, 'pure love' is no longer attractive to people and love is equated with a steaming physical relationship. A drama of 'pure love,' *Winter Sonata* was refreshing" (Hanaki 2007, 286). Laying bare his vulnerabilities, the actor can be seen crying in this melodrama. As a result, some felt free to give full rein to their emotions. Such was the case of fifty-nine-year old Kawabata Keiko who shares the following experience:

> Men are supposed to be strong and not cry, while women are emotional and cry all the time. However, I had forced myself to be strong for so many years that I became more like a man. I stopped feeling, and I also stopped crying, until I saw *Yon-sama* cry. I know men seldom cry in real life, and what I see in dramas is only acting, but seeing him cry and crying along with him made me feel like myself again. (Lin 2012, 172–73)

Further, Koichi Iwabuchi adds to our understanding when he describes the success of the drama in the following manner:

> Most obviously, it is a pure, single-minded, loving, affectionate, and sympathetic interpersonal relationship depicted in *Winter Sonata* that attracts Japanese audiences. Especially admired is the man's magnanimous tenderness that subtly combines embracing leadership and sincere respect for this partner that is attractively performed by Bae Yon-jung. This is something that cannot be found in Japanese TV dramas, and one producer acknowledged that Japanese TV producers would not be able to make such dramas since such pure love stories have been replaced by stories with more ironic twists. (Iwabuchi 2015, 83–84)

A Missiological Look at *Winter Sonata*

A drama like *Winter Sonata* can have a strong missiological component. Carrying echoes of the gospel, this K-Drama is a work of art, and "all great art contains elements of the true story: the story of the good creation, the fallen world, and the longing for redemption" (Barrs 2013, 67). In 1956 C. S. Lewis published an essay in the *New York Times* entitled, "Sometimes Fairy Stories May Say Best What's to be Said." Korean dramas take on fairy tale-like hues, and *Winter Sonata* is no exception. It is a modern fairy tale that captures the full range of the deepest desires of the individual. In his sermon titled "Beholding the Love of God," Timothy Keller (1995) describes the love of God in light of popular fairy tales:

> All good stories, all the stories that we love, all the stories that move us are really about Jesus. The great thing about being a Christian is that every story is two stories, every song is two songs. Think of it this way: Are you a Christian? Then you know what? We are going to fly like Peter Pan. Are you a Christian? Then there is a handsome prince who will kiss us and wake us out of sleep. Are you a Christian? Then someday someone will, a beauty will come and kiss us and though we are beasts make us something gorgeous.

Winter Sonata offers an unfaltering portrayal of pure, unconditional love. This being the case, how should a believer describe Christ to the fans of *Winter Sonata*? I suggest that the gospel should be presented as a love story. Saint Augustine (2014) puts it best when he says: "To fall in love with God is the greatest romance; to seek Him the greatest adventure; to find Him, the greatest human achievement." If there is one lesson to be drawn from the fans, it is that love is and remains an intoxicatingly powerful force regardless of age, or regardless of the passage of time.

> I suggest that the gospel should be presented as a love story.

The drama pulsates with the power of unconditional love. It ripples with sacrificial love. Filled with stirring moments, everything in the series is redolent of the power of first love. These are the intertwined themes to which the fans were acutely and emotionally attuned. They are the lifeblood of the drama. The gospel tells the story of such love. To quote C. S. Lewis once again, "But God will look to every soul like its first love because He is its first love" (Lewis 2007, 640). Just like the fictional character Jun-Sang, who embarks on a mission to recover the memory of his first love, missionaries can present God as their forgotten first love. Television series like *Winter Sonata* can certainly act as a bridge between missionaries and the fans.

There is something unabashedly Christian about this drama. The director, Yoon Seok-ho, imbues the script with illustrations similar to those found in the Bible, deftly interspersing them throughout the episodes. Many fans know by heart memorable lines from *Winter Sonata*, such as: "I will be your guiding star." Jun-sang says this to Yu-jin as he makes reference to the star Polaris. This image grounded in the stellar universe is noteworthy. Also known as the North Star, it is the brightest within the Ursa Minor (The Little Bear) constellation. Now, is not Christ also described as a star? Consider Revelation 22:16c (all Scripture references are NLT unless otherwise indicated): "I am the bright Morning Star." The use of such metaphors cannot be overemphasized. In their seminal book *Metaphors We Live By*, George Lakoff and Mark Johnson (1980, 3) write that "the way we think, what we experience, and what we do every day is very much a matter of metaphor."

Another poignant line from the drama is: "The most beautiful house is the one built in one's heart." This quote is no mere sentimental adornment; for the missionary it can have great illustrative value. Compare this with Ephesians 3:17: "Then Christ will make his home in your hearts as you trust in him. Your roots will grow down into God's love and keep you strong." Or that Jesus is preparing a place for believers (John 14:3). C. S. Lewis (2007, 640) describes this beautifully:

> Your soul has a curious shape because it is a hollow made to fit a particular swelling in the infinite contours of the Divine substance, or a key to unlock one of the doors in the house with many mansions … Your place in heaven will seem to be made for you and you alone, because you were made for it—made for it stitch by stich as a glove is made for a hand.

Another thing to note about the drama is that it attains a spiritual dimension. Professor Kinko Ito (2006, 65; my emphasis) observes:

> One of the reasons why *Winter Sonata* appeals to so many people is that watching the melodrama is a *spiritual or religious experience* … An opportunity to be able to meet again deceased loved ones is one of the most basic desires of human experience, and *Winter Sonata* fulfills that need very nicely.

Do *Winter Sonata* fans know that someone can indeed fulfill such a desire? In John 11:25, Jesus says, "I am the resurrection and the life." With regard to the resurrection, Tolkien remarks:

> The gospels contain a fairy-story, or a story of a larger kind which embraces all the essence of fairy-stories. They contain many marvels—peculiarly artistic, beautiful, and moving … The Birth of Christ is the eucatastrophe of Man's history. The Resurrection is the eucatastrophe of the story of the Incarnation. This story begins and ends in joy … There is no tale ever told that men would

rather find was true, and none which so many sceptical men have accepted as true on its own merits. (quoted in Ryken 2011, 365–66)

It is relevant to our present discussion that the anime version of *Winter Sonata* has a different ending. The animation suddenly turns to real life as Bae Yong-joon and Choi Ji Woo (the leading female actress) reprise their roles in the cartoon version. They happily marry each other, which is entirely characteristic of fairytales. We hear the voice of Jun-Sang in the background softly saying to Yu Jin: "As time flows by, and everything becomes like a dream, will you remember me this way? Your Polaris will always be here." The couple becomes the embodiment of those who, in fairy tale-like fashion, "live happily ever after." The animated series feels like a fairytale (Drama Beans 2009). The imagery of Polaris is significant. We have noted above that Christ is described as the bright Morning Star, and the ultimate happy ending awaits the believers: There will be a wedding celebration as recorded in the book of Revelation.

What exactly did the Japanese middle-aged fans see that was so captivating in Bae Yong-joon? A prince. Earlier I mentioned the following comment by a fan concerning the leading male actor: "There is no man like him in Japan. Have you ever met a man like him? He is like a prince. But he might not be. We might not be able to meet him somewhere. I feel very close to him." Youna Kim helps explain the popularity of the actor in this way:

The hero's *unconditional love* for a woman—faithful and devoted to one lover, sensitive and understanding of a woman's emotional needs—captivated many women in Japan. Fans of *Winter Sonata* in Japan are particularly women in their thirties and fifties, and the depth of their adulation for the hero is striking: 'If ever was ever such a man in Japan, then I wouldn't be suffering like this.' (Kim 2007, 141; my emphasis)

Indeed, no such person exists on this earth. Trying to look for one will only be met with disillusionment. C. S. Lewis expresses it best:

The books or the music in which we thought the beauty was located will betray us if we trust to them; it was not *in* them, it only came *through* them, and what came through them was longing. These things—the beauty, the memory of our own past—are good images of what we really desire; but if they are mistaken for the thing itself, they turn into dumb idols, breaking the hearts of their worshippers. For they are not the thing itself; they are only the scent of a flower we have not found, the echo of a tune we have not heard, news from a country we have never yet visited. (Lewis 1980, 30–31)

However, Christ is the caring, affectionate prince who wants to build a house in their hearts and lead them as the bright Morning Star whose unconditional love never wanes. According to Professor Ito, this drama is basically about love and compassion. It teaches the audience that there are different kinds of love, how important it is to always act and behave out of love, and that you must believe in love. The very ending scene of the soap opera is the triumph of love and fate that Yu Jin and her man believed in. (Ito 2006, 66)

People long to be loved. Such love is ultimately found in Christ, the true prince who displays unconditional love and compassion.

Conclusion

Should missionaries in Japan make references to this drama as a springboard to talk about the unconditional and sacrificial love of Christ? Can they employ a K-Drama like *Winter Sonata* to talk about Christ, the ultimate Prince who is always faithful and tender? What if someone told the above viewers that Prince Charming does indeed exist? That someone loves them sacrificially and unconditionally? The Cinderella and Prince Charming figures often reflected in K-dramas provide powerful imageries that can be used in a sermon. This is important if the missionary seeks to preach to the heart. To preach in a way that engages the heart, Timothy Keller encourages pastors to: 1) preach culturally, 2) preach from the heart, 3) preach imaginatively, 4) preach practically, 5) preach wondrously, and 6) preach Christo-centrically (Ortlund 2015).

> Missionaries can clearly use a drama like *Winter Sonata* to talk about the unfailing, unending, and unchanging love of God.

Winter Sonata left an indelible mark on many Japanese middle-aged women. In addition to being instructive in familiarizing viewers with Korean culture, the drama reminds them of their first innocent love. Watching a K-Drama is much like reading a Western fairy tale, particularly Cinderella, a genre that shares significant similarities with the gospel. The heroes of fairy tales bear a strong likeness to Christ. Missionaries can clearly use a drama like *Winter Sonata* to talk about the unfailing, unending, and unchanging love of God.

References Cited

Augustine of Hippo. 2014. "15 Augustine Quotes That Helped Shape Modern Christian Thought." *Relevant Magazine*, https://relevantmagazine.com/god/15-augustine-quotes-helped-shape-modern-christian-thought.

Barrs, Jerram. 2013. *Echoes of Eden: Reflections of Christianity, Literature, and the Arts*. Wheaton, IL: Crossway.

Crowell, Todd. 2005. "In Japan, Korean Actors Set Hearts Aflutter." *The Christian Science Monitor*, http://www.csmonitor.com/2005/0408/p15s01-altv.html.

Drama Beans. 2009. "Yonsama and Ji-woo-hime Together in Tokyo." http://www.dramabeans.com/2009/06/yonsama-and-ji-woo-hime-together-in-tokyo/.

Faiola, Anthony. 2006. "Japanese Women Catch the 'Korean Wave.'" *Washington Post*, http://www.washingtonpost.com/wp-dyn/content/article/2006/08/30/AR2006083002985.html.

Hanaki, Toru, Arvind Singhal, Min Wha Han, Do Kyun Kim and Ketan Chitnis. 2007. "Hanryu Sweeps East Asia: How Winter Sonata Is Gripping Japan." *International Communication Gazette* 69, no. 3: 281–94.

Hiebert, Paul G. 1985. *Anthropological Insights for Missionaries*. Grand Rapids, MI: Baker Books.

Hirata, Yukie. 2008. "Touring 'Dramatic Korea': Japanese Women as Viewers of Hanryu Dramas and Tourists on Hanryu Tours." In *East Asian Pop Culture: Analysing the Korean Wave*, edited by Chua Beng Huat and Koichi Iwabuchi, 143–55. Hong Kong University Press.

Ito, Kinko. 2006. "Middle-Aged Japanese Women's Love Affair with Winter Sonata and Its Social Implications." *Japan Studies Review* 10: 59–72.

Iwabuchi, Koichi. 2015. *Resilient Borders and Cultural Diversity*. New York: Lexington Books.

Japan Times. 2005. "Fans Follow Suit after 'Yon-sama' Tsunami Donation." http://www.japantimes.co.jp/news/2005/01/07/national/fans-follow-suit-after-yon-sama-tsunami-donation/#.V_lRjLwrKYU.

Kamiya, Setsuko. 2004. "Korean Love Heats up Japan." *The Japan Times*, http://www.japantimes.co.jp/culture/2004/04/07/films/film-reviews/korean-love-story-heats-up-japan/#.WEGyBWQrJsM.

Keller, Tim. 1995. "Beholding the Love of God." https://www.youtube.com/watch?v=_LjjcW1KoTg.

Kim, Youna. 2007. "The Rising East Asian 'Wave.'" In *Media on the Move: Global Flow and Contra-flow*, edited by Daya Kishan Thussu, 135–52. New York: Routledge.

Korean Culture and Information Service. 2011. *The Korean Wave: A New Pop Culture Phenomenon*.

Lakoff, George, and Mark Johnson. 1980. *Metaphors We Live By*. Chicago: University of Chicago Press.

Lee, Hyangjin. 2010. "Buying Youth: Japanese Fandom of the Korean Wave." In *Complicated Currents: Media Flows, Soft Power and East Asia*, edited by Daniel Black, Stephen Epstein and Alison Tokita. Clayton, Australia: Monash University Publishing. http://books.publishing.monash.edu/apps/bookworm/view/Complicated+Currents/122/xhtml/chapter7.html.

Lewis, C. S. 1980. *The Weight of Glory*. New York: HarperCollins.

Lewis, C. S. 2002. *The Complete C.S. Lewis Signature Classics*. Grand Rapids, MI: Zondervan.

Lin, Ho Swee. 2012. "Emotions, Desires, and Fantasies: What Idolizing Means for Yon-sama Fans in Japan." In *Idols and Celebrity in Japanese Media Culture*, edited by Patrick W. Galbraith and Jason G. Karlin, 166–81. New York: Palgrave MacMillan.

McCurry, Justin. 2004. "Korean Heart-Throb Helps Detente." *The Guardian*. http://www.theguardian.com/world/2004/jun/30/japan.northkorea.

Mori, Yoshitaka. 2008. "Winter Sonata and Cultural Practices of Active Fans in Japan: Considering Middle-Aged Women as Cultural Agents." In *East Asian Pop Culture: Analysing the Korean Wave*, edited by Chua Beng Huat and Koichi Iwabuchi, 127–14. Hong Kong University Press.

Norbury, Paul. 2011. *Japan*. London: Kuperard.

Onishi, Norimitsu. 2004. "What's Korean for 'Real Man'? Ask a Japanese Woman." *The New York Times*, http://www.nytimes.com/2004/12/23/world/asia/whats-korean-for-real-man-ask-a-japanese-woman.html?_r=0.

Ortlund, Gavin. 2015. "Why Sermons Often Bore." *The Gospel Coalition*. https://www.thegospelcoalition.org/article/why-sermons-often-bore.

Prideaux, Eric. 2005. "Japan's New Wave." *The Japan Times*. http://www.japantimes.co.jp/life/2005/12/11/to-be-sorted/japans-new-wave/.

Ryken, Leland. 2011. The Christian Imagination: *The Practice of Faith in Literature and Writing*. New York: Crown/Random House Publishing Group.

Shoji, Kaori. 2004. "Japan Gripped by Obsession with Pure Love." *The Japan Times*. http://www.japantimes.co.jp/life/2004/12/30/language/japan-gripped-by-obsession-with-pure-love/#.V_UoBrwrI1g.

Tickle, Phyllis A. 1997. *God-Talk in America*. New York: Crossroad.

About the Editors and Contributors

Editors

Marcus Dean (PhD, Trinity International University) is professor of Intercultural Studies and Missions at Houghton College (Houghton, New York). For six years he was book-review editor for *Evangelical Missions Quarterly*. Before coming to Houghton College, he pastored and then served for fifteen years in theological education with the Wesleyan Church as a missionary in Colombia and Puerto Rico.

Scott Moreau (DMiss, Trinity Evangelical Divinity School) is Professor of Intercultural Studies and the Academic Dean of Wheaton College Graduate School. He was editor of *Evangelical Missions Quarterly* and general editor of Baker Books' Encountering Mission series. He has written or edited over twenty books and three hundred articles, and received numerous recognitions for his writing, teaching, speaking, and service to society.

Sue Russell (PhDs, UCLA and La Trobe University) is Professor of Missions and Contextual Studies at Asbury Theological Seminary. Prior, she was Associate Professor of Anthropology and Chair of the Department of Anthropology at Biola University; and for seventeen years she was with Wycliffe in Southeast Asia working with national pastors to complete the translation of the Tagal-language Bible.

Rochelle Scheuermann (PhD, Trinity Evangelical Divinity School) is an ordained minister and former church planter who has been involved in higher education for over ten years. She currently serves as Associate Professor and program director for three master's programs at Wheaton College. She has co-authored/co-edited three books and authored multiple articles, focusing on preaching and culture, disability and mission, and theology of mission.

Contributors

Jared E. Alcántara (PhD, Princeton Theological Seminary) is Associate Professor and the Paul W. Powell Chair in Preaching at Baylor University's George W. Truett Theological Seminary. An ordained Baptist minister, he has pastored in Illinois, Massachusetts, Oregon, and New Jersey. His research interests include minoritized preaching in African American and Latino/a church contexts, intercultural studies, and preaching pedagogy.

John Cheong (PhD, Trinity International University) has served in three mission contexts in Asia and North America, ministering among the Chinese, Malays, and diaspora Muslims. He is a senior lecturer, writer, and consultant in missiology and teaches in Southeast Asia. He has co-edited/published six books, and researches on Islam, world Christianity, and globalization.

Song (Joseph) Cho (DIS, Western Seminary) is Associate Professor of Interdisciplinary Studies at Liberty University. His research interests include biblical allusions in literary texts, Korean pop culture, and Japanese anime/manga. He has published in various academic journals, including *Persuasions: The Jane Austen Journal*, *Flannery O'Connor Review*, *Willa Cather Review*, and *Evangelical Missions Quarterly*. He received an MA in English in 2021.

Phil Davis (PhD student, Columbia International University) was previously involved in holistic community ministry in the Middle East for seven years. Before his work overseas, he served in the United States in pastoral ministry and community development for eight years. He has master's degrees in business and intercultural studies.

Robert L. Gallagher (PhD, Fuller Theological Seminary) is Professor Emeritus of Intercultural Studies at Wheaton College Graduate School in Chicago, where he has taught since 1998. He served as the chair of the Intercultural Studies department (2011–18) and as an executive pastor in Australia (1979–90). He is currently the teaching pastor at Lombard Bible Church (C&MA) in Illinois.

Kara Garrison (DTL, Bakke Graduate University) spent twelve years in Southeast Asia, discipling Myanmar Christian women. While doing development work, Kara increasingly focused on creating space for women to discuss developing trusting relationships amid their honor/shame context. Since returning, Kara researched women's communication patterns, graduated with a Doctorate in Transformational Leadership, and continues to serve with Cornerstone International.

Timothy Hatcher (PhD, Assemblies of God Theological School) served with Wycliffe Bible Translators for twenty-two years in Bulgaria, Russia, and Central Asia. Tim is chair of the Applied Anthropology department of Dallas International University and leads the Scripture Engagement Research Initiative with SIL, the Summer Institute of Linguistics.

Matthew Henning (PhD student, Trinity Evangelical Divinity School) centers his research on college students as they relate to the Muslim and Christian understanding and interpretation of law in modern society. Matthew has been on staff with Cru for fifteen years, both internationally and stateside, and currently serves at the University of Illinois Chicago.

Theon Hill (PhD, Purdue University) is Associate Professor of Communication at Wheaton College, where he researches and teaches on the intersections of race, politics, and faith. In addition, Theon is an ordained minister who desires to use the gifts and opportunities that God gives him to advance the mission of the church locally and around the world.

Joy Kim (MA, Dallas International University) studied piano, church music, and music education before graduating from Dallas International University with a master's degree in World Arts. She currently works as an ethnodoxologist in Clarkston, Georgia, with Proskuneo Ministries. Joy works with diaspora artists from diverse backgrounds to engage in global mission through building multicultural worshiping communities.

Michael Hakmin Lee (PhD, Trinity Evangelical Divinity School) is Assistant Professor of Ministry and Leadership at Wheaton College. Michael is ordained and has presented and published papers in the areas of the theology and philosophy of religions, race and ethnicity, and religious mobility. He wrote his dissertation on the experiences of former evangelical missionaries and pastors who abandoned the Christian faith.

About the Editors and Contributors

J. T. Matthews (ThM, Dallas Theological Seminary) is a long-time development worker in restricted-access contexts. He has worked primarily with Muslim, Hindu, and Buddhist communities in Southeast Asia, but he has also consulted with indigenous-led organizations in the Middle East and North Africa. J. T. holds graduate degrees in theology and economics and paid for his education by working as a computer programmer.

Hannah Nation (MA, Gordon-Conwell Theological Seminary) serves as the Managing Director of the Center for House Church Theology and the Content Director for China Partnership. Her first book, a collection of sermons preached by Chinese house-church pastors during the COVID-19 pandemic, was published in 2022. She is also publishing the house-church manifesto of Wang Yi in 2022.

Linda P. Saunders (PhD, Columbia International University) is passionate about missions and racial reconciliation. She and her husband served in Venezuela. Linda serves on the leadership team for EMS, is a research advisor for NAAMC, an adjunct faculty professor at CIU and Liberty University, and a multicultural consultant for Wellspring of Hope, Lynchburg, VA, and Community Faith Partners of Ithaca, NY.

Rochelle Scheuermann (PhD, Trinity Evangelical Divinity School) is an ordained minister and former church planter who has been involved in higher education for over ten years. She currently serves as Associate Professor and program director for three master's programs at Wheaton College. She has co-authored/co-edited three books and authored multiple articles, focusing on preaching and culture, disability and mission, and theology of mission.

Jessica Udall (PhD candidate, Columbia International University) is a professor at Evangelical Theological College in Addis Ababa, Ethiopia, and an adjunct professor at Columbia International University. She is a member of Equip International and the author of *Loving the Stranger: Welcoming Immigrants in the Name of Jesus* and *Loving the Stranger* blog, offering encouragement and advice for welcoming immigrants.

Index

A

African American 108–109, 137–138, 141–142, 144
agreement(s) 61–63, 143
Anglican 68, 73–74, 76–78
Arab 58–60
Arab Spring 167, 179
artificial intelligence 171, 180, 182
Asia 85, 87, 96, 187, 192, 194
Australia 67–68, 72, 77, 80
authoritarian 179, 183–184
authority 19, 23, 58, 63, 69, 72, 75–76, 87, 95, 101, 117, 131, 172

B

backyard missions 137–138, 141, 146–147
belittling 88–89, 92, 94, 97
Bevans, Stephen 5
bilingual(s) 31–32, 34, 37, 45
Black church 137, 139, 141, 144, 147
blues sensibility 122
Brainerd, David 118
Burmese 47, 86, 95–96

C

Cary, Lott 138, 142
Center for House Church Theology (CHCT) 128, 132–133
China 85–86, 127, 133, 135, 183
Christendom 178, 184, 186, 188
Christian women 91
Coe, Shoki 5, 140
collaborative 20, 49, 75
collective 60, 64, 87, 143, 194
collective identity 56
collectivism 59, 71, 85
colonialism 10, 56, 116–117, 119, 121, 123, 143
colonialist missions 147
colonial legacy 117
colonial mindset 117
communication
    challenges 57
    cross-cultural 15–17
    nonverbal 20, 57
comparison 91–92
competition 91–92
conflict 41, 43, 54, 56, 58, 76, 87, 94, 96, 173, 177
conflict avoidance 95
Confucian 86, 88, 94
Confucian hierarchy 96
contemporary crises 137
context(s), restricted-access 177–178
contextualization 5, 7, 9, 11
covert maintenance mechanisms 94
Craddock, Fred 12
critical contextualization 4
cultural superiority 117–118
culture(s) 17, 19–20, 42, 57, 61, 69, 76, 89, 96, 100, 117, 131, 138, 157, 166, 168

D

diaspora 44, 47
Doerre, Sharon 57, 60

E

Eastern worldview 85
egalitarian 71–72, 74–76
entextualization 22
Ethiopia 149, 156
evangelism 77, 79–80, 107, 116, 191

Index

F

face 166, 194
Facebook 131, 167–168, 170, 182, 186
face-saving 94
facial recognition 180, 182
famine 149–150
firewalls 186
Flemming, Dean 11
Forsyth, P. T. 3
fundraising 152
    and social media 186
    Christian 150
    communication 151–152, 154, 158
    emergency mode 154–155, 158
    emergency model 152

G

giving 149, 153–158
global village 179
gospel 3, 11, 29, 38, 74, 77, 79, 83, 108, 116, 119, 127, 133, 139–140, 142, 170, 177, 191, 198
gospel, decolonized 117, 119
gospel message 192
gossip 87, 89, 92–93, 97
Grace to the City (恩典城市) 127, 133
Graham, Billy 170, 179

H

Hesselgrave, David 5
Hiebert, Paul G. 4–5, 194
hierarchy 59–60, 86, 89, 91, 94
high power distance 59, 61
homiletics 3, 6, 15–16
honor 56, 59, 61, 63, 72, 85, 89, 93
honor-shame 193
hospitality 7, 45, 157

house church 127–128, 132–133
hybrid 29–30, 33, 46, 99, 108

I

identity 45, 70, 80, 85, 99, 127, 144, 172, 179
    African 142
    American Christians 131
    China house church 135
    collective 48, 87
    crisis 41
    God's image bearers 172
    language 32–33, 44
    Muslim 104, 109
    national 67
    relational 64
    religious 181
    social 29
    social media 167, 180
    unique 1
imagination, prophetic 120
immigrants 45, 67, 70, 77, 100, 107
imperialism 10, 117, 119, 143
incarnation 16, 18, 26, 81, 150, 178, 198
inculturation 5
indigenization 5
indigenous 23, 38, 69, 77, 80, 82, 116, 130
injustice 47, 95, 104, 115, 120–123
Islam 100, 108
Islamic feminism 103
Islamophobia 100, 104–105

J

Japan 191–192, 195
Jesus Act 129–130, 136

K

K-Drama   191, 197, 200
Keller, Timothy   6, 135, 169, 197, 200
kingdom of God   134, 151, 155, 188
King, Martin Luther, Jr.   115, 117–118, 121
Kraft, Charles H.   5, 16
Kurzweil, Ray   173

L

leadership   55, 61
   Arab   56
   church   53, 130
   hierarchical   73
   intercultural   59
   theological   133
Lewis, C. S.   197–199
Liele, George   138, 141
loss of face   60

M

marginalization   128, 133
mateship   71, 74–75, 78–81, 83
McLuhan, Marshall   163–164, 166–167, 171
media   163–164, 193
medium   164, 166, 170
message   16, 47, 49, 77–78, 99, 120, 164, 167, 186
messages   42, 119
Middle Eastern   53
mindset, colonial   120
multicultural   15, 43, 45, 47–48, 78, 99
multilingual   29, 31–32, 34, 37
music   29, 45–46, 108, 195
Muslims   104
Muslim youth, American   99, 106
Myanmar   46–47, 85, 88, 94, 115

Myanmar Christian women (MCW)   85–86, 88–89, 92, 96

N

Newbigin, Lesslie   4, 9–10, 25
North America   8, 11, 99

O

obligation(s)   61, 86, 94, 129, 194
oppression   69, 122–123, 137, 141, 147

P

Parish, Teresa   15
Parker, Sean   182
partners   15, 21, 25, 53–55, 61, 63–64, 186
partnership(s)   44, 53, 56, 59, 61–62, 64, 115, 155, 157
patronage   61, 63
people groups   16
perspectives, local   130
Pitt-Watson, Ian   8
pluralistic world   12
pop/popular culture   11, 191–192
preaching   3, 6, 9, 11, 15, 19, 24, 38, 80, 117, 127, 186
Priest, Robert J.   7
progressive ideology   103
Proskuneo Ministries   41, 43, 45
Protten, Rebekka   138–140

R

racism   10, 115, 120, 123, 142
reciprocity   43, 47
relationship(s)   23, 43, 47, 60–62, 85–88, 95–96, 99, 131, 157, 163, 166–167, 169, 174, 181, 184
   broken   57, 94
   historical   59

interdependent   63
interpersonal   75, 86
Muslim-Christian   109
natural   108
post-colonial   61
socio-cultural   16
religiously plural   99
Robinson, Haddon   9

S

Sanneh, Lamin   5, 10, 23
scholarship, rhetorical   119
Schreiter, Robert J.   5, 60, 64
shame   43, 60, 85, 109, 194
shaming   87–89, 92, 94, 97
Sheppard, William Henry   138, 143–144
Shryock, Andrew   56
Simon, Herbert A.   182
Smith, Amanda Berry   138, 145
social face   63
social media   131, 163, 167, 170–171, 177, 179–181, 183, 186, 188
South Korea   41, 193, 195
South Sudan   43, 115
storyteller(s)   45, 49, 92, 94
Suchan, Jim   57–58
surveillance   178, 181–184, 187
Syria   43–44, 57, 100, 115

T

technology   164–166, 168–169, 172
tetrad   166
textual community   127–128, 130–134, 136
theological resources   151
Tisdale, Leonora Tubbs   3–4
tradition, prophetic   120, 122

translanguaging   30–34, 37–39
translation   15–17, 24, 37, 134
Turkle, Sherry   167

U

unreachable people groups   140, 151

V

values   16, 19, 48, 55, 57, 61, 69, 121, 165, 169–170, 173
American   102, 117
core   123
cultural   12, 42, 64
egalitarian   59
individualistic   63

W

Wadud, Amina   103
Walls, Andrew F.   128
Winter Sonata   192–193, 195, 197, 200
witness, prophetic   121
worldview   9, 16, 19, 47, 69, 76, 85, 87, 137, 143
worship   10, 29, 43, 45, 89, 139
worship music   170
Wu, Jackson   85

X

xenophobia   115, 120

Y

Yon-sama Syndrome   194

Visit us at missionbooks.org

Ephesiology
A Study of the Ephesian Movement
Michael T. Cooper (Author)

Ephesiology looks at the journey from the inception of the church in Ephesus as it became a movement grounded in God's mission and led by those who multiplied generations of disciples. Michael T. Cooper focuses on Paul and John as missiological theologians who successfully connected Jesus's teaching with the cultural context and narrative of the people in Ephesus. Through this study of a movement, discover how the Holy Spirit still changes lives, cities, and the world.

Paperback & ePub

Mission in the Way of Daniel
Empowering Believers to Live into God's Plan
Edward L. Smither (Author)

This book probes mission theology and practice in the Old Testament, exploring the well-known story of Daniel through the lenses of mission history and mission practice. Providing relevant application for contemporary issues like diaspora, power encounters, and divine favor in mission, the themes in *Mission in the Way of Daniel* advance the ongoing conversation about how to do mission.

Paperback & ePub

www.ingramcontent.com/pod-product-compliance
Lightning Source LLC
Chambersburg PA
CBHW071237070526
44583CB00017B/2220